THE

PUBLICATIONS

OF THE

SURTEES SOCIETY

VOL. CXCVII

THE

PUBLICATIONS

OF THE

SURTEES SOCIETY

ESTABLISHED IN THE YEAR
M.DCCC.XXXIV

VOL. CXCVII

FOR THE YEAR M.CM.LXXXV

At a COUNCIL MEETING of the SURTEES SOCIETY, held in Durham Castle on 3 June 1986, the PRESIDENT in the chair, it was ORDERED –

"That the edition by Dr. Joyce Ellis of Henry Liddell's letters to William Cotesworth be printed as the volume of the Society's publications for 1985."

A.J. Piper, *Secretary*
The Prior's Kitchen
The College
Durham

THE LETTERS OF
HENRY LIDDELL
TO
WILLIAM COTESWORTH

EDITED BY

J. M. ELLIS

PRINTED FOR THE SOCIETY BY
JAMES HALL (LEAMINGTON SPA) LIMITED
1987

CONTENTS

INTRODUCTION

In most respects the life of Henry Liddell, c.1673-1717, fitted neatly into the pattern prescribed for younger sons of gentry families in the early years of the eighteenth century. The Liddells of Ravensworth traditionally relied on the expertise and sheer hard work of junior members of the family in managing their business affairs, particularly the collieries that provided the bulk of their income. And in Henry Liddell's case this destiny as his father's business manager was rendered inescapable by the ineligibility of his two elder brothers, one of them being physically handicapped and the other having inherited an independent estate in Yorkshire. In 1701, therefore, Liddell took over from his uncle Thomas as supervisor of the family's extensive interests in the Durham coalfield, becoming by virtue of this role one of the leading figures in the coal-trade. Movement to London ten years later, although it involved handing over the routine management of the collieries to his younger brother George, did nothing to free him from his overall responsibilities to the family firm. Loyalty to the Liddell interest was expected to come before both private profit and personal comfort: even in his last debilitating illness, he was negotiating for the acquisition of new coal deposits to ensure its future prosperity.

Liddell's involvement in the coal-trade, however, brought him friendship as well as responsibility when it introduced him to a rising local entrepreneur, William Cotesworth of Gateshead, c.1668-1725. It was at first sight an unlikely relationship: in contrast with Liddell's privileged background, Cotesworth was laboriously working his way up from humble beginnings as an apprentice tallow chandler when they first came into contact and was never fully accepted by many of the north-eastern gentry families. However, shared business and political interests provided a foundation for the close and enduring friendship that is reflected in the 171 letters written by Henry Liddell reproduced in this volume, the surviving examples of what seems to have been a notably voluminous and confidential correspondence that flourished after Liddell's move to London in 1710.

The choice of letters for publication has therefore been made by the recipient rather than by the editor and this naturally influences the character of the collection. In all probability, Cotesworth preserved these particular letters to protect himself against the claims of Liddell's widow, the formidable Ann Clavering, who had never trusted his business dealings with her husband (or anyone else). As a result, the most significant letters deal with the coal industry, providing the reader with a vivid picture of the labyrinthine workings of the Newcastle coal-trade at a difficult time in its history. Rising costs and heavy capital investment created an almost irresistable pressure to maximize production, but increased production in a period when the market for coal was limited merely led to intense competition in which both the quality of particular collieries and the favour of London coal dealers were of vital importance. The only realistic method of achieving greater profits in prevailing market conditions was to combine to cut back total production, which was the aim of the cartel known as the Regulation which the Liddells helped to form in 1708 and which employed Cotesworth as a principal agent. The operations of the Regulation dominate the earlier letters in this volume: they reveal not only its hard-won successes but also that it chose to operate by cutting back the production of those outside rather than inside its ranks, contributing to the general atmosphere of distrust, emnity and litigiousness in the industry. In these circumstances, Liddell was bound to encounter severe personal difficulties in his efforts to balance the interests of his family against his duties as guardian of young John Clavering and therefore of Clavering Stella colliery, not to mention his natural wish to earn an independent income through his partnership with Cotesworth. The resultant quarrels, recriminations and legal entanglements help to explain the deliberate obscurity of many passages in the correspondence — even confidential letters could fall into the wrong hands.

Extreme caution was also needed when touching upon the friends' other main interest in life, politics. The Liddells' political sympathies were strongly Whig and their eminence in the north-east meant that they fell under both suspicion and surveillance in the later years of Queen Anne's reign. In their political views, if in nothing else, Cotesworth and Ann Liddell were at one: however, in contrast with his wife's outspoken letters to James Clavering (also published by the Surtees Society), Liddell chose to exercise discretion when commenting on current politics. Thus the main political interest of the earlier letters lies in their portrayal of the non-partisan use of political influence, in this case in defence of the coal trade. The accession of George I liberated the correspondence to a great extent and allowed Liddell to reveal not only his Whig enthusiasms but also the frustrations of political victory. The loyal Whigs, after years in the wilderness, thought that their past sufferings should be rewarded and the present settlement secured by a thorough redistribution of official posts in their favour. However, the promised land failed to materialize, even for well-connected men like Liddell, brother-in-law of the Lord Chancellor; and their disillusion grew as party principle was apparently sacrificed to political expediency by the 'great men' in London. Even the Jacobite rebellion of 1715, which is particularly well documented in this correspondence, failed to recall the Whig leaders to what men like Cotesworth and Liddell conceived to be their duty, and Liddell came to the depressing conclusion that the trade in politics was even dirtier than the notoriously corrupt trade in coal.

Liddell's last years were therefore marked by disappointment in both trade and public affairs, as well as by the painful effects of ill health and contemporary medical treatment. Judging by the prominent place accorded to medical matters in his letters to his greatest friend, the state of his health was one of Liddell's keenest concerns, and his health was not good. The correspondence records remissions rather than recoveries and the gradual build-up of distressing symptoms that resulted in his death in January 1717, leaving his friends with a legacy of lawsuits and keen regret. The depth of feeling and confidence between the two men is not only reflected in their letters: it is also apparent in the stipulation in Cotesworth's will that he should be buried near Liddell in Covent Garden chapel if he should die in London. In the event he died at home in Gateshead in 1725, regretting to the last 'those youthfull and vigorous days I spent in the services of my friend'.

Note on the Editing

In general the editing has been governed by the principle of doing as little violence to the original as possible, while presenting a readable text. All the letters are published *in extenso* except that Liddell's usual forms of opening and concluding complements are omitted after their pattern has been established. The original spelling has been retained throughout, except that certain common abbreviations (e.g. wt for what, ys for this) have been expanded. Where it has been necessary for the editor to intervene to expand other abbreviations or to supply interpretation, these additions are placed in square brackets. Intrusive capitals have been reduced to lower case and '£' before a figure replaces 'l' after it. Punctuation has been cautiously adapted to promote clarity and avoid the ambiguities inherent in long successions of commas. In the interests of conserving space the paragraphing of the originals has been simplified, although not dispensed with altogether. An attempt has been made to identify every person mentioned in the text: this has not always been possible but it is hoped that those referred to most frequently are covered by biographical notes in the index. In the same way, the most commonly-used technical terms are identified in the the text and explained in a separate glossary.

In conclusion, I would like to express my thanks to Frank Manders, who first drew my attention to these letters, and to Gateshead Public Library and Newcastle University Library for permission to edit them. Janice Lidgett and Lorraine Salter also deserve high praise for their patience and the accuracy of their typing.

Joyce Ellis, Loughborough University of Technology

SUMMARY OF MAIN EVENTS FEATURED IN LETTERS

1708 Regulation formed: Cotesworth nominated principal
agent
Liddell Governor of Hostmen's company

1710 Liddell moves to London
First investment in salt industry: already involved in
partnership in Bensham and Brainslope collieries
Tory ascendancy: defeats in War of Spanish succession

1711 Parliamentary enquiry into the coal trade: Cotesworth to
London to defend Regulation
Liddell marries Ann Clavering
Peace preliminaries signed with France (Sept.)

1712 Purchase of Gateshead and Whickham by Alderman
Ramsay on behalf of the Regulation: beginning of
Bucksnook wayleave dispute
Proposed general wayleave bill defeated
Whigs weeded from local offices

1713 Cotesworth quarrels with Liddell over lawsuit involving
Bensham colliery: gap in letters (June-Nov.)

1714 Bucksnook case before York assizes (Mar.)
James Clavering quarrels with Cotesworth about
Clavering Stella waggonway: pulls out of Regulation
Liddell and Cotesworth begin to win Farnacres colliery
Tory ministry under internal and external attack
Death of Queen Anne: accession of George I (Aug.)
Whig ascendancy

1715 Regulation finally disintegrates
Jacobite rebellion (Sept.): Cotesworth organizing local
resistance and sending intelligence to London

1716 Renewed negotiations in Bucksnook dispute
Alderman Ramsay dies (Apr.): Cotesworth inherits estate
Liddell and Cotesworth begin to win Felling and
Gateshead Park collieries

PRINCIPAL SOURCES USED IN COMPILING
EXPLANATORY NOTES

Bean, W.W., *The Parliamentary Representation of the Six Northern Counties* (Hull, 1980)

Calendar of Treasury Books 1672-1718

Carr-Ellison (Hedgeley) MSS., Northumberland County Record Office

Clavering Letter Book, Newcastle University Library

The Correspondence of Sir James Clavering, ed. H.T. Dickinson, Surtees Society, clxxviii (1967)

Cotesworth MSS., Gateshead Public Library

Dickson, P.G.M., *The Financial Revolution in England* (1967)

Dictionary of National Biography

Ellis, J.M., *A Study of the Business Fortunes of William Cotesworth, c.1668-1726* (New York, 1981)

Ellison MSS., Gateshead Public Library

Foss, E., *A Biographical Dictionary of the Judges of England 1066-1870* (1870)

Foster, J., *Alumni Oxonienses 1500-1714 and 1715-1886* (8 vols, Oxford, 1888-1891)

Henning, B.D., *The House of Commons, 1660-1690* (History of Parliament, 3 vols, 1984)

Holmes, G.S., *British Politics in the Age of Anne* (1967)

Extracts from the Records of the Company of Hostmen of Newcastle-upon-Tyne, ed. F.W. Dendy, Surtees Society, cv (1901)

Hughes, E., *North Country Life in the Eighteenth Century* (1952)

Jacobite Letters, Newcastle University Library

The Journals of the House of Commons

Newcastle Common Council Books, Tyne and Wear Archives

The Register of Freemen of Newcastle-upon-Tyne, ed. M.H. Dodds, Newcastle Records Series, iii (1923)

Sedgwick, R.R. *The House of Commons, 1715-1754* (History of Parliament, 2 vols, 1970)

Surtees, R., *The History and Antiquities of the County Palatine of Durham* (4 vols, 1816-40)

Venn, J. and J.A., *Alumni Cantabrigienses*, part i to 1751 (6 vols, Cambridge, 1922-54)

Sunday night [1708/9]

Dear Will[iam], I have never been tollerably well since my Tanfield journey, but I dont attribute my indisposition which is more than ordnary to that, but to the violence of the weather, which falls att present, and is to come down. This obliges me to request you to add to former favors that of representing me at the Coal Office to morrow, where the Mayor [Robert Fenwick]'s case is to be debated. I will if he reckons a favor allow him not exceeding 70 *tens, to be taken off when we have no throng [of business] and no otherwise. On this account you may alledge that in case of necessary *mixtures from others, the Office must spare us as much as they can etc., which I leave to you. If Tom Allen be taken in [as a *fitter], the sallery must not be near so great as formerly mention'd.[1] These and all other things I leave to your discretion, who can manage much better than, kind friend, yours in reallity, H.L.

1. In 1708 some of the leading Tyneside coal-owners formed a cartel known variously as the Regulation, the Coal Office or the Contract, which was designed to raise prices primarily by controlling the output of their collieries and agreeing with the principal London dealers to manipulate the market. Regular meetings were held to share out sales between members' collieries, to supervise the activities of fitters and to compensate members who closed down part of their operations.

Wedensday afternoon [1708/9]

Honest Will[iam], I inclosed you last Monday my father's [letter] by John Wattson which I hope you have answer'd [in] those parts which I could say nothing too. I have rec[eived] 17 doz[en] of bottles, part of the hogsh[ead] of lost clarett; your cooper tells Hugh [Ridley] there remains but 5 odd bottles. I am affraid that man abuses both you and me. The wine is hugely improved so that it would vex me to loose att least 3 doz[en]. I have att last gott Jos[eph] Blaky's computation of profitt for Bensh[am colliery] next year which am[ounts] to £117 and no more. This I believe is true. He computes 770 delivering *tens to be wrought att Bensham out of which this £117 profitt will arise, with 100 tens *pan coal. The other 400 tens are to be wrought out [of] Whitefield but I am ag[ainst] that, choosing rather to *lye in that part and recieve off the Office £400 [compensation] for as many tens, provided Mr Rogers will agree to itt. 'Tis I am sure his interest as well as that of the Office. I am sorry you could not conclude att your last meeting. Herin inclose for your perusall my uncle [Robert]'s which you will return, and when you see Poyen acquaint him with the contents. My legs are so inflamed since my last journey that I am extreemly uneasy; the last night I never slept till 5 in the morn[ing] and then very disturb'd. I have not bin so much out of ord[er] a great while, which obliges me to rules and avoiding company. I am ....

3

July 29th [1]710

Dear friend, on Wednesday 7 night[s ago] in the evening I was taken with a shivering cold fitt, which obliged me to hasten to a warm bed. I added a blankett to my number, but after 1½ [hours] sleep I waken'd in a fire, which lasted all that night. The next day I was invited [to be] bearer to my cosen [Thomas] Liddell's mother in law, but finding my illness increase, sent back my tickett, and desired they would pitch upon another. In short they had no time to provide, so it fell to Sign[or's] lott to supply my place. The d[octor] pronounces me in a strong feavor; this confin'd me 6 days to bed and has so weaken'd me, and my head is so light that I can scarce use a pen, further than to tell you I had your last. Lord Presid[ent Somers] is perfectly well appriz'd of our case.[1] Lord Ch[ancellor Cowper] has bin dangerously ill of the strangury for many days, and is this [day] gon into the countrey for a little relief from business, as well as benefitt of air. As to the overstocking the river [with coal, that] is a danger that may divide us among our selvs; but as soon as the *keelmen are gott again quietly to work, then will be the time to lessen [production] when no apprehension can be of their joining [another strike]. By the Cap[tain] I percieve we have but 3 *ship coal pits going, and that is but what the worst of years will carry off. You will consider well before you lower, and not to do it unless of utmost necessity. You have not sent the paper of Sunderland['s coal] price to the Master [of the

Rolls, Sir John Trevor], and the comparison with ours. You may depend there was (upon the hearing att Councell) an order given for one regim[ent] or more to be sent to the town [Newcastle]'s assistance. Your method of treating with Capt[ain] Scott was perfectly right, and much more may be compass't with fair than foul means. We shall hear by to morrow's post how they fettled to their work. We hang an arse yet [*i.e.* hesitate] as to the purchase. Money indeed is very hard to be come by, and times ticklish.[2] Nothing can be don with the Towlers while D[avid] D[ixon] is concernd. Indeed I can't advise your going much further than £30 a year for Jemmy [Clavering]'s exp[enses] least as Lady Ann says the whole should be scrupled, but for this present year he is att liberty to bring in as he pleases.[3] I hope Trumball will stand steady to you; I find G[eorge] V[ane] does not care for renewing his [lease] with Lord W[iddrington] since the sis[ters] will first be p[aid] their dem[ands] out of the coal mine [Stella Grand Lease]. There is no prospect of my coming into the countrey shortly, att soonest will be next spring. Lett your age be what it will, your aptness to business will not I dare say fail you. It should not att least till you have bred up a good apprentice. A dissolut[ion] is talked off as if to be next Sep[tember].[4] This balks my father's fancy chiefly as to the 2 mannors. I have communicated your opinion of this matter to her [Ann Clavering?], and she is perfectly for itt, and hath spoke off it ofter than once. I have writt till my head is runing round, so am obliged to dropp my pen, and hasten to bed, which is the only place that is fitt for me. I am with all sincerity in all circumstances, your most aff[ectionate] friend, Gov[ernor].[5]

1. The Regulation escaped official notice until June 1710, when Tyneside keelmen went on strike and presented a petition to the Queen in Council protesting against the restriction of their employment. A committee of the Privy Council examined their complaints and called the coal-owners to defend themselves: it was clear that the cartel would soon have to face a major attack in Parliament or the courts.

2. The lease of the manors of Gateshead and Whickham on the south bank of the Tyne, together with the freehold of Newsham in Yorkshire, was being sold by order of the court of Chancery on behalf of the creditors of the current lessee, Francis Bassett. Cotesworth and the Liddells were interested in using the lease to regulate the amount of coal coming onto the market from the new 'western' collieries opening up around the river

Derwent. Negotiations proved protracted because the uncertain political
situation raised interest rates and discouraged investment in illiquid assets.

3.   Ann and James Clavering acted as trustees for their young relative John
      Clavering of Chopwell, and their management of the collieries known
      collectively as Clavering Stella was closely supervised by the court of
      Chancery.

4.   A dissolution did indeed take place on 28 September but Sir Henry Liddell
      chose not to stand again for Newcastle, which he had represented since
      1700.

5.   Henry Liddell became governor of the Hostmen's company of Newcastle
      in 1708 and retained the title among his friends for the rest of his life. Such
      nicknames were common in the Liddells' circle; thus George Liddell was
      often called the Captain, while James Clavering was the Vaudois and
      Cotesworth was Mr Mayor of Gateshead.

                                    4

Aug[ust] 15th [1]710

   Kind friend, I have yours of the 8th and 10th are with me. Am
sorry no better success attended your own tryall, tho' the fine
was very inconsiderable. However you have this happiness of
being reconciled to the lady [Elizabeth Bowes], whose favor you
don't a little value for the sake of her husband.[1] The spiriting
away of a jury man is a practice I never so much as heard of
before. My father had most of your letters during my illness and
answer'd them. As to the contents I then gave him my opinion
as well as I could so that discoursing him upon those heads will I
believe be suffic[ient]. No wonder that endeavours should be
used to present the Contractors; we have friends enough in your
town to putt the judge upon such a project, had he no orders
from court. I am and always was of opinion that a bank of £500
should be raised and kept for extraordinary uses. I proposed it
before I came out of the countrey but no notice was taken of itt.
Nay when I came to town I mention'd it to young Wortley who
seemed to approve. I can't imagin the reason why the last year's
*groats are not yet collected. Are they affraid of trusting itt?
Sure a safe hand might be found out to lodge itt in. Indeed I
apprehend as I formerly wrote and of late to Mr Poyen, that
the consequences of not keeping touch with the dealers would
prove very dangerous and occasion such a confusion as would

shake the agreem[ent] more than all other artifices that our enemys could practice. I design for the Gate to morrow to see if I can stopp their mouths by fair promises, but I doubt I shall not succeed since they are a sort of people that will not be fed with words only. 'Tis worth the consideration of the Five and that speedily too, therfore I desire you will earnestly recommend that matter to them.[2] I think you have assessed Jemmy's allowance very moderately and what no body can object against. Certain it is that now he must be att a greater expence, considering the disposition of the trade, and this I have not failed inculcate when ever had a proper opportunity. My feavor hangs still upon me and preys upon my spirits. I don't indulge itt for I go abroad 3 hours every day into the air. I have no news to send you. I am intirely....

To Mr. Will[iam] Cotesworth, to be sent by the postm[aster] of Durham.[3]

1. At an early stage in his career, Cotesworth had been employed as an agent by Sir William Bowes. His relationship with the family later became less cordial, as this court case suggests, and he was accused of having been a 'menial servant'.

2. The arrangements and operations of the Regulation were supervised by local representatives of its most influential members, known as the Five or the Gentlemen: George Liddell, John Ord, James Clavering, Matthew White and John Wilkinson. Cotesworth kept the minutes of their meetings.

3. The inconvenience of collecting letters from Durham was outweighed by the trustworthiness of the postmaster, who was a dependent of Sir Henry Liddell. The Newcastle postmaster, John Bell, supplied information to Robert Harley and the Liddell interest made several attempts to eject him from his official positions.

5

Lond[on October] 28th [1]710

You were resolved not to putt me to a sixpenny [postal] charge whilst att Bath, but you might be assured I should not have scrupled any for such favors from you. I am now safe return'd but in no better plight of health than when I went; I have a continued cold pain that settles about my kidneys and allows me no rest night or day, but especially against change of weather it is not to be bore. This induces me readily to comply with any prescription, be itt never so troublesome; and God knows if ever I shall see the end. I must submitt tho' the burthen be never so great. I was extreemly concern'd at poor Will[iam] H[eslop's?] death; the loss was great to the publick and no less to the private concerns of his family. Pray how doe you hear he has left matters? I have seen a letter to Sign[or] which gives but a melancholly account. Whatever you write shall be kept secrett. In relation to trade, I am vext you should have so great a stock a fore hand of a commodity that will grow so much worse by lying and not a little concern'd to hear from you that the Moorgate seam should prove so ordinary. I must confess I suspected that all the new pickings would prove such for they were formerly left by some extraordinary extremitys, such as *dykes, and there I am sure the coal can't be good. Both masters, dealors, and consumers exclaim heavily and will not on any terms touch them. I wrote last post my sentiments to Jemmy to be communicated to you and wish for your improvem[ent] on them. No private advance of *praemium will doe if the coal will not in it self answer the markett. As the year went I doubted not your meeting with considerable rubbs in your own private *vend, yet all things consider'd you are come off with neighbour fare, and what by experience you find amiss in this year's proceeding you will mend in the next. You will continue to keep dunning the salt owners that are in arrear; they will bear itt and doe expect itt. As the demand is great for salt, they will be in time enabled to give you a large supply. One would be apt to think now that *carriage is laid off and the *pans like to goe till Christmas, that those sort of coals should naturally advance in price, but that you can best judge off.[1] Char[les] S[anderson] is transacting what he thinks necessary in relation to the mannors. I see him 2 days agoe and tells me that he now doubts if £6000 will carry them. I think 'tis the full price or rather more considering that since the last bidding, part of the [lease's] term is expiring. On another hand the ticklishness of the times ought to be weighed as also the indifferent title to Nusam [*i.e.* Newsham] estate. Manlove talks of raising to some thousands more than the above mention'd summ. Your thoughts pray on these severall heads. I am in trouble about poor Jemmy N[icholson's] bad success and that he should loose it by so great a majority. Did his friends stand true to him to the last? For your part I know how much you value the censure of the c[hurch].² Pray what is become of Daniell? I have not heard from him almost these 3 months and tho' I wrote to him from Bath, yet it produced nothing but silence. Pray give me a particular account of your election when over. I shall long to know how it has gon and how the generality of the magistrates menaged on that occasion. Here are no times for news.

P.S. Att long run I have rec[eived] a letter from Daniell with the inclosed vend of the river till the 30th Sep[tember] last. Shortly will be sent down the late order in Chancery for working Whitefield. You will remark that we are to keep the account of disbursm[ents] and neat produce of that colliery distinct from all others. You will consider if it would not be proper that Mr Barns should write to Mr Cole that he can procure his lord [the Duke of Newcastle] a tenant for what remains of Hedley Fell, and that if not accepted of now it must lye for ever, by reason our *branch from Chopwell must shortly be pull'd up, after we have gott the small quant[ity] of coals and lead taken away. I wish 'twixt this and [Christ]mas you would when at leisure draw out an account of moneys rec[eived] and [the] produce of any of the collierys. My head is very giddy and warns me to conclude being with sincerity....

1. The conjunction of salt water from the Tyne estuary, coal from the mines further upstream, and convenient river and sea transport had produced an extensive salt industry at North and South Shields. It was the largest concentration of salt-works in Britain and made over 10,000 tons of salt a year. Coal-owners found the salt-pans a particularly useful market for poor quality coal. This letter also demonstrates the seasonal nature of Tyneside's industrial activity.

2. In the election for Durham city, where the influence of the church was naturally strong, the Whig candidate James Nicholson (who had voted for the impeachment of Dr Sacheverell) was defeated by two high church Tories, Thomas Conyers and Sir Henry Belasis. The result reflected a national trend and not simply the peculiar electoral conditions of Durham.

6

[November] 10th [1]710

I have yours of the 3rd before me. It would be absurd to repeat what you know to be true, that your letters are as wellcome as any bodys. I thank you for your complim[ents] and must assure you that my distemper does so load my head that I am unfitt for any conversation, and that a garrett or a dark room would be the properest place for me, by which means I should be only burthensome to my self while my friends happily escape. As to my return into the countrey 'tis uncertain when; it depends on the d[octor's] success, but this I will venture to say that the satisfaction I always found and still propose in your conversation is what proves a great temptation to me. I thank you for your exact account of the proceedings att Newc[astle] during the days of battle. I am not surpriz'd att the rude menagem[ent]; it would have been a greater [surprise] had it bin otherwise, for tho' we be att the tail of the kingdom yet we follow the fashions of our metropolis. I can't but rejoice that my father had the good fortune to decline, for the insults would have fallen thickest upon his head. If one may be allowed to doe justice to our good cousen Mr M[ayo]r [William Ellison], he has not acted the cleverest nor genteelest part in this tryall of skill. What could induce him to desert his relation?[1] Well honest Will[iam] there is nothing like fair dealing above board; I can't forget Percivall's words which he writt when my father desired to see what sort of a hand he wrote, they were these, *Honesty is the best pollicy*. The man was certainly in the right, for that will carry him hansomly off the stage. By last post I hear you have two vacancys in the gown [*i.e.* among Newcastle aldermen] one by death, the other by voluntary resignation: will not the filling up of these put that great and powerfull body into a new ferment. Will it not be apt to divide bro[ther] against bro[ther]?[2] Tho' thunder be very terrible while it lasts, yet itts advantages are afterwards felt by the purifying of the air and none knows what good may be produced by our intestin divisions. Providence governs the world and to its divine decrees we must submitt.

You must not be surpriz'd att our proceedings about the [Gateshead and Whickham] mannors; I had a path chalked out to me to be pursued and that I have don. From the very first I wrote word that I was willing to come into the menagem[ent], as far as I was able: I was order'd to take Mr F[reke]'s advice and follow itt, which I did. He desired to know how the money could be raised for now on the best land security none can be had, creditt is so sunk. My father would have bin disappointed of half the summ that a gentleman promised to lett lye in his hands had he bin the purchaser. You see times look but with a sullen prospect; in short if you should see the directions given me you would say I had acted only a part that was unavoidable.[3] It is supposed that before the confirmation [of the sale] Manlove will appear and bid more than has bin already, which will lengthen the time to another term and then my father will be up to give his personall directions. If the news of the 3d victory in Spain come amply confirm'd it will mightily revive our spirits; there is a great probability and I know no tydings would be more acceptable to you.[4] When you have discoursed Weatherly on the operations for the next year you will lett me know; what ever you doe, contrive to work good coals. Pray my humble service to Mr Barnes and tell him that I have made particular enquiry after a place for his daughter, but can find none fitt for his purpose and a publick school I know he would avoid. I still employ one to make further enquiry, and if she can find out what is required he shall certainly hear from me. I doubt not your care in taking acquitt[als] in full when ever you make any paym[ents] to your landlords. This must be don. Pray in what condition is the High Fellon [colliery] in att present and how stand Mr Trumball's concerns? A little information of these and such like matters may be use to ....

1. In the Newcastle election, the Tory candidates Sir William Blackett and William Wrightson easily defeated the sitting member William Carr, who had represented the town since 1690. The mayor was Carr's and Liddell's cousin but put the ties of party before those of kinship. Polling took two days and was hotly contested, the Tories using Sacheverell's portrait as a standard and 'Queen and Church' as their motto.

2. Vacancies were created during the civic year 1710-11 by the deaths of Nicholas Ridley and Robert Eden, who were replaced by Richard Ridley and Henry Reay. A system of co-option ensured that power in the town remained in the hands of an oligarchy drawn from a wealthy mercantile elite, united by business and family ties but divided on political issues, as the 1710 election demonstrated.

3.   Henry Liddell was in the difficult position of managing the affairs of the
     Liddell family and those of the Claverings of Chopwell as well as his own
     private estate. He was therefore liable to accusations that he favoured one
     or more of these interests above the rest and had to behave with great
     caution. In this case he was hampered by the collapse of business
     confidence and scramble for liquidity that accompanied the Tory election
     victory.

4.   The Whigs were disheartened by the fall of their ministry in August and
     their crushing defeat in the subsequent general election but their spirits
     were raised by news of Stanhope's victories at Almenara in July and
     Saragossa in August. Liddell's report of a third victory was mistaken.

7

[November] 21th [1]710

Yours of the 11th inst is now before me. The Vaudois had
given us an account of the disappointm[ent] in the Misses
[Claverings'] journey; as it can't be helpt we must have patience
till the spring when both roads and weather will be more
seasonable. You were very kind in affording my father your
company so long; that alone were sufficient to ease, att least
make him forgett his complaints. Sign[or] went yesterday for
Stamford whence he is to conduct him up and on Saturday
barring accidents we expect him here. Itt was not amiss that you
took notice of my being concern'd with you and I hope he took
itt well to be informed.[1] The *pan coal seams are really not
worth your search after, and yet to make the *ship more
markatable you must convert part to that use, but the less the
better; and depend on't unless your coal be right good, I doubt
no interest you can make att this markett will be able to carry
them off. Since my former to you, Mr Manlove and Bassett
have bin bidding against one another and at present the first
seems to stand fairest for the purchase, att £6400. My father will
be here sometime before that is concluded so that he will have
time to consider, but assure yourself that as circumstances both
publick and private stand att present, I can scarce believe he will
ingage. However I shall not fail to putt him [in] mind and if any
way feasible shall promote it to the utmost. The number of
*keels you propose will be sufficient but how to menage the men
is a difficulty; is it that the generality of them have combin'd not
to enter into bond and what pretence have they for so doing?

You will act as others doe under the same circumstances. Can't the Hoastman's company frame a severe law that no *fitter shall employ his neighb[our's] keels on any other pretence than by leave of the chief owner [of that colliery]? I think ther is such an order but I mean whether can't it be made more effectuall?[2] Your press affords nothing but choice ware; I had a ballad since sent me and very orthodox it is. That of yours plainly tends to the keeping up of a turbulent spirit among the poor thoughtless crew, whilst no reall advantage seems to be designed them. I wish some people may not have a different view.[3] Jemmy in his to Lady Ann only tells the results of your meeting, that Weather hill ought to be sett on without loss of time, but as to the circumstances of that concern we are perfect strangers; you will be pleased to oblige me with the particulars. And pray enquire of the Vaudois how the lease that his father and Dav[id] Dixon had of [Lord] Widdrington stands, I mean in relation to the latter whether his *part be anyways ingaged or assigned, and what he thinks the reall value of that interest may be worth? I mention this because in all probability Dix[on] will offer it [as] a security for the money he had belonging to the Infant. It seems highly reasonable that the indifferent coals, belong to whom they will, should be *mixed off with the better sort belonging to that proprietor and that another should not hazard his reputation for this man's service. When I write shall mention to the Capt[ain] the taking notice of the generall *viewer and pray desire Jemmy Clav[ering] from me to doe the like. Your m[istress] as you term her is intirely pleased with your conduct in her concern and doubts not your industry in propogating any thing that may have a tendancy of advantage in regard to itt. I have don with news. This weather keeps me low and under the hatches but I think in the main I am not so bad as I used to be. If my health should continue to improve, you may expect to see me next spring. I long for an occasion on those terms....

[P.S.] I wrote to Mr Barnes last week having found out a place for fixing his daughter. My service to him. I have redd over Jemmy's to Lady Ann about Weatherhill; he does not mention in what condition that colliery is but that you design to proceed to work her if D[avid] D[ixon] being a partner should not be an obstruction. You must know 'tis none, so we wish you to follow the ord[er] of court and success attend.

1.   Liddell and Cotesworth had gone into partnership to work the upper
     seams of Bensham colliery and Liddell was apprehensive about his father's
     reaction.

2.   The charter granted to Newcastle in 1600 gave the Hostmen's company a
     monopoly over the coal trade, thus enabling it to regulate trading practices
     on the Tyne. By the early eighteenth century this control was beginning to
     break down but it had not disappeared entirely.

3.   The keelmen had set up their own hospital and relief organization in 1699,
     only to have control wrested from them by the Hostmen's company as
     soon as its potential as a strike fund was realized. Their determined
     rearguard action was aided by a press campaign which gave the coal-
     owners' cartel unwelcome publicity.

8

Dec[ember] 4th [1]710

Since my last to you I have seen Cha[rles] Sanderson, who
tells me that Mr Manlove's goldsmith has bid £7000 for the
mannors etc. but is backward in filing the report; that Jackson
designs to move the court to oblige him to file itt and pay part of
his money as usuall in those cases. This goldsmith, the person
that has bid, is a man of little or no substance and Cha[rles]
thinks that he will be obliged to drop itt att last. Nay in all
probability your friends may take the bargain off his hands in
case they approve of itt, for he will never be able to go thro' with
it, and before all parties be brought to consent (which must be
first obtain'd) much time will be spent, att least a twelve-month.
So that if you have any thoughts, if you will either write to me or
Cha[rles] (but he will be the properest to satisfye any scruples or
clear objections) he promises to doe all the service he is capable
off. The summ that is generally paid into court on this and the
like occasions is about £400 or £500 in the nature of earnest and
to satisfye the court that the party dos design to proceed. The
two objections you raised in your last are the chief that can
affect the contractors. I shew'd my uncle [Robert] your letter,
but as he was going out of town we had not an opportunity of
seeing the originall. When that is don I shall press a resolution
and I believe it will be thought convenient to cancell itt [the
Regulation], for in effect if the dealors should make a breach I
don't see that the owners ever durst venture to sue their

covenant, least it be thought an illegall one and then it turns upon themselvs. If the partys could be brought to lessen their numbers of waggons as also their winter works, it would effectually remedy the complaints under which the trade groan'd this last year and this may be don without any exception. The abate[ment] of *keels will likewise contribute to make matters go more glibly in severall respects. 'Tis to be hoped that by your prudent menagem[ent] below [on Tyneside], the keelmen will be brought to reason and see what is their true interest, which I take to be the joining in with their owners and endeavoring to serve their interests with zeal. Had you any discourse with Dan[iel] D[ef]oe when in the countrey? What sort off spiritt possesses that man, who seems by the print of which he is suspected to be the author to encourage modestly speaking a refractoriness among that sort of people?[1] Pray will you putt the Gentlemen in mind of providing against the evill day by remitting a convenient summ to be lodged in any hand they think fitt. The sooner this is don the better for we don't know how soon we may be attack'd. Be pleased to acquaint the Capt[ain] that the *bill of forty pounds he *return'd me before I went to Bath from Starkin is not yet paid; the person on whom it is drawn has but twenty pounds of the master's in his hands and will not disburse a farthing for him. Lett the Capt[ain] discourse Starkin about itt. I mention'd thus much to him some posts agoe but now the party is positive he will pay no more than he has effects for, which is as above.[2] I am heartily glad J[ohn] Johnson is like to doe well again. This rainy weather accompanyed with storms of wind little inferior to the great one has much disturb'd my corporation.

P.S. Dec[ember] 5th. Last night I had one from you and another from the Capt[ain] who tells me he has spoke to Starkin. Wortley is not yet come to town but I must tell you unless that money for the menagem[ent] be not remitted speedily, I believe you will find the two gentlemen [the Wortleys] very backward in pursuing the cause. Pray therfore press a supply without loss of time. I shall acquaint Mrs Clav[ering] that you design to furnish the markett with choice coals this next year. I heartily rejoice that you have defeated Sir J[ohn] Clavering] etc. but am concern'd poor Marly should be dismissed, since his crime can be no other than an intimacy with Rav[ensworth].[3] If any post should offer that may be fitt for him, you will have him in view. Adieu I am in hast .... I should be glad of your tittle tattle; it would entertain us extreemly att a time when publick news is not so gratefull.

1. Defoe visited Newcastle on several occasions and spent some time there in 1710 on an intelligence mission for Robert Harley. He became a vigorous champion of the keelmen's grievances in his paper *The Review*, highlighting the inequity of placing control of their relief fund in the hands of their employers and attacking the Regulation.

2. The coal trade was largely conducted on credit. Shipmasters paid *fitters for coal with bills of exchange or other credit instruments drawn on one of their own creditors, and the bills were then dispatched to the coal-owners for collection or further circulation.

3. Sir John Clavering and his associates were attempting to frustrate the efforts of Cotesworth and the Liddells to restrict mining operations in the Derwent valley. The dispute dragged on for decades and its progress can be followed in this correspondence.

9

London Dec[ember] 9th [1]710

This day I have bin to wait on the two Mr Wortlys with both yours. My father would have accompany'd me but has bin a housekeeper since Thursday, being confin'd by his usuall illness, and indeed I can't but say by fitts he is worse than ever. After those gentlemen had perused yours they proposed severall able practitioners for counsell, but as they design to wait upon my father the beginning of next week they postpon'd fixing on any till that time, but as to a sollicitor all sides agree that Charles Sanderson is the properest person. When they have come to a resolution upon their meeting you shall have the result. In the next place I must inform you that yesterday Mr Manlove came hither along with his sollicitor; told us that he had bid £7000 for the two mann[ors] and Nusam, that Jackson presst hard for his filing the report, that for a very small advance my father should be wellcome to the purchase. We could give him but little encouragem[ent], save if we could hear of a proper chapman [*i.e.* buyer] would recommend him to treat with him. This pleased him and as he went off he said he did not care if he left his money in the party's hands for some time, nay perhaps might accommodate by seperating Nusam from the 2 mann[ors]. Now friend, if those you lately mention'd to me think of treating, they would do well to bestir themselvs without loss of time and Cha[rles] Sanderson would certainly be as proper an agent as any they can employ. Who is it that succeeds Brummell in the menagem[ent] of Stella? As to ours [Clavering Stella], pray lett care be taken to supply the spring trade with a flower; and that they may continue in tollerable perfection [in] the summer season, as little should be winter wrought as possible, but more especially at Coalburns where you know the weather does influence for the worse.[1] You will contrive matters best by consulting with the *operators how to bring matters to bear. We were strangely allarm'd this last post by a letter as is said from your town to Mr Wr[ightso]n, giving an account of an infectious distemper with you, brought over by a Dantzick vessell. Pray is there any grounds for that report? I have had severall people this day with me to know the truth.[2] Whatever novells your countrey affords, the communicating of itt [by] so good a hand as yours will be very acceptable to....

1 The coal trade was still predominantly seasonal, with fewer ships operating on the dangerous east coast during the winter months and less mining being carried on.

2. Plague was spreading across Europe in the wake of the war of Spanish Succession, giving rise to fears that it would cross to England and leading to the passage of a Quarantine Act (9 Anne c2). This particular report seems to have been malicious and on 18 December the Common Council of Newcastle ordered a certificate to that effect to be sent to the Lord Mayor of London, the *London Gazette* and other newspapers.

10

Dec[ember] 16th [1]710

I am [twice] in my good friend's debt, who loads me so with obligations that I must never gett out of itt. You may be assured I have acted to the stretch of my commission in the case of the mannors and further I could not goe; I found it would not doe, and it was folly for me to persist where no prospect of success. I shall recommend to Mr Manlove your capacity of serving him by way of menagem[ent] preferable to any other. I have

acquainted your m[istress] with the state of D[avid] Dixon's
case, who is obliged to you for itt, as also for your kind
remembrance of her. I believe this afternoon she and I shall
have a consult how to engage the Oldn[ers] more effectually in
our interest this next year. I am sensible something of that
nature must be don or otherwise your endeavors in the countrey
will be vain and fruitless.[1] You did well in writing to Cha[rles]
Sanderson; we shall be assisting to him what we can. This
morn[ing] I sent Hugh to the carrier's, who returns with a noble
pott of charrs [*i.e.* hill trout] without the least damage. He is
extreemly obliged to you for them and [it] is the most acceptable
of any thing to him; he desires you to accept of his best thanks
by my pen till such times as he can doe itt himself. You say they
are not good meat for batchelors; may be so, but if they chance
to come in my way I shall have no regard to that. I have
communicated to my father the Fenham proposalls. He thinks
that since 'tis to be in partnership with Wortleys, you would doe
well to start such a thing att a distance to J[ohn] Ord, for if we
should doe it here to them they must recieve instructions from
the countrey and will be guided accordingly; therfore I think
there can be no harm if you should feel Ord's pulse. I should be
extreemly sorry that the Recorder [Douglas] and Mr Procter
should compass their ends. I shall long to hear if F[rank]
B[aker] make a discovery of their secrett. Upon what grounds is
itt that Sir J[ohn Clavering] refuses to pay in his *groats? Does
he complain of falling short of his *quantity or what is the
matter? If it be that he thinks himself att liberty, much good
may itt doe him. Bromell if he *fitts for him can't think of being
concern'd in the Regulation. As you remark, in all probability
Will Harrison's business will devolve upon R[obert] Fenw[ick]
and if so how can he act in the Contract, unless he will make
himself one person and his man another, to act in two
capacitys?[2] Bowman has bin here twice offering of his service;
doe you think it safe to trust him when an officer of your own
appointing reckons with his masters, or can be he of use to the
Contract, or of what disservice if he be left att liberty to shift for
himself? Your thoughts as full on this head will be very
acceptable to my father by the return of the post, for he is prest
to give an answer. I could readily guess att the enemys to
Chowden in your liberty [Gateshead] and doubted not your
maugh's [*i.e.* brother-in-law] zeal in that affair. For my part I

don't apprehend any thing prejudiciall can be don either by the lord [of the manor] or your neighbors [Newcastle]. Trouble and disturbance they may give.[3] By last post I wrote to the Capt[ain] and as J[ohn] Carr has the menagem[ent] of Stella, I should think the *pan coal workers might be easily brought to an understanding both as to price and quantity, which could not be while Brummell was concern'd. Success attend your undertakings. I am....

1. Only the chief dealers could prevent inferior collieries being driven off the market and unless they supported a colliery the coal-owners' efforts to improve the quality of the coal and the management were useless. It was therefore vital to secure an "interest at the Gate" with one or more of these dealers.

2. The Regulation controlled only two-thirds of the coal sold on Tyneside and, as Liddell's comments suggest, the presence of collieries operating outside the cartel made its provisions much more difficult to enforce and encouraged existing members to leave.

3. The deliberate obscurity of this passage is, as so often in the letters, a precaution against their falling into unfriendly hands. In this case it was felt necessary to conceal the moves being made by William Ramsay, Cotesworth's brother-in-law, to acquire the lease of Gateshead and Whickham, because his connection with the Regulation and the Liddells was too well known. Chowden or Chowdene lay on the eastern border of the Liddell's manor of Ravensworth but was claimed by the Bishop of Durham for his manor of Gateshead.

11

Dec[ember] 21st [1]710

'Tis a pleasure to have the account under your hand that the report of the plague att Newc[astle] is groundless: in all probability the first rise of this must have proceeded from the spring yours suspects. God be thankt for itt. Jos[eph] Blakiston sends me the particulars of the All Hallows' parish for the last year as well as this, and by itt there appears in six weeks time that this year has increased only five in the burialls in the like time, and that is nothing.[1] I think our divisions att home are a sort of plague, which I wish may not prove 'ere long to be of the worst consequence. Considering the goodness of your *carriage I should have guest your *steath would have *made out att least 15 [*chaldrons], take *ship and *pan [coal] together. But in all probability your steathman has bin obliged to humor or rather court the trade by giving better *measure than usuall. Your presence frequently and inspection of the workings even during the winter will be a check upon your *operator Ant[ony] Pattison and keep him to his duty. Your project of making salt for Mrs Milburn att a price certain ought to be well weighed, but particular regard must be had to ingage an honest person to inspect who has understanding in those matters; and first of all let the pans be *viewed that they be in good repair, and kept so, otherwise a much greater quantity of coals will be required for the making of the same quantity of salt. By this means you will be able to dispose of all your pan coal without being obliged to any of those gentlemen of Shields.[2] You can't doe better than ingage G[eorge] Iley's servant in your service; he must needs have a very good acquaintance among masters and may readily deserve the sallary yours mentions, therfore slip him not. Manlove begins to grow sick of his bargain and upon Bassett's counsell alledging that Manlove's goldsmith, who bid for the mannors, was a bankrupt, they have sett him aside as I hear, and so Bassett remains the best bidder; but I suppose Cha[rles Sanderson] will give you the best account of itt. My father had a letter last post from Ra[lph] Brandling, informing that he had satisfied both you and the Capt[ain] of his demands on Mark Riddle's share of Bensham and had sent a copy of the deed Mark executed in October last to Mr Hebdon. He says there is £350 and above in arrear. He tells me you assured him that Brandling had no real claim, so desires you will give him what information you can of your own or that Hebdon or Jo[seph] Barnes can help you to, that from thence he may frame an answer accordingly. Brandling presses to know if the arrears will be forthwith paid or the reason why they are detain'd. You may send for Blaky if [you have] occasion to know what is due to Mark.[3] Your care in this will much oblige my father, who continues by fitts very much out of order. The dealors have bin with uncle and me and are dissatisfyed that the *notes promised to be given them last Mich[aelmas] are not yet come. They desire the Gentlemen would take into consideration the last letter they wrote to Mr Poyen, so as they may have an answer to their demands one way or other. This must be don or I shall have no peace. Lett the answer be sent to some of their body.[4] Poor Lady Ann has gott a deflusion of rhume upon one side of her face which obliges her to keep house; indeed this uncertain weather tryes all constitutions as well as that of .....

1. Burial figures from the more populous urban parishes were frequently used in this way to measure the incidence of disease and were sometimes published to warn prosperous citizens of the onset of epidemics.

2. As this letter suggests, Cotesworth became involved in the salt industry to provide a dependable outlet for poor quality coal, but his ambitions soon transcended his original object and within ten years he had become the largest single manufacturer in the north-east.

3 The coal industry was bedevilled by the sub-division of mineral rights which could result in proprietors completely losing trace of their landlords or even of their nominal partners and becoming involved in lawsuits for non-payment of rent. The Bensham case reached the court of Chancery in 1713.

4. The Regulation's directors believed that the dealers had failed to push the sale of its coal on the London market and therefore withheld the payments which had been promised to them for their assistance. Liddell feared that this would provoke the dealers to encourage an official attack on the cartel; hence his anxiety about 'our divisions at home'.

12

Dec[ember] 23th [1]710

In answer to yours by yesterday's post, you have fully satisfied us, so that we shall give Bowman liberty to provide for himself and we must depend upon our own and Clav[ering] Stella *fitters to help off with Bensh[am] coals; and if any further assistance be needful, the Chamber must lend itt when requir'd. Itt must have bin the largeness off *measure that contributed to the greatness of his *vend, more than his menagem[ent] att the Gate. As the [coal] fleet is now arriv'd in the river and the weather very open, I believe the price of coals will not exceed 30s the best, which is no great incouragem[ent]. And in all probability there is more stock than will serve the consumption, especially since Candlemas, the time of your north countreymen's fitting out [their ships] draws near, so that I do apprehend that tho' next year's trade may be pretty brisk in the main, yet not very incouraging to the masters. Wherfore unless Enoch Hudson's coals be good in nature, round and in no great quantity, I would not advise your medling with them on any score, for you may depend on't, unless the commodity be choice in the above mention'd respects, you will never be able to make an interest att the Gate that will carry them off. They [the dealers] may indeed promise you and will expect performance from you, but you are to hope for little from them. My father is sorry he can't oblige Mr Rogers in the acceptance of his recommendation, he being ingaged elsewhere severall weeks agoe, as I wrote word to George Bowes, who had join'd with his bro[ther] the D[octor] in behalf of a friend of theirs about 3 weeks agoe. Had Mr Rogers spoke early enough, I am sure my father has that regard for him as that he would not have fail'd of obliging him, but as matters are att present he can't possibly disingage. This you will be so kind as to acquaint that gentleman with, and at the same time make a tender of our humble services to him.[1]

I thought Lord B[arnard] was so much pleased with your countrey air, which was so agreable to his constitution, that he would not have entertain'd such sudden thoughts of quitting itt, but his reasons are best known to himself. The offer [of a lease?] indeed may be advantagious to Frank [Baker] but may not be of any long continuance; besides he must consider that the times are more likely to [grow] worse upon our hands rather than better, and consequently where there is little or no trade stirring the rents will infallibly fall. He has however this advantage of succeeding a landlord that gave little quarter to tenants, so that lett him be never so strict and sharp upon them, it can be no reflexion upon him. Doubtless he and his friends will weigh all circumstances before he ingages. As to Bensham my father desires Mr Rogers would appoint a proper person and the Capt[ain] another to take a *view of her jointly; after which by both their consents lett them make cosen Baker their offers off *keeping the *way and wagg[ons] and inspecting the workings, and if possible letting to him the drawing off the water either by the day, so many shifts of horses, or by the great [i.e. at a fixed price for the whole amount] (for I doe suppose the [quantity of] water is now pretty much att a certainty). Pray what ever be don lett Mr Rogers' concurrence be had and use your own discretions, to which my father leaves matters. You upon the spott must be the best judges, therfore 'tis referr'd to you to act in every respect. As to our Team waggon way you know we have improv'd itt much within these 3 years last past, by raising [the ground] where necessary and by easing of the runs as much as the situation of the ground would admitt off. I remember about that time Will[iam] Rowe offered to keep her for 14s a *tenn, but when I came to discourse him about a conclusion he flew off itt; however doe you and the Capt[ain] talk this matter with cosen Baker and see if you can article with him. I think this proposal a reasonable one: to keep the way and waggons etc. in repair att 10s a tenn in the low ground, that I call from the waggon bridge as farr as the ditch which is above the *engines, and all beyond that att 15s. I think with Frank's good menagem[ent] he may save handsomly by the year. We shall not stand with him for trifles, and shall not *lead but in cases of necessity when the weather is indifferent.[2] The Capt[ain] and you have the same power of concluding but it ought to be on that foundation, high ground and low [a] different price. We generally lead 1200 tens a year. I need not inlarge, you may guess our meaning. The fitters have taken the properest measures with the *keelmen from whence I can't but expect the desired success, and as you intimate, 'tis much better that the owners don't appear in't; there seems to be no occasion for itt. How will the town of Whit[e]haven be ever able to retrieve that prodigious loss in shipping? 'Tis a vast summ for a place that was in a manner but falling into a trade that was considerable.[3] I can't imagin why your magistrates should not have thought fitt to have made an earlier publication of their being free from that infection; had it bin att another time of the year, theyr town might have suffer'd considerably by their backwardness. When does Mr C[ar]r leave you? Were I in his circumstances I should not think it worth my while to spend so much time in a place where I had bin so indifferently treated. I percieve you made Surtis decamp in hast from the coffee house; was it not time when he found himself attack't in front and rear? Now good friend of mine do you and the Capt[ain] hasten to make the above mention'd bargains; you have full power and act as you both judge meet. I wish you success in that and all your undertakings and a merry Christmas, and remain....

[P.S.] My father is generally every other day extreemly out of order. Thise frequent returns [*i.e.* relapses] must of necessity spend nature. The d[octor] however gives hopes of relief as soon as the sun gets a little force. God grant him success.

1. Although Sir Henry Liddell was no longer an M.P., he retained a great deal of political influence and his support was valued by many people seeking official posts for themselves or their dependents. Since demand always exceeded supply, the maintenance of his interest demanded considerable tact.

2. Waggonways were still constructed of wood rather than iron and were easily damaged if heavy loads were run down them in bad weather. They were particularly vulnerable on higher ground, since the engineering problems posed by steep gradients were both difficult and expensive to solve.

3. At this time Whitehaven rivalled Liverpool as one of the fastest growing ports in the country, exploiting the coal and colonial trades to rise to a position of considerable importance. Liddell's comment suggests that its growing merchant fleet had been badly damaged in a storm.

13

Dec[ember] 30th [1]710
½ hour past 10 att night.

I was resolved not to loose any time but sent Hugh with a line to Mr Manlove, desiring he would come hither that I might discourse him about the mannors; but I found by my man that the gentleman was out of town (I mean both he and his agent, whose name is Manlove) and would not return till Monday night. The letter was left att his house so that I expect to see him on Tuesday and hope to give you some account of our transactions by that day's post. In the mean time shall send for Cha[rles] Sanderson and discourse him in the matter. My father returns you his thanks for your advice relating to Brandling, to whom he will write a line or two to the effect yours mentions. Mark [Riddell] should assign or [with] what safety can we pay anything? My father has not bin able to consult the state of the title Mr Hebdon sent him; it was packt up with other things in a box which came in but by this day's carrier, but he will take the first opportunity of consulting on that head. We both rejoice that Brommell's project is like to prove abortive. Had it succeeded, the consequences would have bin very destructive to the present trade of the river. Am sure the prevention is intirely owing to your diligence and indefatigable industry, and for which each particular [coal-owner] are indebted to you.[1] My last would give you full authority to transact with the Capt[ain] what was thought necessary to 'be don in relation to the menagement of Bensham. You have a vast of trouble daily accruing by other people's business that I can't but admire how you gett time to attend your own; but ever since I had the happiness of your friendship I always found you ready to sacrifice or att least postpone your own interest to that of your friends. We are all sensible of itt but how to make a suitable return putts us to a stand. I speak my mind freely and without complim[ent]. I must tell you that the dealors were promised that Daniel [Poyen] should give them *notes att Mich[aelmas] for the last summer's *premium; they are very uneasy and believe would gladly be att liberty. Some answer must be given by order of the Five, and till that be don we can't pretend to treat with the Oldners in private for advancing the creditt of our Stella. I should say retrieving, but that is a word that has not rellished with me for many years. Our affairs in Spain have a most dismal aspect. How subject to changes are all things under the sun. Poor Stanhop who was triumphing but a few months ago att Madrid, now a prisoner in the same place.[2] The subject is to melancholly to dwell upon. Am sure what with this news and the bad weather, my consitution suffers not a little. The bell calls and warns me to conclude. Believe me att all times the same....

1. Thomas Brumell wanted to build a waggonway from Bucksnook colliery that would carry the coal of several other 'western' concerns across Whickham common to the Tyne. Far from being deterred by the imminent sale of the manors, he obtained a *wayleave from Basset and pressed on regardless.

2. The Whigs' hopes of a successful conclusion to the Spanish campaign proved short-lived. By 27 November Madrid had been evacuated and on 9 December Stanhope was defeated and captured at Brihuega. This was the final blow to the allied cause in Spain and Stanhope himself remained a prisoner for nearly two years.

14

Jan[uary] 4th [1]710/11

Mr Manlove coming not to town till Tuesday night, I could
not gett speech to him before. I discoursed him to this effect,
that I could recommend him [someone] I thought a good
chapman [*i.e.* buyer] for the 2 mannors, and whatever should be
agreed to, he might depend upon punctuall performance. He
was not prepared to make a demand but he thought £5000
would be a reasonable one for them. I told him that if £4[000]
would doe the bargain would not be long a-striking; perhaps
£100 more might be added. This I gave as my own thoughts only
but recommended him to goe to Cha[rles] S[anderson] who was
the attorny you employ'd and he might with him talk over the
matter; he promised he would. I wrote to Cha[rles] to advise
him of itt and that he would write to you after Manlove had bin
with him. Lett the 5 doe as they think fitt but don't you meddle
with any project with Lady C[ar]r on your own score.[1] If the
dealors be not gratyfied, you will see a strange disorder att the
Gate this next year; I know they deserve little but it ought to be
well weighed what confusion they can bring the trade in. Am
glad Marly has gott so good a post. I shall readily excuse his
letter of complim[ent]. My father is not fully satisfied about
Bensh[am's] arrears. How comes there to be £30 yearly for law
charges? He desires that may be explain'd to him. I thank you
for your advice in relation to my own little concern. I shall take
an opportunity of speaking about it to my father but must watch
a time and [speak] when he is in right temper, otherwise all will
be to no purpose. If things don't goe according to your
expectation neither doe they [go] according to mine, I will assure
you. If you have a mind to be a little freer than ordinary in any
of your letters, pray direct them inclosed to Mrs Clav[ering]'s in
Bedford Row and they will come safe; others about business
direct as usuall to me in Red Ly[on] Street. I am heartily
concernd for your great loss; I this day see your man['s
bankruptcy] in the Gazette. Is there no thoughts of recovering a
good part?[2] I shall be overjoy'd to see you and the honest
councellor [Joseph Barnes] here in town. He wrote me word
sometime since he did not know but that he might come up with
his daughter in the spring, and yourself for his additionall
companion will I dare say make his journey very pleasant to

him. Now that you have gott Stella *way in good order, hope shortly to hear the same character of those coals which will be very necessary towards the keeping up a tollerable trade att that place. I am sorry to hear you are so full of grief on several accounts. I wish you eas'd of your complaints. Mine increase with this foggy nasty weather; it kills my legs and puts the whole frame much out of order. I am....

[P.S.] Shall be glad to hear of Fr[ank] Ba[ke]r's success of his journey.

1. The Regulation was anxious to bring Lady Carr's Fieldhouse colliery within the cartel. Cotesworth may have considered leasing it himself but Liddell discouraged him and the lease went to Robert Fenwick instead.

2. The financial crisis of 1710 caused a wave of business failures as confidence in the credit system collapsed. Cotesworth was caught out because his London factor supplied a large consignment of tallow on credit to a man already deeply in debt. Composition was finally settled in 1712 at 10s.3d in the £ and about £275 was lost on the deal.

15

Jan[uary] 11th [1]710/1

This must answer both yours of the 5th and that by yesterday's post. Since you only mention a projected design of electing the May[or] into the governm[ent] of our company, I conclude the old one was continued and the exchange of Swaddell for Johnson [as *fitter] is much more to my rellish than it was before.[1] I all along was of opinion that Fieldhouse would fall to Fenw[ick's] share, and the lady [Carr] is beholden to you for keeping up her price. But as the benefactor is unknown to her, she will be att a loss how to return the obligation, tho' were she privy to it yet am apt to believe she would tread in her husband's steps and reward for your good deeds as he formerly has don.[2] I hope the Regulation will not suffer much by the ald[erman Fenwick?] going into another service; they will spare an extravagant sallary by itt. I find you are like to be the chief sufferer, by parting with the fitter you proposed to have had, but in my thoughts they ought to consider some method of assisting you in your *vend att a reasonable price by way of acknowledgem[ent] for your good

services. With most people you know 'tis customary to christen
their own child first, and as the world goes I don't see why you
should not practice that rule. You would doe well to write to
some of your correspondents to treat about an interest att the
Gate without loss of time.[3] I may assure you that till matters be
settl'd for this last year's *praemium I can't pretend to discourse
them about Clav[ering] Stella. 'Tis to be own'd that coals from
severall *steaths have bin sent so very bad that it laid them under
great difficultys; however I tell them they might have kept the
prices more upon an equallity if they would have exerted
themselves, lett their pretences to the contrary be never such.
After all, 'tis worth the Gentlemen's while to consider if the
Contract can be upheld if these people be not gratifyed. Can
their opposition distress us? I am of opinion they can, and even
to a degree bring us into confusion and a breaking among our
selvs, by giving an extravagant preference in price to one or two
concerns. We must consider that we sell for 11s, that is about
9s 4d neat [i.e. net], and [it] can't be imagin'd this price can be
upheld but by our unanimous agreem[ent] among ourselvs and a
friendly correspondence with those necessary evills att the Gate.
This ought to be well weigh'd and an answer must be given the
dealors without loss of time. 'Twixt you and me, they told me
that Mr M[ontagu's] agent had promis'd that his share should
be paid them tho' others did not. Don't take direct notice of this
but by way of supposition the question may be put. I think the
dealors in strictness meritt a --- but the only quaery is if we can
subsist and keep together without their assistance.

My father approves in everything of what you have writt
concerning the future menagement of Bensh[am] and has
signified as much to the Capt[ain] by this post, whom he desires
you will assist with your advice. He thinks Jos[eph] Clark may
as well be left out and be no *undertaker but may be made
usefull as a check upon them. More needs not on this head, he
having writt word formerly that Grayson would be better outed
[i.e. dismissed] than continue, but it must be don with as good a
grace as can be. Now about the 2 mannors. Mr Sanderson was
here and designs to write to you shortly; in the mean time am to
acquaint you that this very day Mr Gibson bid anew £5000 for
them and the freehold [i.e. Newsham] and presst to be reported
the best bidder. Your agent offer'd £4000 for the mannors and
Mr Manlove att the same time £1500 for the freehold. An

argum[ent] arose for not seperating the purchase, but it was carried that they might go to the best purchaser either by the lump or distinctly. Then it was presst to have part of the money paid into court which was agreed to and time given till this day 3 weeks for making the report. Cha[rles] would be glad to know the utmost you would goe and he will menage as warily as he can; there will be bidding one above another to be sure till the very day of report, so that you may send him full instructions. He thinks £2[00] or 300 ought to be *return'd him in case he be approv'd the best purchaser, to deposit in court. And as we agree that Mr Willson's name would be the properest to be made use off, he must be writt to by the Ald[erman] to desire [him] to send an order under his hand authorizing Cha[rles] or the attorney Cha[rles] thinks fitt to employ in his behalf to act for him. You will hear further particulars shortly to which I referr and am ....

1. The election of the mayor, William Ellison, as governor of the Hostmen's company would have aided the Regulation as he was more sympathetic to the cartel than the current governor, Robert Fenwick.

2. The Regulation seems to have paid the London dealers to favour Fieldhouse coal, perhaps to encourage Lady Carr to join the cartel. Cotesworth's unpopularity with the Carrs dated from 1709 when he was assaulted upon Sir Ralph Carr's orders during a *wayleave dispute.

3. Cotesworth had used his London factor in this way in 1710 but the task proved to be too arduous and unrewarding for an amateur.

17

Jan[uary] 27th [1]710/1

By the last post you would have a short one from me with an addition from Charles; since which he has bin with me, and as Wednesday will be the last day allowed by the court for bidding, I have given him his full powers after having consulted my father, to this effect viz: to try to bring Manlove for the freehold to £2500 att least and not to exceed £4500 for the mannors, and in case Manl[ove] should not come up to that summ, to bid for the whole any summ not exceeding £6500. But if he found it could not be carried att that rate, I gave him liberty to add discretionally as farr as £7000 with this caution to watch and

time his matters so warily so as to compass the design at as easy
a purchase as possible. Were it my own concern I should readily
strike if Manl[ove] proferd for the freeh[old] as above, for I
apprehend that will be subject to most difficultys.[1] The scheme
you put into Jo[seph] Barns's head has a prospect of great
advantage to the publick, therfore wish success to itt.[2] 'Tis no
wonder Calv[erley Bewick] shews himself in his naturall colours;
att this time of day people of very great figure are apt to doe the
same. The Capt[ain] and you will best judge what sallary is
fitting for Stark[in] after considering the time of his absence and
expences there. Jemmy has once mention'd the purchasing of
Almond Garths to Lady Ann who will comply if he thinks it
may be had at penyworth, and for my part I think £450 is its full
value, especially considering what advantages may be made of
money att this time. But we must first obtain an order of court
which may easily be had if you think that summ would fetch itt.
I have from the best hands that £425 is the summ already bid
and that you may depend on. I am sorry that you are like to be
plung'd in law, since you desire the opinion about a learned
person proper for the Excheq[uer] barr to be employed. You
have your choice of Mr Dodd, Mr Turner and Mr Ettrick; I
should choose one of the two first were it my case. Your town
will suffer much by the loss of the late alderman, yet doubt not
the prudence of the corporation in a new choice. My father is
your humble serv[ant] and none more such than....

[P.S.] Poor Cha[rles] Sand[er]son had his cellar doors broke
open last night, lost 2 doz[en] of excell[ent] claret that Capt[ain]
Cotesworth formerly sent up of the condemn'd wine and all his
stock of brandy.

1. Establishing a proper title to Newsham did indeed cause difficulties when
    Cotesworth tried to sell the estate for £5,000 in 1720.

2. Barnes and Cotesworth were instrumental in preparing the Regulation's
    defence against the coming official investigation of the coal trade and
    Cotesworth persuaded the directors to send Barnes to London to plead
    their case. When Liddell suggested that Cotesworth should join him, they
    at first refused but by late March Cotesworth was in London to give
    evidence to a committee of the House of Commons.

18

Feb[ruary] 6th [1]710/1

You would by last post hear from Cha[rles] of the last transaction which he promised to doe without fail, so I need not repeat nor have to add on that subject. I believe Bowm[an's] bond is here but shall be sent down. Is the fellow mad to ingage with such a number of *keels when in appearance he knows not of coals to keep ⅓d employed? I will again speak to my uncle about his trusteeship but he is very loth to be concern'd, being a wary person. You do well to put Mr Wortley in mind of the admeasurem[ent] of the Sunderland keels but we shall be att a loss to name proper commiss[ioners]. That [matter] of opposing any attempt from the Duke of Rich[mond] must be watched by the two Members [for Newcastle] and Wilkinson's letter will be of use. If we learn when it comes on, shall indeavor to possess the Members of our acquaintance which are few in number.[1] I have askt some Members when the additional duty on candles takes place but they could not yet inform me.[2] I shall be glad to hear of your election how it goes; surely this will raise feuds that can't be of any disservice to by standers. I am glad that Fr[ank] Baker has agreed with Lord B[arnard and] hope 'tis to his satisfaction. 'Tis much [to] mine that he will not be obliged to leave our part of the countrey where he is so usefull and so ready to serve his friends. Is itt not possible for you to contrive your business so as to accompany Mr Barnes to town; it might on several occasions be worth your while I should think, especially you would have opportunity of settling an interest att the Gate, while they will not allow a contractor to speak to them on such an account till their last year's demands be satisfied. I have proposed honest Peter coming up but have no direct answer as yet. When I hear any certainty from Jo[seph] Barnes] I shall give notice to have his daughter's room fitted up for her. By this post I have writt to the Capt[ain] not to be too forward in striking in with a subscription to the Contract for another year, and he will discourse you on that head. Who can putt the keelmen upon this new expedition? A contre petition may balk their design.[3] When do you think Bensh[am] will be a thorough going colliery, free from fire and profitable? You will inform yourself of Hebdon what writings he has relating to Bensh[am] and what in Mr Ord's hands that are materiall; my father would be glad to see them that he may be satisfied fully of the title. He desires they would intrust them with Mr Barnes who will take particular care of them. You will likewise inform yourself of Mr Hebd[on] where the originall lease of Bensh[am] is, whether in the hands of the court or a sollicitor and who he is. He desires likewise you will gett information if Mr Mark Riddell's wife levyed a *fine of the quarter *part as is pretended in the case sent up and where it was don. I am....

[P.S.] My father sends you his service and Mr Bowes who is here bids me tell you that he bid his man Wilson write you word that he had spoke to Kitt Pinkney who would acquaint his man to impart to you. Young George Vane is your s[ervant].

1. During the Privy Council investigation of the keelmen's grievances in 1710, the Tyneside coal-owners had complained that their rivals on the Wear were stealing trade and defrauding the customs by exceeding the statutory *measure; see letter 3. This accusation was now to be the subject of an investigation on behalf of the customs' administration and the coal-owners were preparing their case and mustering their political influence. The Duke of Richmond had an interest since he collected 12d on every *chaldron of coal shipped from Newcastle in the coastal trade.

2. It was proposed to clear the revenue deficit which was one of the main reasons for the financial crisis of 1710-11 by floating a series of lottery loans and taxation had to be raised in order to secure them. The first Loan Act, which received the royal assent on 6 March 1711, was charged partly on duties on home and imported candles for thirty-two years from 1711.

3. This probably refers to the petition later printed as the *Case of the Poor Skippers and Keel-men of Newcastle*, which Defoe sent to Harley in June. From the coal-owners' point of view, the revival of the struggle for control of the keelmen's charity was very ill-timed and a counter-petition duly emerged.

19

Feb[ruary] 8th 1710/1

By last post you would have myne att large in answer I think to all former particulars as farr as I could. Have since made further inquiry of some Members about the taking place of the additionall duty on candles, but they tell me that the bill is not yet brought into the House and when it is a blank is left for the time. However one has promis'd me to ask Mr Lownds that question and if he will resolve I shall know itt and then you may depend itt shall be communicated. I referr'd you to Cha[rles] for particulars of the business in his hands; I think it remains as when he wrote, Mr Willson the best bidder att £6400. As there will be occasion to advance att least a brace of hundred pounds in court and money being very difficult to be had, my father has promised to goe to his goldsmith, examine his cash and if he finds sufficient will advance for the present; but care must be taken to remitt itt him speedily, least his occasions should require. Both my father and I made an exception against my uncle's letter and therfore stopt itt a post; we represented to him the jealousy it might give our partners as then expressed but he said there was no harme in itt. You will guess in the main the scope of the letter and what is meant by itt, and itt would not doe amiss if you should by word of mouth discourse the substance so as not to give offence.

You know every additional duty is a burthen upon a trade and this lately laid on will contribute to make itt goe heavily this next year.[1] This will make the dealors more absolutely necessary to us than otherwise, who must exert themselves in the Regulation and for that service only to make things goe smoothly on; ['tis] the only way to free us from generall complaints which the last year had like to have brought us into troubles, which where they would have ended God knows. Should you quarrell with the dealors att this time, you may guess att the disturbance and interruption they would unanimously give to the trade. And tho' you were to ingage all the other dealors in your interest, yet they are most of them people of little or no substance for which reason they can't force a trade; if they doe it must be by the creditt you give them and what sort of reckning you will have with them att the making up your accounts you may judge.[2] When an answer is given to the dealors it must be don with great caution, least if they be discarded their naturall malice and spirit of revenge will readily prompt them to produce the letter and probably may bring us into trouble. For instance were itt expressed that some of the Ten had received £50 for sale of Fieldhouse coals contrary to the stipulation [of the law], if this letter were exposed, as certainly it would be by them if disobliged, the Review would lay hold of itt and handle us as last year, that it was a plain proof of a design'd monopoly; so that what now seems to sleep would be raised up against us and a prosecution would certainly be sett on foot. What then you will say can be don? We think a cautious letter to them must be framed, but particular instances of their false dealing should be represented to my uncle in a letter to him and that he may charge them with by word of mouth. I think it would not be improper if the generall answer to the dealors be first inclosed to him that we may peruse and alter if thought necessary. Believe me we can't be too cautious as the world seems disposed. My father writes on this head to the Capt[ain] by this night's post, by the help of which the meaning of this may be explain'd where itt wants. I doubt the proposal of [paying] £2000 att Mich[aelmas] next and £1000 after will scarce goe down, but when the 5 have come to a general result lett it be dispatched as above. As to an interest for your own concerns att Gate, 'tis time it should be looked after and you must employ some friend of yours to transact for I must not appear nor can be of any service. Itt seems necessary Mr Ord must keep back his *leadings whether wc keep up our interest with dealors or not.[3] The sexton's adventure made me smile and reflections upon itt are such as I should guess att. I have now tired myself sufficiently and the more because this weather does indeed sensibly affect me who am....

P.S. I desire you will send me an account of what money I advanced on the [Bensham] upper seam service. I remember not perfectly well now Brainslope concern was to be divided; as I take itt I was to advance the charge of half that concern for the Capt[ain's] use as we agreed att Percivall's. If I be wrong sett me to rights and direct your answer to this postscript inclosed to Mrs Cla[vering] in Bedford Row. Adieu I am....

1. The imposition of further coal duties from 1710 for thirty-two years was another element in the financial backing for the March 1711 lottery. There is evidence supporting Liddell's contention that the high duties on coal dampened potential demand: see Ellis, *Business Fortunes*, pp.76-80, 86-87.

2. Liddell's letters support contemporary accusations that the Billingsgate coal market was dominated by a ring of ten powerful dealers whom he called the 'great Dons' and who easily outweighed the rest.

3. Coal-owners inside the Regulation were allotted shares of the estimated demand for the coming year and were expected to adjust their sales so as to keep within their quota or 'quantity'. Coal from the Wortley-Montagu collieries managed by Ord was much in demand and was often subject to restrictions.

20

[February 13th 1710/11]

This evening both Mr Wortleys were here, and it was agreed I should write to desire upon the reciet of it you would gett Mr White, Mr Ord and Mr Barnes and who other you think necessary to a metting if possible with Carr (if thought safe to consult with a person so well verst in that business but so much a friend to a great man of the other river [Lord Scarborough]); therfore doe as is judg'd convenient. You will consider and draw up such a clause as may be thought of most use for adjusting the Sunderland river and naming the commissioners. It must be return'd by the first post or 2d at furthest, least it come too late. You will give your opinion of what Mr Hedw[orth] communicated to you. We can't so much as guess in what respect the union must be or what tendency.[1] We again press the determination of the 5 and that with speed. If they don't agree to satisfie the dealors, which is the unanimous opinion of all here concern'd that they should, they will send their reasons. But I pronounce a bad trade if they be not complimented to their minds. Air and Calder can't be assessed as yours proposes. Young Wortley has had all the points of yours communicated. He can't inform if the duty be upon 36 bushells or our New[castle] measure.[2] Indeed as the world goes scarce any cares to give themselves the trouble of attending the House.[3] I thank you for your repeated favors and accounts of what passes, among which that of your new merch[ant] Gover[nor] is not the least pleasant.[4] Cha[rles] has answerd fully yours. I am....

1. The Sunderland coal-owners were basically hostile to the Regulation. The threatened inquiry into the coal trade and the actual inquiry into their *measure temporarily revived interest in co-operation between the rival ports but proposals to improve the river Wear remained a source of friction.

2. A duty of 9s per ton imposed on rock salt exported to Ireland formed part of the financial package behind the lottery scheme but it also represented a concession to makers of white salt. The size of the measured ton was crucial here because white salt was reckoned in tons of 40 bushells rather than 36 bushells for rock and less for imported salt and this affected their liability for duty.

3. The parliamentary session had been unduly lengthened by protracted debates about the new financial measures, which the average backbencher found tedious and unpalatable; this led to dwindling attendance in the Commons.

4. Later letters suggest that George Liddell had been elected Governor of the Merchants' company.

21

22th Feb[ruary 1]710/1

Tho' I have bin in a perfect feavor and for severall days confin'd to the house, and have just wearyed myself with a long letter to Ald[erman] White, yet I am willing to satisfy you that your 3 *bills came safe to hand. The 2 largest I shall send to Cha[rles] Sanderson and take his reciet for the use you design them and he will press that business [the manors] as much as the nature of itt will admitt. I wish with all my heart you could putt your business upon such a foot as to be able to leave it for 3 weeks; it is the opinion of Mr Wortlyes, my father and uncle that if you came up to town with discretionary power, the dealors might be brought to reason. I beg of you therfore not to refuse in case the 5 propose it to you. You will have the advantage of treating personally for your own concerns at the Gate and likewise look after your other concerns, besides a singular satisfaction that I should have in itt, whose company would doe me more good than the d[octor's] phisick. Don't therfore admire I press you so much to itt since I have my private end in itt. I have in the ald[erman's] letter taken notice that I knew you were a great sufferer by *way leaves etc. for which you paid *dead rent, which was thought very unreasonable by all the gentlemen here; since they were taken with a view only of publick service I recommended the consideration to them. My father thanks you for yours last post; bids me to tell you that Mark Riddle is in town [and] presses for money, therfore would gladly know your sentiments what he ought to doe in that case. I am just jaded so you will excuse me since I am.....

22

Mar[ch] 6th [1]710/1

Your 2 of the 27th are now before me. I find since [then] your
suspicion that no invitation from the 5 would be given for you
confirm'd by Ald[erman] Wh[ite] last post. I must own it were
not seasonable at this juncture to appear with the people of the
Gate or to have any transactions with them; however this I will
venture to affirm, that the insight and assistance you might give
us here in case we be obliged to oppose the bill might richly
deserve the expence of a journey as also a gratification. My
father has bin very ill and this is the first day he has gott abroad
to take the air, and for my part I have a lurking feavor hanging
upon me that dispirits me to a degree and unfitts me for
business. What is design'd by the bill is kept a secrett among
those that bring itt in, so that we can learn nothing of itt till we
gett a copy, which can't be till it be presented; yet I think the
reall intent is to call in question the partys att New[castle]. A few
days will discover and then we shall move as upon consultation
may be thought most expedient. I foresee plainly there will be a
breach and then the *fitters will obtain their ends and the
Lond[on] markett will be supplyed with a worse commodity and
on dearer terms.[1] My father is very difficult to resolve, therfore
if you should write to him and state the business of Fenham with
the prospect of future advantages and see what he says to itt. I
must own my own circumstances will be such as not to allow of
hazarding any thing. Mrs Barnes is arriv'd safe and I have
order'd Mrs Evans to call for what she wants. The clause your
Gazette affords is much of the same nature with that I sent the
Capt[ain].[2] Jemmy [Clavering] has taken a prudent course with
the fitters; to have complyed with their demands would have bin
destructive to the last degree both as to making good
proportionable price as also seperating the two coals [from our
pits]. Your alder[men] trip off apace and the mayor is no less
successful in his windfalls. We have this day taken Mrs Bayles
and her bro[ther] Preston's joint bond for pay[ment] of the
arrear due. I hope we shall be in the main secured[3].....

1. On 3 March leave was given to bring in 'A Bill to dissolve the present, and
   prevent the future, Combinations of Coal-owners etc'. It was presented in
   the Commons on 15 March, had its first reading on 4 April, its second on

10 April, its third on 18 May and received the royal assent in June. Liddell here produces the standard apologia for cartels in the coal trade, arguing that unregulated competition would drive many collieries out of business and leave consumers at the mercy of those that survived.

2. Newcastle was one of the first provincial towns to establish its own newspapers. The *Newcastle Gazette* was first published in Gateshead on 29 July 1710 and appeared three times a week for at least two years. In April 1711 the Tory *Newcastle Courant* was launched in competition.

3. Mrs Bayles owned three salt-pans at South Shields and had undoubtedly run into debt with Cotesworth and Liddell over the supply of coal, the largest single element in the production cost of salt. In 1713 Cotesworth leased her pans himself to avoid this sort of incident.

23

Mar[ch] 14th [1]710/11

I have often since the reciet of one of your letters some time since reflected upon the contents and now by experience find them true. There are some people in the world endeavoring to tripp up my heels or rather to cutt my throat with a feather, how justly I know not. I thought I might have deserv'd better att their hands when I formerly stood in steed of a father, but 'tis likely former kindnesses are effaced and forgott. 'Tis with very great grief I must tell you that I am suspected, att least to me itt seems so, of having raised a considerable summ out of the colliery more than was fitting for my own use and therfore I am refused a request of working 50 *tenns for the supplying the *quantity allotted me by the Regulation. A small favour demanded God knows to be rejected; and methinks the gain of about £2000 in twelv years' service is no very extravagant allowance for one's service and pains, not to mention the intire ruin of a man's health, which att this time is a savage rent charge. But all this I am resolved to bear with patience. The lossess att Bensham are all attributed to my neglect; all losses by *fitters or others in the way of trade in my time are not directly but by a side wind levell'd in some measure att me. If I have bin guilty of any advantagious thing to the family, that is not noticed or looked upon to be an incumbent duty. My friend we live in an age of generosity; little did I expect such usage, but since I am deprived in effect of being a collier att home, I shall take leave of trade and desire not to be concern'd any way relating to itt. My service has bin pernicious, therfore I will prevent it for the future; I desire if you have any thing to recommend or propose, lett it be don directly by letter to my father. Then you may have an answer but I may sollicitt weeks without numb[er] before a resolution can be taken on which a certainty may be relyed on. Wittness this business of Fenham; I have formerly discoursed that point over and over, yet I believe you may have thought my answers very superficial because I could send you no other. Indeed my father is so ill now that he can't think of business, but depend upon't when he is better I durst venture a wager he will have so many objections that before they be answer'd a vast time will be spent. Therfore herafter when you have any thing to communicate do itt directly to himself. Pray inclose your answer to this to Mrs Cl[avering] in the Rowe under a cover and I conjure you not to signify the least of the above mention'd to any person living. I foresee in a little time as things are menaged there will be great feuds among us, which I can't but bewail. Pardon the freedom I take but since 'tis to so particular a friend as yourself I venture to doe itt.[1]

My father is something better, returns you his thanks; he apprehends the length of the *way [from Urpeth], the trouble of securing *way leaves thro' so many different proprietors and the uncertainty of the lease makes him wave thinking of itt. Doe you think J[ohn] Hedw[orth] might not be willing to admitt of a partner or two and lett the coll[iery] come down his way? You may if you think fitt try his pulse, suppose Jemmy, you and myself should stand to a half. This I only recommend to your thoughts. To the rest of your letter I must give an answer when my father is in better plight and myself too, for what with these northerly winds and vexations of one sort or other I am almost off my leggs. This day I rec[eived] a letter from the 4 directed to Mr Ed[ward] Wortley and me desiring we will employ Nevill Ridley as a sollicitor to watch the bill and recieve instructions from us. Don't you think him so great a friend to Wrightson as to communicate anything we shall entrust him with to that gentleman and that Ald[erman] Fen[wick] will be inform'd from time to time? Doubtless they will. Adieu my good friend and lett me be in favor or out you shall allways find me according to former professions...

[P.S.] Was not the Capt[ain] to have had a share in Brainslope after won, as we agreed att Percivall's; was not I to be att a part-charge in *winning and what might she cost? Your answer to these. I almost think it would be worth your while to come up on your own account to settle your own private concerns as well as those att the Gate for yourself. I shall be willing to contribute out of our joint concern att Bensh[am] towards the charge and right glad should bee to see you.

1. Despite his caution, Liddell had not been able to avoid accusations of putting his own interests before those of his family. He may have suspected his younger brother of encouraging these attacks: George Liddell had taken over the running of the family's affairs in the north when Henry moved to London and it is noticeable that the Captain is referred to in a much less affectionate tone than friends like James Clavering or Francis Baker.

24

Mar[ch] 17th [1]710/11

We are all extremely beholden to you for your indefatigable industry for the service of the publick where you are, as allso for the frequent and most intelligent accounts you give us of transactions below. I can't give you a fuller answer than by last post; have only time to tell you that I am extreemly rejoiced att the prospect we have of seeing you shortly, when we may settle severall of those points you want to be satisfied in. My uncle was this day with old Mr Wortley, who told him that Mr Ord was coming up upon their private affairs but that it was absolutely his opinion that your presence would be of singular service, and therfore gave him his hand that he did join with my father and uncle to desire that you would hasten up on the publick account without loss of time. So that since the Gentlemen of the countrey think it also advisable, my request is that you will comply and putt your business in order that you may post away without delay. Depend upon't as the bill is actually brought in, there will be occasion for heads nay of the best and I am certain none will be of such use as yours. Young Mr Wortley promised to procure us a copy of the bill, which might have bin had this morn[ing]; we relyed upon his promise but he has fail'd us, a thing that can't be forgiven. However depend upon't the

Capt[ain] or you shall have it as soon as comes to our hands. Sir J[ohn] Cl[avering] had a very proper answer return'd him about his *way leaves.[1] The produce of your ¼ of an hour's thought might by its elaborateness be supposed to have bin a consideration of many days. We will remark itt and according as we see occasion shall push those heads [*i.e.* points]. You must pretend your own affairs bring you up and no publick business, but I must again repeat nay press your departure for believe me time is precious. My father att this juncture is in a rack of pain; it grows upon him almost dayly and decays him sensibly. This morn[ing] Count Guiscard dyed in Newgate.[2] I am still much out of order but a sight of you will extreemly revive....

1. Sir John Clavering had approached the directors of the Regulation about their plans for the current shipping season only to be informed that their meetings had been suspended. In fact meetings continued to be held until at least 1715 but it had become impolitic to admit their existence to anyone who might use that admission against the cartel.

2. On 8 March Antoine de Guiscard attacked Harley with a penknife while being questioned by a committee of the Privy Council on charges of high treason. He was taken to Newgate, where he resisted attempts to treat wounds received in the struggle and died on 17 March. The attempt on Harley's life increased his popularity; meanwhile Guiscard's body was pickled and put on show for ten days until the Queen ordered its burial.

25

Mar[ch] 20th [1]710/1

You would hear from me the 2 or 3 last posts so that I have little to add, but since have seen Mr Edw[ard] Wortley who shew'd us yesterday morn[ing] a copy of the design'd bill. That gentleman told me that he hoped to see you here shortly, that your presence seem'd more necessary than formerly when I wrote by their joint order. Thus sir, you have the repeated requests of your friends here, who are sensible of your capacitys to serve them and jointly press that you would hasten up without loss of time; and as the time of year has better'd the roads, don't you think that easy stages by post would be the cleaverest conveyance? We think that itt will be about 3 weeks from the first bringing in of the bill and the last reading. I need not trouble you with my remarks since you are so much better

att making than any I know. I have bin twice down att the Gate
where I found poor John Walker att his witt's end; he could not
dispose of his Clav[ering] Stella tho' offerd [to accept] 6d under
the markett. Pray will you acquaint Mr Clav[ering] of this and
tell him that my opinion is that the master ought to have some
consideration for the loss of this voyage, and lett him have a
bulk of the best this next [voyage] if he can be perswaded to
load. Indeed you must send nothing but what is very good this
beginning of the year, and about midsummer when the masters
are used to the *steath one may venture to putt in a larger dash
of Coleburn. Pray what are your thoughts of our new tryall att
Bucksnook, is she like to be of any continuance? Is it feasible to
putt the smallest of Coleburn to the *pans, while the rest went to
ships? I mean can any small profit be made of them that way,
for when the other sort is gon (which I apprehend to be
shortlived) what will become of the trade? Could not you prevail
with Jo[seph Barnes] to write to the Duke [of Newcastle]'s agent
about Hedly Fell? Mr Coal told Cha[rles] Sanderson he would
not [let] under 20s [a *ten] rent, which is not to be thought off.[1]
The Speaker [Bromley]'s son is dead and the House adjourned
till Monday, after which will be a small recess during the
hollydays which will give a little respite, so you will regulate
your journey as the Gentlemen in the countrey and you think
most proper. I am in hast....

1.   Coal marketed under the name of Clavering Stella did not come from a
     single colliery in the accepted sense: in effect all the mines operated on
     behalf of the Claverings of Chopwell were classed as one 'colliery' and
     their produce was blended to suit the demands of the London market. This
     was quite a common practice and several families faced legal problems
     when the Coal Act banned the *mixing of coal from different collieries. At
     this stage, however, Clavering Stella's main problem was that it was
     producing too much poor quality coal and desperately needed to acquire a
     pit that could improve its overall standard.

                                    26

June 14th [1]711

   I am favor'd with both yours. The latter was the most
acceptable since it brought an account of your safe landing att
Gateshead, tho' you had suffer'd in the journey by the loss of
the Red Lyon juices, but as crabs and lobsters are so easily come

att with you I doubt not your speedy recruiting. I have drank the German spaw [water] and you know writing makes it fly into the head, therfore must be short and so shall fall to business. Mrs Smith is uneasy till Mrs Barnes's business be concluded, she having oblig'd her friend to fitt up an apartm[ent] for her on purpose. You will discourse Jo[seph] and let that matter be made an end off one way or other speedily. Mrs Smith is a woman of experience and doubtless if she will be free in giving advice in any sort, she wants not capacity. We are both of opinion that the overplus summ remaining in the hands of your dear Peggy [Ramsay] belongs to herself, and should you contest itt, Mrs Smith would comb your head for such a presumption were you within her reach. As the world goes I don't admire people's being called strictly to account.[1] I think your *vend is extraordinary considering how the season has bin for *leading; if you can add 2 *keels more to your number, it can't fail of doing well for there are no stocks att *steaths, as the masters inform, even Clav[ering] Stella was grounded. I believe you will find the trade grow worse every year after this therfore recieve the advice you formerly gave to another person, make hay while the sun shine. Gett what *carriadge you can and lead what is possible; both ships and *pans will swallow what ever are brought down. This day I was att Gate and see Capt[ain] Oldner, who told me the town was more than half supplyed. He had sent up the river Lord W[illiam Powlett]'s coals this day. Price is Team from 25½ to 26[s], Hutt[on] and B[enwell] 28[s]. My father desires cos[en]] Baker, Bullock and Hutchinsons might take a *view of Fenham, that their thoughts might be imparted to the Capt[ain] and yourself and that you would send him an account what steaths they might be brought to and about what charge; and if not to advantage but thro' Mr Montagu, by what means could that be compassed. You and the Capt[ain] must draw up a scheme and that will give us an insight. Bowman is here and presses an end of that lease to be made. I have not heard a syllable of the project of widening of our *way but what yours mentions. I could not gett a penny of money att the Gate this morn[ing]. Capt[ain] Oldner was wishing that he had had a list of the ships that loaded of your coals sent him, meaning that he would have bin serviceable to you. I am rather better than when you left me tho' not much; this hot and sultry weather is burthensome to me and were I not *refreshed* with some cool breezes in the [Bedford] Rowe, I fancy I should cease to be.[2] My father desires your acceptance of his best services and so does Mr Honywood who is by. Hugh has bin almost every day att the custom house without effect; he grows very peevish on't. I have writt a letter and sent it to Lord W[illiam] to sign to Sir Mathew Dudly, one of the commissioners, by which hope for some success. Did you borrow a blue coat from the master of the Gun Tavern and if you did, where was it left? Capt[ain] Oldner was making enquiry after it. Mrs Smit[h] makes a tender of her devoirs to her beau, who she says writes such plain lines as she can't venture to read unless in a corner by herself. Pray pay my complim[ents] to the cash keeper and the honest Alderman [Ramsay]. I remain....

[P.S.] When will they begin to lead from the new work att Whitefield Stella?

1.   This may be a veiled reference to Tory attacks on prominent Whigs like Walpole for alleged misappropriation of funds during the last ministry. In 1711 the Commons revived the Commission of Public Accounts, a move which led to the censure of Marlborough and Walpole in January 1712 and explains Liddell's dislike of strict accounting. His caution is explained by government surveillance of the post.

2.   Liddell's courtship of Ann Clavering was now approaching a conclusion and they were married towards the end of July.

27

June 25th [1]711

I have yours of the 17th which should have answered last post, but being in a long arrear to the Vaudois and [as] the waters won't allow me to write above one att a time, therfore chose to pay the debt of the longest standing and that I know you will excuse. I must begin with the young lady you design'd to place out and must tell you: that this morn[ing] Mrs Evans was here and told Mrs Smith and me that her lodger removed last Fryday to Mrs Wait's, that she was not att all displeased att itt, that the lady told her you did design to have placed her att a painter's in Lincoln's Inn fields (a person that was a stranger both to her and yourself), that she did not like the place so well as where she now is. I doubt the whole mystery has bin reveal'd, which sort of proceeding is very unaccountable; however poor

Mrs S[mith] is reconcil'd since the young lady is in a place that perfectly pleases her. She knew well that her friend Mrs Richardson would scorn to recieve any money for the charge she had bin att in fitting up the apartm[ent], therfore chose rather to send her in your name ½ a p[ound] of best tea, 2 lb coffee and 2 loaves double refined sugar, the whole charge £1 12s, as an acknowledgm[ent]. She told Mrs S[mith] that itt should occasion no breach of friendship 'twixt them and [was] glad the lady was better provided to her mind. Such usage as this will be a caution to you and her how you ingage yourselvs herafter.

I am sorry that when you had so great a stock att *steaths, that not a ship of the last fleet should fall to your share. I had the Capt[ain] and young Dick [Oldner] up here to diner the other day: he assured me that he had not rec[eived] a letter from you but that giving an account of the coat, which is now found. He had no list of your ships neither did they know your *fitter's name. I told them that Dick was his name; oh, says the nephew, I had a load of them the last fleet which prov'd extreemly small, and indeed I percieve he gave a price answerable. The[y] would not ingage otherwise than to try a few bulks and if they prov'd to their mind, the[ir] dispatch should recommend ships to you. I shall be down att the Gate to morrow and then shall make further inquiry. They desire a meeting of the 5 might be [held] speedily and some resolution taken for their service of last year. This my father desires, that in case the owners can't agree in opinion, then the money that is collected should be refunded to each owner and they may dispose as they think fitt. My father, uncle and self are of that mind and I can assure you that if this was don, you would find a new life att the Gate and better and more equall proportions of price observed. Certainly our people of Chopwell endeavor all they can to ruin the creditt of that concern. Is it not downright madness, to say no worse, to press off in the time of a fleet's loading the wettest, smallest and worst of your coals? Can't be expected that the dealors will ever more take a tryall or encourage the ships to go there, when after repeated assurances of the goodness off this fleet, they will find them worse than ever. My reputation with them will be forfeited and herafter if I should assure them more positively, I shall not be believed. Sure never was such menagem[ent]. Pray when will Whitefield be ready? When it is a quantity of those choice [coals] must be *ledd down, which will be the only way of

retrieving; nay and even that can't be done but towards the
latter end of the year, yet there will be this advantage that for
the next it may leave the fragrant smell of a good name. Pray
what did you agree when here to pay the Capt[ain] O[ldner]?
Lett me know; I will make it good and *draw on you for itt.
Hugh has repaid me the 2 guineas I lett him have for the
d[octor]. If itt can be proved that Robinson has kidnapp'd a
p[air] of your wheels, he ought to be prosecuted to the utmost to
expose such a villanous act, wherby the like for the future may
be prevented. I have acquainted my father with what you write
concerning Harry Hudson and J[ohn] Cay. The latter's wife is
come up to sollicit about a bond that her husband enter'd into as
security for Mr Abrah[am] Dashwood to the Government, as
also perhaps to settle the affair of recieving with Mr Gold. I
should not think Jos[eph] Milburn att all a person qualified for
such a post.[1] The weather is hott enough as you remark for the
trying of a new experim[ent].[2] Mrs S[mith] is of opinion that
nothing will cool a man so much as going into the Thames; are
you of her side?
Tuesday noon. I am just return'd from the Gate whe[re] I see
the Capt[ain] and young Dick; the former told me his wife has
sent after him to lett know that there was a letter from you,
wherin he supposed might be a list of your ships. I putt both of
them in mind of serving you. They promised faintly, pretending
they could not doe as they would since the ships coming in so
quick upon them, they have overglutted the markett and their
customers finding they can be served att any time, putt off the
evill hour of parting with money as long as they can. This is
matter off fact, and if you will take my opinion you will be
better served by your petty dealors such as Godfrey etc. (to
whom I am a stranger) than by the great Dons, therfore would
advise you to write to them. Besides the less I appear, the better
I can assure you on severall accounts; for instance this only, it
may give umbrage att home. I must again recommend an
immediate meeting of the 5 and an order for the moneys due for
last year to be *return'd , without which I doe positively affirm
that the whole trade will suffer to the greatest degree in
inequality of prices. And that ought to be prevented for the sake
of shipping. I have nothing more save my father's and Mrs
Smith's best services joint with mine to you and your dear sister
Peggy.[3] Adieu I am....

[P.S] Hugh is gon down to Greenwich with the *bill; the success
I know not yet.

1. The salt duties were paid to local collectors who arranged for their transfer
    to London by bills of exchange obtained from a credit agency. The sums
    involved were large enough to attract the attention of prominent financiers
    like Gould, who is here choosing a salt proprietor to receive the duties on
    behalf of his agency, a position which would give the proprietor concerned
    considerable influence over the collector. This was not the only method of
    putting pressure on local officials since the Salt Board demanded
    substantial securities on their appointment and the proprietors were only
    too willing to supply them.

2. This may be a reference to the Act establishing the South Sea company,
    which received the royal assent on 12 June. It was designed to consolidate
    the Government's floating debt and was disliked by Whigs both because it
    threatened the interests of the Bank of England and because it effectively
    pledged the Government to make peace.

3. Cotesworth's wife Hannah had died in 1710, whereupon her sister
    Margaret Ramsay moved to Gateshead to supervise the household.

28

July 12th [1]711

I am 2 in your debt but we are so busy in settling and
exam[ining] the writings [*i.e.* marriage settlement?] that I have
not bin able to write to any save a few lines to Jemmy and the
Capt[ain]. This is an excuse so just as I know you will readily
allow. I have rec[eived] £30, part of the *bill you sent Hugh; the
rem[ainder] is promised this week. There is no dependance on
any of the great men att the Gate, their promises are like
syllibubs, seemingly great and yet nothing in them. I have
sufficiently experienced them by their managem[ent] towards
poor Giles Conyers, who had an extraord[inary] loading of all
Coalburn. The 3 Oldn[ers] assured they would despatch him att
curr[ent] price, and yet when my back was turn'd they told the
mast[er] they knew nothing of the matter and did not take a
coal. Such usage wearies me out of my life and makes me sick of
the business, so I have don with them since I find my endeavors
are intirely useless. I have procured you 5 doz[en] of Florence
wine. It is tollerable and I hope not much inferior to the last but

durst not venture of a hogshead, being in apprehension that it
may prick [*i.e.* become sour] this hott weather. 'Tis putt on
board John Smallwood. I shall pay for itt. Mrs Richinson is so
much obliged by the present made to her that probably it may
produce a letter to you from Mrs Smit[h]. I am sensible you
have bin a vast sufferer in all those respects you mention but am
the more supriz'd that the Gentlemen with you, whose cause you
have bin pleading, should not think fitt to gratify you in so small
a point as that of helping you off with a small number of *keels,
but the business is over and the services to them partly forgott.
Another thing I can but observe to you is this, I percieve 'tis a
crime for me to be concern'd in the upper seams [of Bensham];
tho' not in direct words, yet [it] seem'd levell'd att. Mr Rogers
was here and that point was touch'd upon att some distance and
I discoverd they design'd to work the upper seams themselvs,
therfore I would have you be cautious how much you lay out
money in *ridding off shafts, as also to lay aside thoughts of a
*trunk, for that would be imprudent where the title is so
precarious. I only touch on these heads for your timely
consideration as also leave you to judge from whence this arises.
I am the person chiefly aim'd att, but 'tis hard you should be a
sufferer on my score. I will quitt all my pretensions rather than
make people here uneasy. It has certainly bin represented that
great treasure is yearly gott and that it would be better in any
hands than mine. I am satisfyed to purchase peace and quiett att
any rate. I could now wish myself with you for a shank of an
evening that I might open my case fully and have your advice.
The main business draws to a conclusion but severall rubbs are
mett with and delays in the drawing of the writings; we conquer
one difficulty after another. All together make me very uneasy
as you may guess, added to the infirmitys of a bad constitution
which the late great rains and now the hott weather have much
disorder'd. But have not in the least alter'd the respect I always
shall have for my good friend, to whom I am....

[P.S.] My respects to the good Ald[erman] and sis[ter] Peggy.
What does the 5 design to doe in regard to the dealors?

29

Aug[ust] 2nd [1]711

I thank you for your kind wishes of all sorts; I venture to direct this to Richmond, where your zeal to serve your friends has carryed you. This is your misfortune to be endowed with a good will as well as capacity.[1] My father writes to you by this post and directs to Gateshead; he has secured you a tickett, the number he knows not. I seal'd it up and it is left in Mr Freek's hands; if you like you shall have itt, if not my father will, so pursue your own inclinations. Only lett me know by the return of the post what you design, because the lottery is actually drawing and the first class was finished last night, but if your tickett be drawn or not we know not. If I don't hear from you by the return of the post, shall conclude you don't like itt and then it falls to my father's share. He has paid £25 the first paym[ent] and about 6s over and above. The 2d paym[ent] must be made the 15th inst[ant] without fail and that is £25 more.[2] I shall be ready to recieve your commands in relation to this or any other business wherin you shall judge me capable of serving you. My best respects attend my good lord, all our friends att the Green [the Yorkes?] not forgetting the weazell tail. This is a busy time, so I can't allott you more lines than to assure you that I am....

1. Probably on the recommendation of the Liddells, Lord William Powlett had engaged Cotesworth as agent for his lead mines and mills in Yorkshire, which had been losing money.

2. The lottery authorized in June 1711 consisted of 20,000 £100 tickets which were paid for in instalments. The tickets were divided into five classes, the prizes being slightly different in each, but even those who drew a blank rather than a prize stood to regain their money within thirty-two years and receive six per cent interest in the meantime. The unrealistic generosity of these terms led to competition for tickets even among staunch Whigs.

30

Aug[ust] 11th, late att night

I thank you for your very obliging and kind letter. I must be short, therfore you must know that last night I see my uncle Rob[ert] who told me that the tickett sealed up was 9480, to which I wish good success. I don't hear that 'tis yet drawn; when it is you shall have an account. The £25 *bill was paid Hugh today and I shall give it to uncle Rob[ert] in part for that tickett. My father and Mr Freek went for Blenheim yesterday morn[ing] where they part and the former goes for Bath I believe. I shall pay Hugh for your wine etc. and give you an account as desired. Your Streatlam adventure with the barr[onet's] answer diverted me extreemly.[1] I wellcom'd honest Geo[rge] Bowes to town with it, who is hugely recruited by the Bath. He stays about a fortnight in town. I foresee the trade will run into distraction, doe what we can. I had from none an account of the *fitters' plott. I [s]hould have bin glad of particulars. However am glad their mine blew up without effect. What can be the meaning of the Capt[ain's] strangeness towards you? I don't admire that of the Justice's att all. Mrs Smith wrote to you a week agoe and desired I would acquaint you as much. Honest Peter [Bernardeau] leaves us next week. He has settled matters in dispute 'twixt the two bro[thers Baker] to mutuall satisfaction. My legs have bin very troublesome these 3 or 4 days past so must hasten to bed, but believe me I am with all sincerity, honest Will....

1.   Lady Bowes was determined to refuse Sir John Clavering's and Brumell's
      demands for a *wayleave through her land at Fawdonfield and defended
      her rights with vigour.

31

Sep[tember] 10th [1]711

Methinks the time of my confinem[ent] very tedious, both as to the length of itt (which is now near 5 weeks and may be as much longer for ought I know) as also being debarr'd the use of my penn, which was wont to be a diversion to me tho' perhaps a nusance to those I corresponded with. However I would venture that with my friend, as I do att present to transgress my d[octor's] rules by stealing a few short lines in part answer to your last favor of the 28th ult. First then, I find that some people with you are masters of the secrett off getting off bad coals in quantitys, and 'tis certain that there has seldom come up more trash to a markett than by this last fleet. I freely own I could have wished that our Stella *fitters had not bin so much strangers to that mistery. I think their comodity was not inferior to the [Black] Burn or some others, which have disposed of a considerable quantity while our people stood with their arms cross and seemed like Solomon's sluggard; they apprehended a lyon to be upon your key [*i.e.* quay], so durst not venture abroad to sollicitt. Strange perverseness in mankind. The distemper is visible and deeply rooted; we have sufficiently suffer'd this year but there it is not likely to end. Pray good friend turn your thoughts as my d[octor] does in the case of my body pollitick; when an application has bin once tryed (which he hoped would have succeeded) and that fail'd, he rested not till he tryed another. And as I have the greatest opinion of his phisicall performances, so I justly entertain the like of yours in this business. You are upon the spott and know the severall parts of the trade that are affected and can give the best guess att the cause, and when that is known pray who can prescribe better. I must own I doe expect no redress but from your endeavors, yet even those can avail little unless the chiefs concern'd, that is the 5, should cotton better together than att present they seem to doe; and doubtless the dealers are not unacquainted with the divisions and will improve them by setting distinguishing marks upon some particular concerns. As to the upper seams, spare no industry to gett off in this last fleet, tho' att a less price; they will be infinitely worse for lying over year, increase your dead stock and ten to one but after Christmas 2 or 3 in the [score, *i.e.* *gift coal] will open the trade. I see no help for itt. Sunderland grows upon us while we lessen, yet every Tine owner is not I suppose willing to abate one *chalder of what his *vend has bin for years bypast and this must needs occasion strange distraction. Would it not be worth your while to postpone the raising of a *trunk till we see what turn both the trade and the owners of that concern think to take? Cha[rles] Sand[erson] has bin out of town near a month and not yet return'd, which occasions his silence in your regard; when I see him shall acquaint him etc. My father's offer of taking the tickett was with no other design than hopes of serving you without prejudicing himself. I paid uncle Rob[ert] the two £25 for the first paym[ent]. Mrs Smith has writ to sis[ter] Peggy which she says quits scores with you; sends her services, as I do mine also to her and the honest Ald[erman].

Kind friend, we are now busy furnishing our little house from

top to bottom; and lett us contrive as well as we can, will cost us
new beginning housekeepers a handsome summ of money,
which will drain more than I am att present master off. And as
you intimated in one of your former that you would remitt me
some towards the latter end of the year, I desire it might be
sometime next month if you can possibl[y], for it will be then
that we shall enter upon our new quarters and I shall have
severall bills to discharge. I must further beg of you to watch
John Linskill and desire him to deliver you for my use the bill of
sale of a 1/16th *p[art] of his ship, which belongs to me and the
man has never had the manners to do itt as yet.[1] If he be not in
the ship, pray desire Frank Rudston to write to him for it was
partly att your neighb[our's] instance that I adventur'd with
him. Pray likewise acquaint honest Jemmy that considering the
circumstances of our Stella trade, it seems absolutely necessary
that we should have orders from the court how to proceed and
then we act securely. To this end a state of the colliery as it is att
present with all its difficultys must be drawn up and
represented, as also a prospect of gift this next year; and of
another hand if that colliery should not be carried on, the
inconveniencys that would ensue as first the decrease of rents
for want of employ[ment], the loss off the *way which would in
a manner be entire by rotting upon the ground, the certainty of
*steath rents etc. to which we are confin'd by lease. After this
the court must judge what is fitting for us to doe and we must
pursue the directions given, and then come on't what will, we
shall be kept indemnifyed and blameless in the eye of the world.
This must be thought of and returnd me up so as to be presented
this next term, so pray lay your heads together. I have no more
to add, being in an uneasy posture with my 2 legs on a stool
almost as highly elevated as my rump. I can't give you authority
to drink any new health; I know nothing of the matter further
than that the means is frequently made use off for obtaining the
end.[2] No more but due respects to friends in your
neighbourhood....

[P.S.] My d[octor] has order'd me to drink punch in
moderation, a pint a day. I want some good brandy; pray use
your endeavors to procure me some and may disperse 3 or 4
bottles with one master and as many with another. Lett them be
sealed and tyed down. You must also get my madam a table suit

of huckaback from Darlington, which I remember is very fine
and good of the sort. Adieu. Harry Waters has some money in
his hands of mine, £6 14s 6d, the ballance of Tom Walker's
profitt which you will recieve for me and reimburse yourself for
these commissions as farr as will go.

1. This was not just a question of manners: there were contemporary
   complaints that masters held onto bills of sale for as long as possible to
   preserve their operational and financial independence.

2. Henry and Ann Liddell remained childless.

32

Sep[tember] 25th [1]711

Yours att your return from Richmond I had yesterday. By itts
speedy answer you may guess I am more att ease than for
severall weeks past. By tomorrow we hope to root out, I should
say eat out, the last and deepest part of the slough [*i.e.* scab] and
then adieu to those racking pains that gave me no quarter. We
shall heal up quickly; I could wish those animositys among the
coal owners were no longer liv'd, but while they are kept on foot
I expect no good. Yours mention a breach threaten'd among the
4 families. I doe imagin that Lamesly does not sett up his horses
with any of the other 3 but surely Greencroft and Rav[ensworth]
keep together, though I fancy the old people and your late
visitant don't cotton well together.[1] Should be glad to know how
these matters stand but rather to hear of an intire union, the
more necessary att this time of day than ever, otherwise the
publick will suffer as well as private familys. What should be the
meaning that Bensh[am] *steath have sold scarce a coal these
two fleets? Is it the dealors that give the word of command?
And how comes the steath att M[ain] Team to be so much
slighted this voyage; the Capt[ain] writes me word they have not
above 3 ships in the whole fleet. Strange it is methinks since that
concern has stop'd the mouths of the dealors by making good
the *praemium for last year; but as I told my uncle my
apprehensions [were] that as soon as they had gott last year's,
they would never bee att rest till he paid them for this allso, and
so I suppose are resolved to sitt upon our skirts and so give a
specimen of their arbitrary power. Helas! When I see poor

Sign[or's] letter with an offer of service, I could not forbear
smiling to my self. For my part I can't see of what use he can be
in the least; they would provoke him to the uttmost, would putt
him into passions and ten to one would toss him into the river or
use him very scurvily. I doubt not he would doe his best, but it is
not in the power of any one I know to undertake such an affair
except your self and I am sure not worth any body's while.
Cha[rles] Sand[erson] promised to write by Saturday's post.
Least Hugh should suffer in his ears, I send you an account of
my disbursem[ents] on your account. Thanks for your care of
my brandy as also of a *return. We drank your token att home;
I took your crown and gave Ned [Mawson?] a dish of meat one
evening and a bottle of better wine than the King's Head ever
afforded. I prevail'd with Mrs S[mith] to be one of the company
and very merry we were. I doubt not your putting my Lord
[Powlett]'s affairs into a good posture and hope he will be so
sensible of the advantage as to keep them so. They are expected
in town on Thursday night. Then must I sett apart one week
intirely to hear Sign[or's] novells. Is it usuall to install
gov[ernors] twice? They had that formallity many months agoe
when Ralph Gowl[and] came over to assist att the ceremony. I
pity poor Jemmy with all my heart; it must make the place very
disagreeable to him. My best services attend him. Now having
secured H[ugh's] ears I beg you will accept of a tender of our
joint services as also mine to Mrs Peggy and honest Ald[erman].
I remain....

1. The four families are probably the closely related Ellisons of Hebburn,
    Claverings of Greencroft and Lamesley, and Liddells of Ravensworth.
    Lamesley was a Liddell estate but was occupied by James Clavering.

33

Oct[ober] 4th [1]711

I don't know if I am indebted to my kind friend or no but be
that as it will 'tis no matter; I don't stand upon ceremony,
which allways ought to give way to business. And as this is the
criticall time for deciding the fate of the trade and on the
resolutions taken depends wellfare or ruin, I long to know what
steps have bin taken on that head. I have repeatedly

recommended both to Jemmy and the Capt[ain] to have an understanding in this weighty matter and tho' either party should suffer a little, better so than the whole goe to distraction. Two posts agoe I had a letter from the latter, who gives me an account of his installation, thanks me for my thoughts of the renewall of the Regulation, which to him seem the most naturall. He adds a computation of charges [for] laying a *way from Urpeth to join our own way, as also those of working, and so draws itt into a scheme of profit and loss. The quaerys I desire to be satisfied off are whether the lease is to commence att present or after old Tom [Bewick]'s death; whether there be a possibility of obtaining *way leavs through Kibblesw[orth] grounds and through Rav[ensworth] town fields where are so many different propertys? The rent is easy enough. And B[lack] B[urn's] wain *trunk might be converted into a waggon on that occasion very conveniently. He leaves it to me to communicate to my father if I think proper. Accordingly I did in the gross; had I not, perhaps some exception might be taken which I will industriously avoid. I can't yet have his answer. But if the concern were actually taken, she would fall most naturally both for working and *leading down Mr H[edworth's] way, if he could be prevail'd to be content with a share of her and contribute to part of the laying charges thro' his own ground. This would certainly turn to best account. But of that you can best judge and inform. This fleet is come up. Att their arrivall coals were 26[s] 6[d] the best, but then the markett was att a stand and since that I hear [it's] occasion'd by the Yarm[outh] men refusing to sell but att 29s. I must own I think them in the right. I have wrote to the Capt[ain] this post who will discourse you on the points above. I heard you were out of order; pray write particularly to the d[octor] or send itt to me, for without particulars the d[octor] will not prescribe. I hope Mrs Ramsay (to whom my humble service) will oblige you; there is nothing like taking things in time. The youngest of Mis[ses] Clav[ering] I doubt will scarce hold out 3 days [with] a violent feavor in her head; poor creature, she has no less than 9 blisters on att this time and is not sensible. If our d[octor] recovers her he may work miracles. Poor Mrs Smith has likewise bin much out of order for a week by past. She keeps a foot and is to begin to morrow to take some of our d[octor's] sweetmeets. Adieu I am....

[P.S.] Just now the Sig[nor] is come in, who in his travells this day hears that our Councill disapprove of the peace as proposed. How true this is time will discover.[1]

1. Peace preliminaries were signed in September, arousing protests from those like Shrewsbury who were reluctant to abandon Britain's allies. There had also been a quarrel between St John and Somerset which gave rise to rumours about divisions within the ministry.

34

[October] 13th [1]711

Be your letters never so long, you give them that handsome turn that one is pleased with reading ofter than once. I have drank a flask of spaw these 2 mornings which does not agree with this paper employ, and business has so fallen out that I was obliged to write to my father [and] to bro[thers] Ellison and Bright upon extraordinary occasions. Yet can't forbear giving you small measure instead of great, with variety of thanks; first for the insight you give me into Urpeth and that neighbourhood, 2dly for the prospect of the meeting of the Five, 3dly for your *bill upon Capt[ain] Oldn[er] which I have given Plumpton this day to present, as also the *note on uncle Rob[ert] which I shall my self tender to him some time next week, and lastly for your kind care of my commissions. To the first: I apprehend you will have more people to treat with in crossing our Rav[ensworth] town fields than what you mention and doubt those will be upon the high horse. 2d: I expect little from the meeting of the 5. If some must think of adding to their *quant[ity] while all others lessen, [it] is what I never expect will be comply'd with and methinks an understanding is not cordially search'd after. There needs no futher argument than Wortley's supiness in lying att Durham when he should be upon the spott to assist and promote so good an understanding. You remark right, he is puff'd up with a notion of the wonderfull feats the people att Gate will doe for him, but after all I should not be sorry to see them drop his honor's tayle in the dirt. 3d: I have given you cred[it] for the £21 8[s] and shall mark also that of uncle's when I know what it comes to. Lastly: as to the table cloth it must be if in length 2½ yards, bredth 2 [yards] and so in proportion. Napkins are in the price. The brandy will be acceptable. This latter I hope will be up before the latter end of next week when we shall remove to our new quarters, and then I shall be enabled to give my friends that come a house warming a bowl of punch. I have spoke again to Charles S[anderson] as also to his clark to putt him in mind of writing to you and give answers in due course to your letters. Mrs Smith is perfectly well recruited by a small prescription of our d[octor's]. She was here this morn[ing]; says you are a perfect wagg and if ever you come to Lond[on] again she will be even with you. Last night Jo[seph] Barnes came from the Bath, not better'd by those nor Bristoll waters. He complains of want of appetite to meat but his greatest affliction is he can't drink either red or white wine. Yet his complexion seems clear. He designs to sett out for the north week after next. My father not expected till toward the middle of that week. We last night buryed the youngest of our Misses after 15 days lying in extremity. This has putt us into great confusion for the present. My spouse salutes you. I am ....

[P.S.] My service to sister Peggy.

35

[October 1711]

Just time to tell you that I have received the [£]21-8 (the ball[ance] of my own disbursm[ents] for you) of Mr James Collier, who paid it to Mrs Smith by mistake but she rep[aid] it me. My uncle hopes to sell your tickett I belive this week; that class sells for about £94 10s. We long to hear of a final conclusion of your meetings. Pray tell Jemmy that if he could send a *bill itt would be acceptable, for the funerall charges, d[octors], apothecarys, mourning for the childer has and will sweep away a great summ. It is an age since I have heard from you particularly. Adieu ....

36

[October] 25th [1]711

I am in hast to answer two of yours; I call itt so since Mr Freek is come in and my company is expected. I thank you for your care of shipping my provisions; I am much obliged to my good

friend Jemmy and yourself for the generous remembrance. No
greater satisfaction could be to me than the enjoym[ent] of your
2 companys over a bottle in our close quarters; such I call them
since our house is so little that one can scarce swing a catt, yet
big enough for our circumstances, and that accompanied with a
contented mind makes it roomy enough and easy. The dealors
were with me last Monday, that is to say the 3 Oldners, all
extreemly offended that no *praemium has bin paid for
Clav[ering] Stella, without which they will not talk of any future
ingagem[ent]. Nay were that bargain performed by us, I
question much if on any terms they would be obliged to ingage,
complaining heavily of the smallness and of their absolute
incapacity to serve us. I promised that this should be
communicated to Jemmy, which I desire you will doe. And as to
Johnson's coming up, nothing can be resolved on till we hear
the result of last Tuesday's meeting. If he should come up, who
knows but by his joint contrivance with the dealers he may make
himself more necessary to us than hitherto and may give them a
further insight, so as to distress a Regulation if any. Therfore
the consideration of this will be deferr'd a little longer. My last
to the Capt[ain] will inform what my father desires should be
explain'd about Urpeth. He is cautious but likes the concern
extreemly, only his apprehensions are the same with mine, that
*way leaves will be of the greatest difficulty to obtain. You will
have his positive answer by the return and we are extreemly
beholden to you for your kind offices not only in this but many
other instances. If the 3 pieces of huccaback be sent up, I believe
we may dispose of what we don't like our selvs. Many thanks to
our kind factoress with her commicall adventure. 'Tis good to
lean to the safest side tho' one should pay a little for itt. I
approve of your offer of the salt *pans and readily accept of itt,
for while under your menagem[ent] I know there will be no
miscarriage. Having answer'd I think fully to the most materiall
points, I wish you good success and must return to the company
who wait impatiently for ....

[P.S.] I forgott to tell you that the Oldners were commending
your Parson Flatt coals yet would not buy them, as they
pretend, because they were not in the Regulation. What dam'd
fellows are these. I was provoked with them beyond measure.
The talk of a peace is much cooler than some days agoe yet I

fancy it will take effect att last. How will that affect your salt trade? My hearty respects to our factress. My father is very hearty.

37

Nov[ember] 10th [1]711

Perhaps my longing desire of hearing frequently from you made me complain without a cause, but I can assure you yours directed to Mr Ashley both came safe and sooner by many hours than if addressed to our own habitation, since in the winter season the post does not deliver our letters till the next morn[ing]. I should in Sign[or's] short postscript have advised you of the reciet of yours but he was hurrying me to save a peny so that in all probability I forgott. I have no objection to Johnson's coming, save that by his cunning he may give the dealers a great insight into the *foible* as the French call itt of the coal trade, which they understand too much of allready. In the next place you will see they will never treat with us for Stella without the *praemiums for the year before as well as this last; both which will am[ount] to above £200, and perhaps should this be granted I question whether they can doe us or at least will doe us any great service. This is my positive opinion before he arrives, which you will communicate to my good friend of Lamesly and lett me know his if we ought to comply provided we have some assurances, which by the by will not be better perform'd than former ones. But when we have made tryall, more cannot be don for the Infant. Our Bucksnook must be wrought to supply the markett with good [coal], nay choice good, the begining of the year or otherwise the laboring oar will lye dreadfully heavy upon us all the year and that can't be born. Pray therfore send us word if we can propose to work a quantity of right good for this ensuing year. I foresee that concern can't be supported but while the coals are extraordinary, Contract or none. Once a fortnight there ought constantly to be a clear pay att pits and in part for *carriadge; the oppression is prodigious by longer delays and gives Weath[erly] and others an opportunity of feathering his nest. Recommend this heartily to our friend, who I am sorry is ingaged in the black trade if the concern be from Tanfield side. I was sensible from your first undertaking the waggon way you would meet with difficultys and crosses in abundance. There was such a confederated tribe of r[ogues] nested together and each plaid into the other's hand, that I could but admire you could make that impression that has bin made. I believe you will find the same game playing in Richmondshire among the miners and the quondam agents.[1] I am att a loss what to fix you for your pains and trouble; if it should be answerable to either, I know the summ would be very considerable. But att this distance must leave it to Jemmy and your self. You will see what the concern has saved by the alterations and accordingly proportion the reward. I am satisfyed £150 is the least acknowledgm[ent] that can be made you by the publick for your signall services this last year: were they as sensible of itt as we that were eye witnesses, they would make itt att least a brace. These are my thoughts and pray communicate them to the honest gentleman of Lamesly, who I know will press as much as possible this affair in your favor.

My father had last night a large account of the last meeting from the Capt[ain]. I have but barely read itt over. His quaery to me was what character those *fitters have that are appointed for Bensham. They are all sett up for themselvs since I left you, att least were not of my acquaintance, so was obliged to answer by silence. This good effect the Agreem[ent] will have, that I hope itt will keep both fitters and dealers in a better decorum. Waters's impudence ought to be corrected by the united body. We hear that Byker M[ain] coal is gott [*i.e.* *won]: what is your opinion? If the coal be tollerable, that concern may be a thorn in our side and may incourage the fitters to keep up their heads. We leave all menagem[ent] of Stella to the honest Vaudois with your assistance and he may depend the dealers will never treat about that concern without the full satisfaction for the 2 last years. But you shall hear more of this shortly for my head and stomach are much disorder'd and increased by the badness of the weather. The inclosed is my uncle's account of the disposall of your tickett by which you will percieve he has paid me on your account £45 7[s] 4d for which you have creditt. Yesterday noon dyed old Mrs Blakiston of the gout in her stomach, which had bin there near a month before she sent for our honest d[octor] but he came too late. The Parl[iament] is adj[ourned] to the 27th.[2] Next post my wife designs Jemmy a long epistle. Our young pupill has behaved himself not so civilly as he should to his sist[er] Lady C[owpe]r, which has given great offence and makes me sick of my charge. Did you put on board Ableson the Capt[ain']s wine he presented me? Pray remember me kindly to my factoress. My wife and Mr Genuini present to you their respects and I remain ....

[P.S.] I hear by the by that Brummell pretends to lay his *way in spight of mankind. My hearty respects to my honest Alderman.

1. Both Cotesworth and Lord William Powlett were convinced that the poor performance of the latter's Yorkshire lead mines resulted from collusion between the miners and Powlett's local agents, who had siphoned off the profits. Cotesworth had been brought in to tighten up the management but found it a difficult task.

2. The opening of the second parliamentary session was postponed, ostensibly because both Harley and the Queen were ill but actually to prepare for the Lords' expected attack on the peace terms.

38

Nov[ember] 23th [1]711

Yours inclosed to Mr Ashly came to hand this minute and have sent itt to my father to peruse and give him time to consider of itt. Therfore am now answering off book, having an hour of leisure and free from company. You desire to know my thoughts of a certain concern [Urpeth] but I must first tell you my father's. He you know is very difficult to enter upon any new project which is attended with a present considerable outlay. He is very cautious, which none can blame him for. He sent for me and ask'd my thoughts. I told him that if *way leaves could be had upon tollerable terms and the colliery wrought on such as yours and the Capt[ain's] represented, I looked upon't as a concern that ought not to be slipt by any means. After a few days he repeated the question; I continued of the same mind. Well, says he, will you go shares? Yes sir, said I, my present opinion is such that I will venture ¼, nay to share ⅓ if you please. You are wellcome, said he. Not long after he produces the severall charges of laying the *way and working, which he look'd upon as too small considerably as well as the rent too great. As to the first I agreed with him that to *winn and lay the way, £1160 would not doe itt. To that of working I told him I

thought I could satisfy him to a nicety in that point, for among
some of my papers I was sure of finding a project with the exact
charges of Mr H[edwor]th's att the time that Ald[erman]
Wh[ite] had taken this, and should look out for itt. He was
delighted with this. I brought it to him. And where the
Capt[ain's] comp[utation] makes £1 15s the [*ten of] 22
wagg[ons], the other made £1 13s the 42 *fother [of] 7 *bolls
each, so that the wagg[on] tenn would be near upon 50s
work[ing], draw[ing] water etc. Well, says he, proceed and sett
down every article what you think may doe. Accordingly I
promised I would doe itt very liberally, so sett down 20d a gate
[for *carriage] and twice a day made 3[s] 4d for man and horse,
which was as much as his own waggon men could addle [i.e.
earn]. I reckond the way longer by a good mile than Norbanks,
however sett down 18s a tenn while Mr M[ontagu] paid but 12s,
yet I would not be positive but that M[ontagu] had but 20
wagg[ons] to the tenn. I charged 5s p[er] tenn for all charges att
*steath, which is more than will doe itt, perhaps pay the
steathm[an] and under-steathm[an's] wages into the bargain.
The way leavs, steath rents, *viewers and all salarys I think £250
yearly, including satisfaction for the liberty of his [Sir Henry's]
steath and of the way from the Cowclose to the steath. £2000 for
winning the colliery and laying the way and wagg[ons]. All these
summs except the last I thought would each overdoe; and
allowing 16½ [*chaldron] *making out and *double coal att
11s, *fittage, [*keel-]owners' wages and dealers at 6d p[er]
ch[aldron], there would remain £600 neat upon 600 pitt tenns.
The chief dispute with me was whether the way over Urp[eth]
dean could be effected without casting the way so much to the
east as that it would be of the utmost difficulty to bring the
wagg[ons] up to Kibblesw[orth]. As to the rent he was of
opinion that 10s was full much. I told him that it was not above
7s for a wain tenn and I thought not att all unreasonable. All
this he desired me to draw out in a scheme and send it the
Capt[ain] which I did above a week agoe, and on his answer he
will take his finall resolution. I would not be over forward in
pressing and had rather that things could be brought to bear
under the proposall than upon a tryall to exceed, for that would
make him exceeding uneasy. The next thing that makes the case
disputable is the apprehension that it will lessen Team *vend and
that I doubt is but reasonable to expect. But of another hand I

represented that if these coals went unmixt, [they] might probably yield 11s 6d so consequently £250 more yearly profitt; if *mixt with Team, would help off with many of his small workings. Cav[erley Bewick] was with us this day and will wait till we recieve the Capt[ain's] answer.

Just now our parcells of wine and ale came home safe. We drank all your healths att supper. The former is very good and the latter we hope, tho' a little down, will recover with time. The brandy is safe and extraord[inary] measure. My good friend will accept of my best thanks for his very kind remembrance. The huckaback 2 pieces of 16d and 14d are with us and well approved off; that of 10½d came not to our hands. I have bin large and particular on the first article of this letter, which you will keep to yourself; if hear further shall be sure to advise. The dealers were with my father 3 days agoe. They eat so heartily that poor Mrs Smith could not forbear lifting up her hands, yet would not conclude absolutely for Team the next year tho' my fath[er] proposed doing by them as Mr W[ortley] did for H[utton] and B[lenwell]. For Clav[ering] St[ella] they would not ingage for 2s 6d p[er] ch[aldron] if the coals were such as last summer. And if they were assured that they were never so good this next, they would not touch a coal of them unless first satisfied for the year 1710/1711. What ever you doe be sure not to work any but what is choice good and little of Coalburn, as Jemmy and you shall agree, for retrieving the lost reputation. I wish Johnson does not give us the slipp, as I have advised the Vaudois. I have wearyed my self and my head is confused, but yours is so clear that you will be able I hope to hammer out my meaning. Adieu then and rest assured that I am ....

[P.S.] My wife salutes you. My respects to the honest Ald[erman] and Mrs Marg[aret].

39

[December 1st 1711]
Saturday night past 10

An invitation to Lord C[owpe]r's has kept me till this time. I must be short and referr you to Cha[rles] for particulars. He was with my fath[er] and me this morn[ing]: we all agree that offering a summ to Mr Mead would not look well, but rather that he might be assured of a few doz[en] of good wine when the business is over. Cha[rles] designs to move the court strenuously next Tuesday, that the profitts of the mann[ors] etc. be rec[eived] by an agent of the present possessor join'd to one appointed by the purchaser. That the profitts accruing shall be paid to the Bi[sho]pp's originall rent and interest to the mortgagees; if any surplus, to remain in the agents' hands subject to any future ord[er] of the court. That no lease of *way leave be made for the least term, directly or indirectly. That no lease for year[s] be made of any colliery; but in case the court should say that were unreasonable, and they will have, then say I press that no lease be made but by consent and approbation of the purchasor or such person as he shall nominate. Cha[rles] pretends to excuse himself but I doubt has bin tardy. Has promised double dilligence for the future and he shall not want spurring up. He says Cratchrode misunderstood him and would satisfy Jackson that it was a mistake, but that will avail little. He has promised to give you a particular account p[er] this post of what advice Mr Mead gives and how they design to proceed, and assures ther is nothing don by his concession that can bind you but you are att as full liberty and att large as if nothing had bin [done]. My father has not bin able to stir abroad, and truly I gott such a stitch in my side that I can scarce breathe and would gladly have putt of this day's invitation, but could not well doe itt since the good lady came in her own coach to fetch me. I can't add but that I am in all conditions ....

40

Dec[ember] 6th [1]711

I have two of yours before me. To the first you should have had an answer by Tuesday's post but Cha[rles] S[anderson] was so late in making his motion that I had no account of the success till very late, and he promised to peruse the minutes of the court and give you a full account. My father as well as self are of opinion that he has bin tardy in his former proceedings and wish he were not too free in his conversation with Tom Gibson, to the prejudice of the business in hand. What he has obtain'd by the last motion in my mind is insignificant; that you be privy to all contracts but I don't find that you can overrule any contracts Jackson shall make. He says the court would not allow a lease to be made by the present possessor but only a contract. I putt the question if a contract could be made for a year or longer; to this he could give no direct answer, att least satisfactory one, but assured me Mr Cratchrode, Bassett's attorny, insisted upon no longer term than a year. To this I replyed that was not in court, only by word betwixt you and that he may revoke att pleasure. Att length all he could promise was that he would seek to insert (for the term of a year) in the drawing up the last order of court and if that can't be effected then he will move the court again; but he thinks Cratchrode will not deny itt. I can assure you that both my father and self have labor'd him hard this very day till with teazing him he was almost vex'd. As to the other concern, my father is backward in treating but I proposed this to him; to give your friend a meeting, insisting upon 2 years for laying the *way and other preparations and the 3d year to begin the paym[ent] of £300, work or not. He thinks the quantity too large to be bound too but I hope we shall prevail with him to condescend.[1] I think the Capt[ain] intirely in the right to secure another *way leave; lett the worst that can happen, you have no less than two strings to your bow.

It must certainly be some of Jackson's friends that writes these anonymus letters to your bro[ther] with a design to create a jealousy twixt you and him and that they may therby reap the advantage. Brummell seems very expeditious in his undertakings; what he thinks [is] that possession is a main point. Mr Freek's thoughts are that if a lease for years be not made, those that lay a way may suffer considerably and the purchasor may safely pull up every stick off wood; as if a man builds upon my ground, I being ten[ant] for life, my son will take possession after my decease. But in your case the court will not hinder any thing that may advance the interest of the estate. In the rentall there appears no rent reserv'd for way leave over those wastes. Here comes Brummell, offers the present possessor suppose £200 for full liberty over those commons; this is an advancem[ent] of the estate and the question is whether that can be destroyed by the new purchaser. Cha[rles] gives me shuffling answers: but if you comprehend this quaery, putt it to him in form and more fully and desire he will authentically inform himself and give such further instructions as you judge

reasonable. He grasps after more business that he can goe thro'
with. Your huckaback came carr[iage] free and if the course
piece had come up we would have ventur'd on't; for common
use it would serve, but as it did not come up tis no matter. Pray
lett me hear if Lady B[owes] makes any steps in opposition to
B[rummell]. I have gott a very great hoarsness by visiting ladys
last night in my father's company; towards night it grows sore.
My respects attend all und[er] your roof as well as the honest
Ald[erman]. I am ....

1.   Most colliery leases deferred the first rent payments for two or three years
     to allow the lessee time to bring the mine into production. Rents were
     usually assessed by the modified royalty arrangement indicated here,
     which stipulated a minimum quantity of coal that had to be worked and
     paid for every year, with an additional royalty payment for anything
     above this agreed threshold.

41

Dec[ember] 13th [1]711

I have bin laid up as I may call it for severall days of a violent
hoarsness, which att last is turned into a wett cough. I have not
bin out but yesterday for an hour to wait on T[homas] Bew[ick]
upon the treaty, having before sent our proposalls by
Cav[erley]. My father offer'd 9s rent and 400 *t[ens] certain, to
have a reasonable time for *wining, laying the *way and
providing *way leavs etc. This was the first proposall made by
my father to Cav[erley] but I assured him that if 10s rent would
fetch itt and 500 t[ens], he might depend I should work my
father up to itt. This was given Cav[erley] in writing on Monday
I think; he shewed it to Tom, who immediately cry'd they were
Mr H[edwor]th's proposalls he was sure. No, says the other,
they are not and if you think you can comply with the terms or
therab[outs] you shall see the chapman. Tom being ill of the
gout appointed a meeting att his house last night; Cav[erley]
appeard. After some introductory discourse my father ask'd
Tom his terms. He told him if he lett her it should be att 12s 6d
and to be bound to work 800 t[ens] certain every year; that he
was offer'd £400 certain from the signing of the lease, work or
not, and if they wro[ught] more than 800 t[ens] the rent then to
be 12s 6d. This we thought very extravagant, not to allow time

to win and lay the way and the rent too high; [so] that my father told him, whoever the party was that made that offer had much exceeded any that he could make, since he could advance very little higher than the proposall he had given Cav[erley] in writing. So they parted, wishing each other well. Now what can be don? My father will not give higher than 10s rent and 500 t[ens], after a reasonable time allowed for winning etc. I have used my endeavors to bring it to this length; absolutely dispair of getting further. What is then to be don; could you not write to Cav[erley], or rather the Ald[er]man to him, letting him know that if the coal proves well my father will be able to dispose of a greater quan[tity] in our river than even Mr H[edworth] or any other can in Were, and tho' the rent be less yet in the main the concern will be as heartily wrought, and so forth? And lett him go as from himself and try what his bro[ther] will doe and give us an account, but I find Tom keeps him att a distance.[1] Tom does not know who has made this large offer. I have wrote fully to Cha[rles] and sent Hugh with itt, to desire him to answer what you wish to be satisfied in by this post as farr as possible, and depend on't he shall not want a spurr. But if he has already lett slip the opportunity of preventing them letting a lease, what can be don? If that can't be sett aside, which he does not warrant can be don, had not you best threaten to decline the bargain? But you are a better master than to want instructions from so mean a capacity. The purchase will make but a scurvy figure when the best flower is taken out of it. 'Tis now near 8 att night and I have not gott a mouthfull of vitals. I am summon'd in to break my fast. Adieu, I wish you such success as may answer your ends and the expectations of your friends. You will excuse me to the good Ald[erman] to whom I must now be silent as well as to honest Jemmy. I am ....

[P.S.] Adieu to the profitable part of most collierys in Tyne, if this way proceed. My fath[er] will send you Cha[rles'] letters, they being in his custody.

---

1. Negotiations to lease Urpeth colliery were complicated by the fact that the estate was entailed and would therefore pass to Calverley Bewick's family rather than to Thomas Bewick's daughter. This created a conflict of interests and considerable ill-feeling.

42

Dec[ember] 27th [1]711

'Tis past ten att night. Jemmy is safely arrived and just gon to
see my father. I have *drawn upon you £11 payable to my late
man Hugh Ridley, which I desire you will give it creditt. I sent
privately for Calverly and without consent of my father offer'd
10s rent [and] 600 *t[ens] yearly, the rent to begin after *winning
the colliery which I computed would be about 6 months after
execution of the lease, so that in a year and ½ they would have a
year's rent. [I said that] Though yours works [a ten of] 22
wagg[ons] and 15 *bowls each, yet I insist on 19 or M[ontagu's]
present Norbanks *measure. I represented that tho' H[edwort]h
might offer £400 certain, yet if he complyed to allow Tom £200
out of the 300 for the first year or two, in all probability he
would be reimbursed with interest afterward. Calv[erley] was
convinced and would doe any thing in his power, but doubted if
convenient to mention these proposals to Tom till Swaddell
came up for, says he, my bro[ther] will not conclude till that
time. I left to himself to act but withall told my opinion that he
should broach it before. I find Whitfield is always putting in a
word in favor of H[edwor]th. I hope my father might be
brought to the terms above, tho' with difficulty, and the offer is
very handsome. Make what use you please by getting the
Ald[erman] to write to Calv[erley]. Cha[rles] Sand[erson] is
ashamed to come nigh us. But I will acquaint him with what you
write and he shall be putt in mind of his business. Excuse hast,
'tis near 11. I am ....

[P.S.] Poor Mrs Smith has bin a housekeeper above a week;
proposed to wish you and sis[ter] Ramsay a merry [Christ]mas
and happy new year but is so much out of order that she can't
sett pen to paper, but salutes you both. You will be curious to
know why I part with Hugh. I must own he has behaved himself
honestly and faithfully but happen'd to be invited to my father's
coachman's to a bowl of punch, and whether he gott in drink I
know not, for he did not cast up till next day att 11. I satt up for
him till midnight. He says he was taken up by a press gang.
Perhaps it was so, but he having given me warning before, I
agreed to it and so we parted. Adieu.

43

Feb[ruary] 28th [1]711/12

Your last was extreemly acceptable since it brought particulars of your severall adventures, by which you shew'd a nice menagem[ent], especially considering some of the people you had to transact with; and all this for the service off your friends who upon all occasions will be ready to own the obligations. I am sorry that the honest Ald[erman] should be disturb'd by such frequent sollicitations; could it not be contriv'd that an end might be put to them, by their [the manors] being disposed off to some other hand on a reasonable consideration? I need not say more but shall leave you to hammer out a project. I must own your proposalls by way of addition to Hebd[on's] were a masterpiece and will afford them tow to teaze [*i.e.* cause difficulties]. I am sensible your Lond[on] journey proved very prejudicial to your private concerns, which tho' they suffer'd by your absence yet the publick rec[eived] infinitely greater advantages by your presence. When you sold to the ships att 9[s]6[d] did the master make his way att the Gate or did you allow a *praemium over and above that abatem[ent] att Newc[astle]? The reason I ask is this. I sent a friend to the Gate to speak to Rand and partners to help off with an unknown concern (which was Cl[avering] St[ella]). The answer he brought me was that if it was a good concern they would ingage, and they were att liberty since some whose coals they had taken off last year had dropt them without giving the praemium stipulated. They did not name any person. Now if you found that they had not don their parts and consequently did not deserve, I know it would be in vain to speak to them about assisting you. As to the number 10, you may depend they have undertaken for more than they can perform, and even should they promise there would be no relying. For others, I know not one soul so much as by sight but if you will tell me what the concern will afford, I will employ one; but to appear my self will not be in the least advisable. I know that Wetherly gives 12d by his own confession. The ships are come too early by 3 weeks for the warehouses are not quite empty, so that the price will scarce ever exceed 27s for the very best and God knows how low the indiffer[ent] and worst will be.

Is it possible that Brigad[ier's] *undertakers can be bound to sell 16000 Sund[erland] *ch[aldrons]; which way can they perform? That river has more coals already than will supply the ships. What is then the consequence? 'Tis plain a lowring of price and a fighting trade, and what then? I should think inevitable destruction to the new undertak[ers] and if they can't gett off their *qu[antity] what becomes of them? Indeed were there a prospect that they could lett for the rent or an advanced one to Mr H[edworth], 3 or 400 *t[ens] yearly then would bring their own obligation to a reasonable quantity. I must own as it is, it passes my understanding. I must referr you to my letter to the Capt[ain] by last post, which gives att large an account of what conversation I had with honest Cav[erley]. You will see if you can't gain a little further time till it may be consider'd what course to steer, and have your thoughts along with the Capt[ain's] to my father, who begins to entertain a much more favorable opinion of that concern and speaks with some pleasure of her. If Fieldhouse, Bensh[am], Bl[ackburn] and the [Hedley] Fell should once begin to fail it would ease the trade, but I don't expect any great deficiencys from any of these for some years. My head is still much disturb'd, though I gott by means of a chair as far as my father's this day being the first attempt and din'd with him. He is not well, catching cold after phisick yesterday. Adieu, my hearty respects to the honest Ald[erman]. Grant me another fav[or] which is to hear frequently from you which satisfaction will contribute as much to gain me strength as the d[octor's] prescription ....

[P.S. ...] writes tis a design of the magis[trates] to bring them under a lash which has occasion'd their petitioning, and I hear (says he) that he *keelmen themselvs violently oppose the bill.[1] Adieu.

---

1.   The bill in question represented Newcastle corporation's latest attempt to gain control of the keelmen's charity. It was presented to the Commons in January 1712 but was challenged in March by petitions from the charity's officials and nearly a thousand keelmen and also from twenty-five *fitters, who feared that the corporation's proposals threatened their own independence. The bill was rejected by the Lords in April.

44

Mar[ch] 25th [1]712
past 7 att night

'Tis of a long standing that I am indebted to you and since
you are pleased to allow me that liberty now and then, I doubt I
shall be apt to call custome. Your account of the last elect[ion]
was the most entertaining of any I have mett with. I find your
interest helpt to strengthen that of the church by which you have
curryed fav[our] with the diocesan, and tho' our friend Jemmy
N[icholson] is now allow'd to be a white boy, yet I think you
stand fairer for preferm[ent] while most of your former
acquaintance lye under a black censure; how reasonably I can't
say but shall leave you to judge. My father being never desir'd to
give the little interest he had, resolved between the two late
candidates to stand newter and leave every one to dispose of
their votes as they thought most suitable to their inclinations,
but it seems the doctrine is this, those that are not for us are
against us. This interpretation I suppose is putt upon't and so he
is deem'd an enemy to the person elected and the interest that
brought him in, by which you see how the cloud still hangs over
his head while you are so happy as to enjoy the brightness of the
sun in its full meridien. Long may itt continue to you in that
perfection and answerable to your deserts, still hoping that you
will not intirely forgett your quondam friends, tho' now in
affliction.[1] But I must drop this subject and proceed to another,
which to me seems more materiall. I must tell you that I had the
honor to dine with your honest Record[er George Bowes] att my
father's last Fryday, who intertain'd me with your nice
menagem[ent] of his sister's concerns in protecting them against
a certain person that formerly by force had gott a good yard
within them. We drank the champion's health but alass! I was
mightily dejected when I heard from Cha[rles] that he was
confin'd to his bed. He executed his commission by shewing the
letters wrote by your serv[ant]; and as for your project of
communicating to Mr Pitts, I could not but approve off [it] and
the rather since I find Mr Gibson is so farr ledd by your friend
J[ackso]n that he will recieve no other impression than what he
has from him, especially when so back't as by the insinuations
and representations of another gentleman, who threatens
publickly to tear up all wagg[on] ways that cross a high way or

street and so putt the trade upon a levell.[2] I won't trouble with a repetition of particulars since I know Cha[rles], who was an ear witness, has given you them att large. Only excuse my adding to your proposal to Sir J[ohn Clavering] (for whom Rob[ert] W[right] assured Mr G[ibson] that he would ingage the barr[onet] should lett *way leave thro' his grounds upon reasonable terms) that you insist that he grant liberty for a number of years certain, not for his own life, which considering how free he makes with itt may not spin out the length of your lease, tho' you should not renew.[3]

I have not seen nor heard from honest Calv[erley] since my last to the Capt[ain] on that score; my father went about a fortnight since to wait upon him but mistooke the coffee house that he frequents, so lost his labor. That concern of his is the only one unopen'd in all your river that I should covet to be ingaged in. Pray how goes on Mr H[edworth's] wag[gon] way? Mr Gen[uini] would inform what past twixt him and two of the dealers in relation to your concern. They will not undertake for a *quantity and indeed there are so many of them in such mean circumstances that you would not desire they should. I doe believe these two are the best of that sett but if they will not undertake, I don't see but that if the master undertook for himself, it would be the safest way. But Sign[or] expects your further orders and a ship of the coals for a sample. I am summon'd to meet Mr Freek att my father's. Therfore must conclude with hearty wishes for your speedy recovery and the continuance of a health so usefull to all your friends. Adieu honest Will[iam], I remain ....

[P.S.] A peace very speedily is expected.

1. In February 1712 a by-election was fought for Sir Henry Belasis's seat at Durham, in which Robert Shafto beat Anthony Hall after a short contest: see Bean, *Parliamentary Representation*, p.130. Liddell implies that James Nicholson, the beaten Whig candidate in 1710, failed to stand in order to placate the virulently Tory bishop. Cotesworth's own defection from the Whig cause may have been prompted by the bishop's influence as ultimate lessor of Gateshead and Whickham and was in any case strictly temporary.

2. One of the main charges levelled against Brumell's Bucksnook waggonway was that one stretch had been laid along a public highway in order to evade wayleave payments and controls and that this obstructed traffic. Brummell of course denied that his way obstructed the road and

threatened that he would use a decision against him on this point to attack the many other waggonways that crossed or ran along highways.

3. This may be a reference to negotiations that were certainly in progress later in the year to end the waggonway dispute by transferring part or all of Bucksnook colliery to Cotesworth himself, thus ensuring wayleave through Whickham for a moderate amount of coal from the western collieries. An agreement on these lines was reached in 1716 but failed in its purpose as Sir John Clavering's widow steadfastly refused to come to terms.

45

Apr[il] 5th [1]712

I think I must not begin a letter without acknowledging double obligations, but if you had such disturbing weather as we have had of late, you would guess by your own constitution how much a farr weaker is influenced by itt; and in such circumstances writing is nott allow'd. Itt has affected my father not a little, who had begun a letter to you two posts agoe but not yet able to finish. Indeed what chiefly disturb'd him was his anxious sollicitude about poor Kitt Stockdale, who being att diner 3 or 4 days since att Tom Gibson's, was taken so ill with a sort of convulsion that they were obliged to send three people in a coach home with him to support him, and it was so late before he could be remov'd that the news of his illness came not to my father till near 9 a clock, when good Mrs Smith was detached. She satt up with him as long as she could, being obliged to return to give an account. I can assure you it was a melancholly one since she never expected to see him more. Poor man he lay in such agonys till the next day that he came to himself, that you would admire he should ever gett abroad; however his heart was good, and with some cordialls (wherof a bottle of your brandy was one) he was brought in a chair to Red Lyon Street day before yesterday where he began again to relapse, but God be thank'd, tho' extreemly weak he is gott abroad again. You may imagin considering the dearness there is twixt the two bro[thers] what a confusion my father was in, who gave due attendance to his [own brother] even to the last extremity. This he desired me to acquaint you with and hopes for your pardon to his silence till next post.

I gave the Capt[ain] a full account of what passed twixt honest Calv[erley] and me the day after I received his and your letter, which doubt not he has communicated. Calv[erley] promised that when ever he received any account from the north about Urpeth (the letting of which he did not in the least expect) that he would call upon me in his way to his bro[ther] T[om] and give me an account, but I have not seen or heard from him since. The loss of poor Jo[seph Barnes] is not easily to be repair'd. My wife and I went last Sunday night to sup att Mrs Wait's, where we found poor Mrs Betty Barnes melancholly to a degree and not without reason. I sent your last inclosed immediately away to Cha[rles] S[anderson]. It is a compleat answer to such allegations as one would not admire to see B[rumel]l subscribe too, but for a person of the other rank [Sir John Clavering] methinks tis unaccountable; but one plainly sees that he pins his faith upon some people's sleevs. Cha[rles] and I had talked over the matter in my parlor and I gave him such reasons for your conduct as I was capable off and convinced uncle Stockd[ale] fully, who is a person that is as well heard by T[homas] Gibs[on] as any. But Jackson has laid such a foundation in his opinion as nothing but time and experience can root itt out. Therfore I think you are to blame if you concern yourself further. You have don handsomly and friendlily by Mr G[ibson]; if he will still be led by the nose, much good may doe him. He may smart att long run. I am sensible the weather must have distressed your *vend, as allso that a *trunk tho' never so small would have bin of singular service. You are left to act as you think fitt in relation to that, whose judgem[ent] all ways sways with me. Gett a ship for a sample as soon as you can when the weather is dry; if the coals be roundy, I hope Sig[nor] Projector may be of service, and be sure not to send the worst. Mr Gen[uini] has bin sadly plagued with your Newc[astle] carrier about a box Jemmy Cl[avering] sent up before he came to town, directed to Mr W[illiam] Cotesw[orth] merch[ant] in Lond[on]. Sign[or] sends a letter for the box, which was deliv[ered] with a demand of 16s after the rate of 3d p[er] pound; the paym[ent] was offer'd if he would give an acquittance, but that being refused, the money was detain'd. Now you must know he wrote twice to you about itt to know if his paying 3d p[er] p[ound] for a box so directed would not be to your prejudice and that you would discourse the carrier, but you never took the least notice, so that his back is up and what adds to itt is since he had like to have bin arrested for the money. He has wrote I suppose an angry letter to Jemmy p[er] this post, I suppose on the same subject. Pray if this day's Medly come to your town, read itt; you will think the time well spent. I have nothing to add further save my respects to the honest Ald[erman] and all friends that wish me well. I am ....

46

Apr[il] 22th [1]712

I have bin in sad circumstances of health since my last to you. I was seized on Sunday was a 7-night [ago] while att table with a diziness greater than usuall and this was followed by a little sort of convulsion, which made me falter so much in my speech that nobody could understand me. The d[octor] was immediately sent for and by good luck was readily found. He clapt me a blister of an immense bigness which gave relief by removing of the twitching, but the dizziness still remains. Believe me my good friend I have never wrote two lines since that day, nay and can doe this but by halfs and by stealth. Yet am unwilling to deferr congratulating you upon your delivery out of the hands off the Mohocks. Certainly such a barbarous treatm[ent] in one's own house was never heard off. It was happy for you that you were in a condition to oppose force with force.[1]

This day my father and I waited upon Mr W[ortley] who read us a letter he had received about 3 posts agoe from one of their agents in the countrey, which gives an account of Lady Bowes's being obliged by Brummell['s] people to light out of her coach, since they stopt its passing cross their new laid rails; that the *way was push't on briskly; that Sir J[ohn] had told his ten[ants] that he would lead no coals but with wagg[ons]. Upon which the writer gives his remark that then he thought they would not damage the trade this year, but does not mention a syllable of the apprehensions they had of their endeavoring to pull up other people's ways in case they miscarried in their own project. I was the person that started it to him and desired to know his opinion what were fitting to be don in case such a thing should happen. Nay after some discourse, I told him that in my thoughts it would be but reasonable to be providing against the worst by endeavoring to fence off this blow with safety and by

justifyable means, and could it be amiss if the opinion of some
learned counsell was taken. Oh says he, that will be time enough
when any violence is offer'd. To that I reply'd, it were
impossible to give directions att this distance so soon as
necessary, for if we staid till the first onsett, the damage would
be over before that could arrive. Well then says he, we must
leave itt to Mr O[rd] and Mr C[otesworth] to menage. He
promised to write to J[ohn] O[rd] and desired [the] same to you,
for your joint opinions. By all which one may discover a
s[upineness] which give grounds of suspicion that they had some
secret assurances from Brummell that their concern should not
suffer by any act of violence. Sign[or] has sign'd your pardon.
The sooner you begin your 3 *keelbirths the better, for assure
your self this year will be a dull one to masters especially, for
coals are sold already for 24 and 24[s] 6[d], I mean most off
[the] 11s coals, while M[ain Team] fetches 26½ and 27[s]. Nay
the sole ship the Capt[ain] sent up this fleet, being a bulk of
excell[ent] Washing Wells and for which the mast[er] paid 12s
per *chald[ron], is offer'd by Smith and Blunkett but 24s tho' I
wrote to them both to assist him and I would pay them the
*praemium down. This is scurvy usage from those vile wretches;
therfore I was obliged to give the mast[er] the praem[ium],
which was 4d p[er] Lond[on] ch[aldron] and bid him make the
best of way he could for himself. Pray acquaint the Capt[ain]
with this and desire him that in case the mast[er] should be a
sufferer the first voyage, that he would make him privately some
amends, for on his loading a 2d voyage of those coals depends
his trade. Believe me the dealers, that is the Ten, can just doe as
they please. What you recommend to be kept secrett, depend
upon't shall goe no further. I don't know any person that will
pretend to discourse positively if peace or none, but a little time
will discover. Itt's certain Madam Louise is dead, and I can
assure you it is as confidently handed about this day that her
bro[ther] the P[retender] is gon the same way.[2] I can't add save
that have spoke to Cha[rles] to be speedy in sending you an
answer to what you desire to be satisfied in, and was seconded
by my father, who is as well as my self to you ....

[P.S.] My kind respects to good Mrs Ramsay, who had the
misfortune of being ingaged as well as your worship.

1. The Mohocks were an aristocratic London street-gang that flourished between c.1710 and 1715, but Liddell's use of the term suggests that it was being applied to a broader category of criminals. James Clavering reported in November that housebreaking had become very 'fashionable' in the district and this may be connected with the prescription of stiffer penalties for the offence in 1713.

2. Louisa Maria Theresa Stuart was the daughter of James II and younger sister of the Old Pretender, who defied these reports by surviving until 1766.

47

May 13th [1]712

I am entirely unfitt for this employ therfore must be short, especially since I write by stealth and I know of my d[octor's] being here, who will certainly catechize me if he finds the pen in my hand. What I wrote to the Capt[ain] last was by my father's directions and am sorry itt should have given any offence. The chief objection he has a mind to have remov'd was about the validity of the lease lett by Jackson to Sir J[ohn] and Brumm[ell], for as I take itt he had lett everything that was in his power, and if that stand good what will a new lease avail us? If itt would answer the ends proposed he would be willing to contribute his share among the rest of our brethren, nay even for Bensham it self rather than fail. But we would be glad to be first satisfied what are each man's proportions and to have that objection as above cleared. In the next place as to Clav[ering] Stella, we that transact have our hands tyed up and can't act with safety but by order of court. I have consulted a great person on this head, who tells me that before we were call'd to account before the court, we were att liberty to act according to the best of our judgem[ent], but now that we are before our Master nothing can be don with safety for the trustees but by an order. However I doubt not you might menage the matter well enough if you would indulge honest Jemmy a little, but I beg of you not to mention a syllable of this to any person. As to the charges that may accrew by endeavoring to stop the proceedings thro' what you took off Tom Shaftoe, as itt was don by order of the 5 so it must and shall be repaid and that punctually too, tho' I were to do itt out of my own pockett for our share of Clav[ering] St[ella].[1] Don't take any thing by a wrong handle I

beseech you; that you should imagin that we should either call
your judgem[ent] in question, or your integrity, is all wrong my
good friend. I could heartily wish that my head and hands
would allow me so much liberty of thought as formerly. I would
convince you that we are the same as usuall. But by the by lett
me advise you to state the case plainly and send us up the
particulars in a letter to my father, after which you shall have I
doubt not a satisfactory account to your mind. Now friend my
d[octor] is come and Sign[or] along with him; there is so much
noise I can't tell what I write, excuse therfore all faults and
believe me to be with a cordiall sincerity and true affection ....

[P.S.] I have charged Charles this day with your complaints.
Excuse faults.

1.   The directors of the Regulation not only took exclusive wayleaves through
     Whickham manor but also contributed several thousand pounds to the
     campaign against the Bucksnook way. Both actions were strenuously
     denied in public.

48

June 20th [1]712

'Twas or att least seemed to me almost an age since I heard
from you, and did conclude that some body had attackt you on
the road in your way to Yorksh[ire] or that you had bin seized
during your absence with an untoward fitt of the gout, which
had occasion'd your silence. But was glad to find itt under hand
that you were safe return'd without mention of the least
disaster. We all doe own that your refusing such considerable
advantages offerd by Br[umell] etc. was infinitely more to your
own particular [cost] than the summ demanded [from us], and
that the proposall last made is what I think no one can refuse to
comply with. I wish you would send me a copy of the
proportions and then I will find out some expedient to ingage
my partner to comply to the paym[ent], for if that *way be
suffer'd I am certain we att Chopwell must shutt up shop. For as
itt is, we have all the difficulty in the world to struggle with att
this markett to gett our coals taken off, as well as a great charge,
and yet all will not doe; but to be sure if this other glutt come
upon us we must *lye in or trade to loss. I thank my good friend

for the particular account you gave me of what passed att the first setting on of the waggons.[1] I sent for Charles to discourse him and enquired what progress he had made in your business. He told me he had wrote to you severall times wherin he did acquaint you that he could not proceed regularly or effectually till such times as he had received Jackson's answers to the interrogatorys; that you had given information of their being sent up but without naming by what conveyance, so that he is att a great loss and can't proceed till they doe come to hand. I desired the Capt[ain] to acquaint you to this effect some posts since, that this term might not be slipt. I have *drawn on you according to your ord[ers] for fifty pounds att sight pay[able] to Mr N[icholas] Furrs or order, for which have given you creditt, and if have leisure will draw out your account from the last that I did send you [in] which as I take the ballance due to me was £21 [0s] 8d. Pray send me word on board what ship you load your Tanfield and be sure to send up a choice bulk and I will assist what I can, tho' I must tell you to be sure not to oblige yourself to make good any price att Lond[on]; if you doe depend itt will goe the worse with you, and as for *praemium, I will venture that less than 8d will not doe any service for the markett is overglutted allready. My good friend will excuse my confusedness in writing. I have had a terrible shock with a fitt of the stone in my kidneys, I doubt it is, and not yet gon off. Adieu. I rest ....

[P.S.] A peace is att hand you may depend on't.

1. The official opening of Bucksnook waggonway was celebrated with a procession led by the vicar and Sir John Clavering, accompanying a waggon full of punch down the length of the track. Thomas Shafto was arrested for obstructing their passage across his land and the proceedings were later disrupted by a report that Lady Bowes had called out 200 men to pull up the rails crossing Fawdonfield. Clavering generated a great deal of local humour by riding heroically to the rescue, only to discover that the culprits were a herd of cows which had strayed across the line.

49

July 3d 1712

Yours of the 27th ult. lyes now before me. Itt came but to hand late on Monday evening so that I could not send to Mr Sanderson, but on Tuesday I wrote a line to him to intreat him to come to my house any time that day which suited most with his convenience and bring along with him your two letters of the date yours mentions. He return'd for answer by word of mouth that he would wait on me; accordingly I stay'd below stairs till after 10 att night, att which dispair'd of seeing him, but just as I was undressing for bed some body rattled att the door and itt proved to be my gentleman. I button'd on my cloths and down I went. I told him I had a budgett off complaints to produce against him for his slowness in proceeding in your business. I read to him part of yours. He told me that he had all along told you the reason of his delay was that he could not proceed till he had gott Jackson's answer, a copy of which he had gott out of court that very afternoon and not before, and that now he was prepared to goe thorough stitch [*i.e.* all out] and apprize the court all att once; that as success hitherto constantly attended him, he did not doubt but in less than a fortnight's time to give you an account that would be to your satisfaction, and that he would shortly goe to Sir Joseph Jekyll one of your councell to give him full instructions and desired I would accompany him. I told him that if he thought I could be any ways servicable, on notice I would attend. He shew'd me the 2 letters of the 26th Apr[il] and the other. I explained itt to him as I had don some time before so that he own'd he thought himself perfectly master of itt. Before our conversation ended itt struck 11 a clock, which was the reason why I could not write by last post, and before we parted made him promise me he would write att large to you by this post and give you a particular account. As for the ship off Cliffton's I can't tell what will be don. Sign[or] has bin twice down about him but can't gett a coal off: they offer him but a guinea a *chald[ron]. I went down on Tuesday last to the Gate where I see Capt[ain] Cliffton, who told me he had bin near a month att the markett. I inquired what *praemium he had to give, [*i.e.*] the master; he told me 9d p[er] Newc[astle] chaldr[on]. If I mistake not, said I, Mr C[otesworth] wrote me word he did allow you 12d. No indeed sir, not one farthing more than 9d. Upon this I sent for Rob[ert] Watts and told him that he would oblige me if he would help off with that bulk of Bensh[am] upper seams and should receive 4½d p[er London] cha[ldron] provided he would give 22s, which was the lowest price that any of the 11s coals passed att. He would not ingage further than a promise to help off with 3 or 4 score att the latter end off the ship. I then sent for Arlington, Hartley and Wren; promised them the same praem[ium] but first of all desired the master not to mention whose coals they were, because you had a little difference with the two latter, but only should call his coals Bensh[am] upper seames, which he did. They likewise promised a little assistance; as for the other dealers not one would touch a coal. In short the master does not I find understand the Gate and he will meet with much difficulty. I told him that I hoped to be down once more this week and then shall inquire how those that have promised doe perform, tho' I own I expect little from either the great or small dealers. I am going to make a visitt to our honest Durham Recorder [George Bowes] who leaves us to morrow. Wishing you all health and happiness concludes me ...

P.S. I went down to the Temple where I see Cha[rles] who will give you a full account this post. He likes the affidavitts wonderfully you gave him; was asking me if itt would not be a prejudice to the lord's colliery if that wagg[on] way was suffer'd. I told him that itt would doubtless; for this reason, that the other coals were a much more vendible commodity which would be *ledd down by that *way att a much cheaper rate than usuall and in vast quantitys, and consequently must lessen the *vend of those that had a meaner sort, much as the l[ord's] lessees generally had, and so must throw up their leases etc. He told me it was a very materiall point and wisht you could send up an affidavit to that effect which would be of very singular service. Adieu, excuse errors, I have not time to peruse.

50

July 17th 1712

I have had lately a good hour's conference with Cha[rles] Sand[er]son about your business, off which I doe believe he is perfect mast[er]. He seems now to bestirr himself heartily; has

bin with the Master who I can assure you has no good opinion
off Jackson, and I fancy can scarce entertain a better when he
peruses his answer to the interrogatories. The Master's report
will be made shortly and I doubt not by what I can learn from
Cha[rles] that itt will be a favorable one in your behalf. He
wishes that there had bin an affidavitt made off the prejudice
this *way would be to the l[ord's] mines and leases in being,
which should not have bin made use off but as the learned in the
law should direct. I went down to the Gate last week, where I see
Coltman and partner and recommended to their particular care
the ship that loaded of your Brainslope. They promised they
would take a tryall and this last Monday I was down again to
make enquiry after them; they told me they had delivered the
master, that the coals answer'd the character the mas[ter] gave
off them, which was as to their smallness. I told them that I
could not believe that that seame could work otherwise than
round, that indeed they might suffer by the vast of rain that had
fallen during the time of loading; in short they own they doe
believe them to be very good in nature. Now my good friend
give me leave to tell you that you will find the coal trade draw
near a period for this year. Scarce a master that comes over the
barr that can clear £10 a voyage, even supposing he come and
goe well, very few that can save themselvs and most have made a
great hole in their stocks, so that necessity rather than
inclination obliges them to lye by. Nay the common saylers are
reduced to such a low ebb that they can't so much as feed their
familys with bread and water, for particular instance of which I
will leave you to Hugh. I am gott here with my father and Lord
W[illiam Powlett], who desires me to acquaint you that he has
bin up these 4 nights and that last his lady has father'd a boy
upon him; therfore desires his humble service to be presented, as
does my father. I am ....

51

Aug[ust] 7th [1]712

Tho' I have bin silent yet have not fail'd spurring up your
sollicitor and incouraging him to pursue your cause with vigour,
without which he could not expect success; an account of which
I suppose you have had from himself, but least he fail'd you I

gave itt to the Capt[ain] in short, with a request that he would
impart itt to you. I must confess I am very much unfitt for
business. I am perfectly plagued and distracted with the masters
on one hand and the dealers of another, that I have not a
peaceable hour and what adds to itt [is] there is no prospect of
better days. You observe right that these vermin will prove in
some measure worse than *gift, were itt only on this account
that they squeeze the poor masters as well as the owners. I wish
therfore that any expedient could be thought off to bring them
within bounds. Sure I am that att Clav[ering] Stella where we
give them an unconscionable *praem[ium] yet they do oppress
our masters beyond any concern in the river and I don't see any
possibility of preventing itt this year. I can assure you itt would
doe well if you below as well as we above would turn our
thoughts upon some method of redress. My Lord W[illiam]
came to see me last night and shew'd your short epistle. I went
down to the Gate but could not learn that master Basspoole was
arriv'd. So will deliver his commission over to Mr Gen[uini] who
is now gott abroad but looks miserably thin. Here is a sad sickly
time. 'Ere this my father will be att his journey's end and I am
of opinion that this will meet you att Newton. Excuse shortness,
being in every respect ....

52

Aug[ust] 26th 1712

Your very entertaining letter by yesterday's post has reviv'd a
little my low pulse, which any that feels itt would fancy I was
expiring. For this ten days past I have not bin able to sett pen to
paper but once to Jemmy Cl[avering], and that was a work of
necessity that ingaged me to give him an account of the insolent
behavior of those vile wretches att the Gate, who tho' they knew
I was so ill as not to recieve company yet forced themselvs upon
mee. You will think itt strange how they could doe soe, but itt
was by a mistake in my man who told me they were some
masters of ships who desired to speak with me, and accordingly
were admitted. The first that offer'd himself was fatt Geo[rge]
O[ldner], then his bro[ther] Rich[ard], Blunkett and Coltman.
We battl'd itt for 3 hours till diner parted us: I neither offer'd
them to eat nor drink with us. They insisted upon full pay but I

would not part with a farthing till I had Jemmy's order. I told them that they had almost every fleet bought Clav[ering] St[ella] att 6d below the markett, and I could prove itt upon them by severall of our Team ships as well as others, and that Robinson's and Weatherley's coals which were bought for 10s gott the same price with Clav[ering] St[ella] generally speaking; that as they had not perform'd their part, I hope they would not blame me for keeping such a part of the *praemium in hand to make satisfaction to our masters that were sufferers, etc. They stomack'd this extreemly but I stood to my tackle [*i.e.* to my guns]. Indeed some exped[ient] must be thought of to break into the measures of these great men, otherwise we shall be slaves with a wittness [*i.e.* without a doubt], and this without loss of time. I am turning my head upon a project for Clav[ering] St[ella] which considering the smallness of the quant[ity] hope may succeed; it is among the petty dealers but where there is a quant[ity] that will not doe. However I want such a headpiece as my friend Will[iam's] to assist me or rather to correct my rude notions of trade, whose judgem[ent] I sett no greater value upon than itt deserves.

I congratulate you sincerely upon your late but signall victory [in the Bucksnook case] but be sure not to trust to their hon[ours]. Cha[rles] is att Richmond, however I am preparing a note to your namesake the capt[ain]'s son [Edward Heslop Cotesworth] to dispatch yours away to his master. I am satisfied in conscience that what you have so earnestly and hazardously espous'd and att long run carried, will prove the saving of the trade from ruine, nay beyond all retrieve, and doe you think or can anybody think itt [un]reasonable that an answerable return be made you for your pains? I don't mean what was proposed formerly, because that was only for your friend and mine the honest Ald[erman] but particularly appropriated to yourself. You have bin a considerable sufferer in your own private concerns to my knowledge and might have had terms such as you pleased to have insisted on from those you have now laid upon their backs, provided you would have given no obstruction to their destructive carreer. Sure then there is not a coal owner of any consideration in your river but that will make an offering to your self either in one respect or other that should be in some measure adequate to your sufferings and desert. Were I in the countrey, should be the first that should propose something of this nature and shall in the mean time recommend itt as far as I am capable. Considering that no reall misfortune befell the judges, itt was as lucky and pleasant [a] hitt as could have befallen your antagonists.[1] 'Tis so remarkable that in an age itt can't be forgott. You can't imagin how crest fallen are those mighty dealers upon these tydings. They used to threaten me with Bucks Nook, that the next year we should goe a begging with our Team, Bensh[am] and Clav[ering] St[ella] for those and Hutt[on] and B[enwell] would be able to supply the chief of the trade to this port with the best of commodity, and I should then plainly see the difference in price which should be 2[s] 6d p[er] Lond[on] *chald[ron]. Oh this is a bitter pill to them. I must now beg excuse for breaking of abruptly. My head is sadly disturb'd, and I wish I be able to write a few lines to my father; tho' have no novells of any sort, yet would not be wanting in paying my dutifull respects to him by inquiry after his health, now that the fatigue of the assizes is over. Howere least I have not time, desire you will plead my pardon. My best respects to all friends. I am ....

[P.S.] You must make excuses till next post to my father, for I am not in a condition to write. I see cos[in Ralph] Sanderson who promises to write to you but least he should fail, tells me that no affidavits can be prefer'd before next term. Adieu.

1. Sir John Clavering attempted to use the visit of two influential judges to the Newcastle assizes to demonstrate that Bucksnook way did not in fact obstruct the public highway along which it ran. He sent his own coach to carry the judges and the mayor of Newcastle up the track to Crowley's ironworks at Swalwell but succeeded only in proving his opponents' case: one of the horses fell over the edge of the embankment and nearly pulled the coach down a nine-foot drop.

53

Sep[tember] 13th 1712

I had yours with the affidavitt and inclosed answer to itt in course. As luck would have itt Cha[rles] S[anderson] was come to town 2 or 3 days before, and happen'd to dine att my cosen's [Thomas Liddell] in Bedford Rowe that very day and was ingaged to spend his afternoon there. Upon this notice I wrote a note to him and dispatch'd itt away. I told him that I had by that post rec[eived] a packett with some matter of importance to be communicated to him, that I promis'd he should be dismiss'd in half an hour. Upon the rec[eit] of mine the ladys who were att cards with him were very unwilling to part with him, but upon the promise that he should not be detain'd long they consented. I waited att home all the afternoon and about 8 a clock my gentleman made his appearance. I first produced the affidavitt which he had seen before, then I read to him deliberately the answer to every particular of itt, with which he was extreemly pleased. I asked if any explanation was wanted, he told me no; that itt was couched in such plain, easy and express terms that he could make your counsell as much masters of itt as I was my self. He told me he had bin att the Lord Keeper's severall times to inquire how matters stood, but he was in the countrey and not expected back for severall weeks. Then he went to his secretary on the same inquisitive errand; he was upon his diversions in Kent, which is generally practis'd by the gentlemen of business during the vacation. So that Cha[rles] is positive nothing can be don till next term and is satisfied no alteration of the order will be made, being there has bin no presid[ent] of such a practice in that court. However as Cha[rles] was going out of town to visitt some of his wife's relations for a week or ten days, I charged that he would call again the last thing he did both at the Keeper's and his secretary's to gett information and give you an account, and att his return I shall take care to remind him. All this he gave me his word and hand should be don and every thing else that was necessary. I read him over the letter and desir'd of him to consider in time what further affidavitts were necessary, so that timely notice might be given you. I gave him the answer to the affidavitt. I received half a crown for postage, after which we parted. You have now I percieve drawn your sword and thrown away the scabbard. My best wishes attend you. And doubt not of your success, depending on the righteousness of your cause. In the next place, I must most earnestly recommend to you the giving in your account of the Chopwell wagg[on] way without loss of time, tho' it were but in gross for timber so much, workmanship in another article, so that four or five heads will suffice; and give itt into Mr Clav[ering] for our accounts must be made up off hand and without that of yours they can't close that year's book. I therfore earnestly intreat you will doe itt and I shall reckon itt a particular obligation laid upon[1] ....

1. Cotesworth's prevarication over these accounts angered both James Clavering and Ann Liddell, who found fresh cause for complaint when they did appear since it was alleged that Cotesworth had made excessive claims on the colliery.

54

Oct[ober] 18th 1712

I am infinitely indebted to my kind friend for his obliging letter off a long standing, for which I heartily begg pardon that he has had no sooner an answer. The vast quantity of rain that has fallen for some weeks by past has putt me off the byass off writing and intirely incapacitated me for transacting any business. In reallity I have bin so ill and continue so, that I can with much adoe keep off the bed. However was resolved to trespass a little on my own repose rather than deferr my acknowledgm[ents] for the fav[our] of your last any longer. I must referr you to particulars off what passed with T[homas] B[ewick] and me to the Capt[ain], to whom I wrote by the last post att large what I hinted only to my father [by] that before, from whom I have not heard a syllable for above 3 weeks last past; the meaning I know not, neither will itt be fitt for the inquiry. Whether itt be this new undertaking att U[rpeth] or no I know not. For he has never so much as mention'd itt to me, and only once to my wife that if I had a mind to ingage in such a concern, and so forth. Now my good friend, I must be free with you. All I have in the world off stock is in our joint undertakings; how they stand I must leave you to judge. I would not interfeer with any project that is already on foot. If you think therfore that within a 12 month's time as much money could be raised as will menage this new undertaking for your proportion and mine, I should be very proud of coming into so good a partn[er]ship. And to that end doe recommend to your consideration if itt would not doe well to *lay in your Brainslope, which can't turn to any account, as allso the upper seams att Bensh[am] after this year, and by that means turn our stock into ready money, which I should think would turn to a more promising account than the undertakings we are allready

ingaged in. But I intirely submitt to your judgem[ent] and begg
your thoughts freely, off which I have so good an opinion that
your determination will allways sway mee. I charge you that you
will not divulge the least tittle of what I write to any living. But if
you can discover by any means why my father is so much upon
the reserve itt would make me much easier. 'Tis to me strange. I
am sure att his first getting into the countrey he selldome fail'd
writing to me every other post, and his last was to my wife that
day Lord Scarb[orough] dined with him, which I take to be this
day 3 weeks. I mett with Cha[rles] yesterday, who shew'd me
what he had from you. He thinks himself amply provided with
materialls for a good defence and understands them fully. He is
drawing up his briefs for councell ag[ainst] Thursday next. Last
night att Mr Freek's I mett Sir Joseph Jekyll one of your
councell; I took him to a side, told him that Mr Sand[erson]
would wait upon him shortly [to] in fee him in a cause that my
father wisht well to. He promised to exert himself. Now my
good friend accept of my best thanks for your pleasant
entertainm[ent] which did me more good than any of the
d[octor's] bolus's. Adieu and believe me ....

55

Nov[ember] 1st 1712

You have obliged me extreemly by your two last. Just now I
am sent for to meet Jack Hedw[orth] att the Tavern to drink a
token from Jemmy C[lavering], a place I have scarce troubled
since you left the town. This will oblige me to cutt short.
Therefore you will excuse if I write as a late author does, by
sentences. No longer than yesterday's post, I had in a postscript
to the Capt[ain] an ord[er] under my father's own hand for
taking U[rpe]th upon the best terms. So shall meet Tom and
Calv[erley] both att the Tavern on Monday or Tuesday next in
order to conclude if possible. I thank you for your kind offer in
relation the disbursem[ents] of my ¼. I acquiesce in what you
judge most necessary about working or *lying in the upper
seams, about which you have a vast of trouble and scurvy usage.
I could have wish'd that the terms for W[illiam] Ramsay's *way,
as allso thro' Team had bin thoroughly adjusted, for I shall find
a tedious business off itt if left to me to transact with him [i.e.

Liddell's father]. Itt is not becoming one in my circumstances to object ag[ainst] any thing he may think reasonable etc. I am concern'd that the number 5 should not as yet have rewarded you for your Lond[on] journey. I was an eye wittness to the indefatigable pains you took in a service for which you did deserve a generous recompence and even without a demurr. Methinks it is copying after the publick.[1] I am sorry that my interest should be off disservice rather than otherwise to you att this time: and that a suspicion should be raised that I am playing into your hand when I only recommend to them to be mindfull and not to neglect a person so capable of serving or otherwise distressing them in their business according as he is used.[2] But a word to the wise is enough. Your scheme seems justly calculated about Bensh[am] *way l[eave] and *steath rooms. No objection have I to itt but this; when it is known that you have taken all those and on supposition that you should even lay the Ch[ief] Just[ice Wright?] on his back (which I hope you will be able to effect), yet say I, will not that give a colourable handle for bringing in and obtaining an Act for giving a reasonable compensation for all manner off way l[eaves]?[3] I don't inferr from thence that there is any just grounds to be given for so doing, yet reason does not att all times prevail, nay the best argum[ents] are but indifferently heard in a crowd. I give only this touch for you to improve. I am glad to hear you have had the offer of B[ucks]n[ook]; 'tis a certain sign they grow sick of their undertaking. You would doe well to know the reall terms on which she will be lett, as allso the party or partys that will join in the letting, for I am satisfied Bru[mel]l has the least share and that she is like a bastard whose mother can't give an account off the reall father. In the next place you must be satisfied on what terms Sir J[ohn] and others will lett way leaves and att what price [for] the way as itt now lyes. They will certainly endeavor to deny you as much as possible. It is worth while likewise to consider if feasible to lay a wag[gon] w[ay] from the pitts to the *mount, for as itt is their coals don't intirely answer the expectations off the markett by reason that they don't come as round as formerly. I thank you for your kind offer off letting me be concern'd as a partn[er] in whatever offers. You lay me under deep obligations, which under present circumstances I cann't tell how to rubb out. My time off appoint[ment] draws near. Have but time to thank you for the d[...]'s comicall adventure; to request secrecy in this as far as you think necessary, and therfore gett Mr Ashley to frank [the letter] for me; and so wish you success in your cause which is putt off till Tuesday or Thursday next and to all your family wellfare and happiness. I remain ....

[P.S.] Read this if you can.

1. The Regulation's failure to reward Cotesworth for his defence of the cartel against the 1711 Parliamentary enquiry often prompted Liddell to make this sort of veiled comparison with the Tory administration's churlish treatment of Marlborough.

2. This is probably a reference to Cotesworth's influence over the vital wayleaves crossing Gateshead and Whickham, but he was also in a position to exploit his incriminating knowledge of the cartel's continued and illegal existence.

3. Proposals for legislation that would oblige landowners to let wayleaves at fixed rents were frequently urged on Parliament as a means of reducing coal prices. They were just as frequently condemned as a dangerous attack on property rights.

56

Nov[ember] 4th 1712

I have had a blister on my back since Sunday and never stirr'd out of my chamber till this day, to accompany my father to Tom B[ewick's] where with difficulty we brought him to consent to all [articles] positively except the 2d which is not absolutely determin'd. My father desires you will gett a short copy off a lease drawn up and sent away with all expedition. Tom says he will gett one done here but 'tis no matter for that. In the 3d article with much adoe [we] gott prevail'd to have generall warning allow'd att 6 months; and insisted that in case of *styth, civill war etc. the rent should cease, which they agreed too provided the lease was immediately deliver'd up, to which I could not intirely agree, therfore referr'd that to the custom off Newc[astle] leases. I had this obj[ection] that in case we had bin att the exp[ense] off laying the *way and after a civill war should ensue in the north, which might be quell'd in a little time, itt would be hard that our lease should be given up, and to pay when one is disabled from working is hard. You will consider this and without loss off time gett a form off a lease transcrib'd, with all other usual coven[ants] as mention'd generally in the last line. My father would not att first hear off taking unless 6 months for *wining were allowed, but honest Cav[erley] told me he would suffer in his own interest rather than fail and would refer what that should be to Ald[erman] Ramsay, to which my father att last comply'd. I can't say whether Tom will stand to what was as good as agreed on after all, but the difference can't be great. Ut[recht] Whitf[ield] boys him up and makes him harder upon us than he otherwise would be. I am in great pain: excuse haste. Am sorry to hear you are out of order. I heartily wish you much better than myself and am ....

[P.S.] I wrote Jemmy about what you desired and desired he would shew you my letter.

57

Nov[ember] 5th 1712

On Monday last I sent to Tom B[ewick] to desire a meeting with him and Cav[erley] on account off Urpeth; the time appointed was yesterday. I must own I was much out off order and had bin so for above a fortnight before, and yesterday there struck out a rash all over my should[er], breast and arms. I was strongly sollicited by my better half not to stir over the threshold, least by catching cold should strike itt in again, which was represented off very bad consequence. However was resolv'd to perform my promise, least our friend Cav[erley] should suspect that our design was only to putt off and by gaining time disappoint Tom Foster etc, which I was very loth to give so honest a man the least just ground for. We mett accordingly att the Tavern; I was first, then came Tom and his son in law, and in ½ hour after enter'd Cav[erley]. We went immediately upon the matter off the day, Tom desiring to know what I had to propose. Upon which gave in writing as follows:
1. To be bound to work yearly 900 *t[ens] certain.
2. Each tenn to consist off 24 wagg[ons] Norb[anks] present *measure.
3. The rent to be 10s.

4. To be allow'd 1 year from the date from the signing the lease for *wining and laying *way before the rent took place.

5. That the lessee should have liberty off giving warning [of] not less than 6 months; that in case off excess off water, *styth etc., want off myne or civil warr, the rent to cease; and all other common and usuall coven[ants] in coal leases.

6. To have a year after any determination to work the deficiencys of any of the foregoing term gratis, etc. This was all I determin'd to trouble them with att present.

Objections to the 1st made by Tom: that as he was offer'd 1000 t[ens] certain, it could not be expected that he should comply with a *cha[ldron] less and so positively declared he would not depart from that offer.

2. A long dispute arose; he insisted that the same *undertaker offer'd to be content with 50 *foth[ers] to the ten and that he would not allow any more than 22 wagg[ons] att 18 *b[owls] each.

3. The rent he agreed too, 10s.

4. No time for wining but to commence from the date off the lease and to be paid quarterly.

5. No warning att pleasure, unless for the causes express'd.

6. Was readily agreed too.

To these object[ions] in short I made the following reply:

1st. That itt was a quantity to be bound too that I defy'd them to parrallell itt in the whole river, therfore hop'd that 100 t[ens] would not break squares [*i.e.* matter].

2. That I did demonstrate to them that none off them nor even their grand child[ren] could be prejudiced by the addition of 2 waggons, by reason of the quantity of ground, and to tye up our hands that we should not *lead as much as a horse could conveniently bring down att a time was a hardship such as I had not heard off.

3. Agreed too.

4. That we could not lay out so many thousands as must of necessity be expended in wining, work[ing] and laying the way and other preparat[ions] under a 12 month. Therfore to pay £500 *dead att first when nothing was coming in was enough, with £4000 outlays, to break any undertaker, therfore hoped they would ease us in that point.

5. As to the warning being voluntary att 6 months, I thought itt but highly reasonable, as well as [for] the causes exprest;

because said I, you can't think that we would expend such a summ in winning and laying way etc, suppoz'd to be £4000, and then give warning att 6 months when we have don[e]. No. I appeal'd to Tromantle who was present; he told me plainly he thought what I insisted very reasonable.

6. Answers itt self.

To these Tom and his son surreplyes:

1 and 2. That he has bin offer'd and is courted by the partys to grant a lease for 1000 t[ens] certain, who would be glad to accept of the 22 wag[gons] to a ten [of] 18 b[owls] each; therfore itt appear'd ridiculous in him to accept off a less quan[tity], therfore would not depart.

3. No dispute, save that he was offer'd 11s: this his son affirm'd.

4. In consideration that he was but ten[ant] for life he must loose no time, therfore whoever took the lease should be bound from that very day. If he did not oblige to this, could not answer itt to his own family and even common prudence did oblige him to insist; therfore positive Tom would not hear a word more on this article. After this came upon the stage [the question of] who would be bound; I answer'd I thought the Capt[ain] and [my]self. And will not Sir Harry, says Tom; perhaps not said I.

5. As to the warning (says he) being voluntary att 6 months, itt might be that we design'd to take her only that these other undertakers might be baulk'd off their *way leavs and then we might have her on our own terms, and such stuff as this. That every qu[arter] should be paid 14 d[ays] after demand, otherwise the bond for performance offer'd should be forfeited. In short no reason I could offer would be heard since Tom had one always ready, viz. if you will not another will.

Now my good friend these are hard lines that goe much again[st] the stomack. Nay to find Whitfield so pert and I dare say made his father by much less complying that otherwise. Nay he asserted that he did not doubt to find that 2000 t[ens] a year would be wrought if carried to the Were. Upon which I asked him if he knew what a working ten *made out; if he did or did not I could answer he talk'd without book, for I could affirm that Mr M[ontagu] who was the greatest owner in our days would scarce pretend to exceed 1400 such tens from his Hutton, which was ever allowed to be the chiefest colliery in either river. After all by what I can gather they will allow 22 wagg[ons] of 20 b[owls] each to the tenn; the obliging quant[ity to be] 1000; the rent 10s, to commence from the signing and paid quarterly; no liberty off warning unless [for] want of myne, excess off water, styth etc, or in case the coal should not prove merchantable (which will admitt of many disputes). I should not have disputed the quant[ity] could we but have had the others in my proposall, which certainly were but highly reasonable. Besides they insist that we shall pay damages for way leave to the ten[ants], that we shall not have the least cottage, only liberty on the fell to build. I must own I was shock'd. And before we broke up, considering my father's arrivall was so near att hand, they were willing to referr till Wednesday to have his finall answer, but I can putt them off till Fryday [or] perhaps begining of next week. Therfore haveing time am thus particular, requesting you will gett the Capt[ain] if possible, read my short one to him p[er] last post which perhaps may help clear up this, lay your heads together and consider matters well, and send your opinions by return of the post. You talk'd of a new scheme. Weigh the advantages off the one with the other. If you were concern'd ¼ and could be assured off this other in dispute (Bucksn[ook] on reasonable terms, with way leavs etc. thro' Sir J[ohn Clavering]), this might perhaps prevent their endeavouring to gett an Act off Parl[iament] which Whitfield assured me they thought themselvs secure off succeeding in. This is a random notion of my own, undigested, but as itt occurrs I only hint that if you think itt off any weight, may improve and add your full thoughts. I request off you on the main [issue] what we had best doe. And gett the Ald[erman] to write freely to Cav[erley] on the subject, not to be too obstinate or as you think fitt. Adieu my kind friend. I think I now repay you in your own kind in point of measure, tho' not entertainm[ent]. Adieu, I am ....

58

Dec[ember] 20th 1712

These great and lasting falls of snow will not allow me to alter my tone in regard to health and what discourages me much is itt has affected our honest d[octor] to that degree that he is confin'd to his bed, and none allow'd to see him but the apothecary. However I can't forbear writing a line to my good friend, notwithstanding these afflictions, and inform him a little of what passes in relation to the matter on the anvill. 'Tis near a week since young Whitfield deliver'd a paper book off a lease in form, which I read cursorily over and sent itt to my father, whose indisposition would not allow him to look itt over till the day before yesterday, with which he was not well pleased. The rent is there to commence from Candlemas. The lands he will not on any advanced rent lett to us. Therfore we shall have a troublesome matter to adjust about damages. By this lease we are to pay 40s damage for heap room, with the addition of the word yearly; that we are to make ample satisfaction besides for *way leavs and all spoil off ground for building hovells, stables, cottages and all other necessarys for the colliery, the like I believe was never heard off. In the next place they foist in a new coven[enant] that we shall not lett or assign any *part off the colliery to any without the privity and consent of the lessor first obtain'd in writing, on penalty of forfeiture of the lease; and severall other strange unheard off clauses. On this my father call'd a councill, wherof Dan [Poyen] was one and I the other. The question being putt what was most fitting to be done in this emergency, I proposed to send their paper book as allso your instructions and lease to John Ord, with yours and the Capt[ain's] last remarks copy'd, and those heads that we had agreed to before and was to be the true foundation for a lease, and see if he could hammer out of both a lease that would be most to mutuall advantage of both partys; that the harsh part of their paper book should be softned so as itt may be advisable for the lessees to comply with. This was resolved upon nemine contradicente and accordingly the whole was putt yesterday into Mr Ord's hands, who promised to bring us a copy of such a lease he shall think proper we should insist on by Tuesday next. He says that severall of the lands, as the Ryding and others, are copyhold and consequently the bishop's royalty. By all which you may guess that our trouble is not ended, nay farr from itt, for I doe assure you that Tom is so positive that I doubt he will not relinquish a tittle; therfore must begg your further advice how we should act in this matter and how farr. I don't know but that my father writes to the Capt[ain] by this post, but if he does not I desire you will communicate to the honest Capt[ain] the

contents of this letter. In the next place I must acquaint you that
we had severall meetings with the Billingsgate people but
nothing is yet fixed upon with those vermin. They hang in a clan
much firmer than the coal owners and are truer to each other; I
doubt the harmony among the Gentlemen will not be long liv'd.
My head and from thence to foot are full of pain, therfore
excuse faults and hast from ....

59

Jan[uary] lst 1712/13

Yours of the 23th ult. lyes before me. Have weighed the
account you give about *wining off Urp[eth]. I must readily
concurr with you that the best method will be off attempting to
gett her to the dipp [of the seam] as farr as you can, but with this
caution that you be sure off a good roof (which may be easily
discover'd by the *boring); otherwise you may depend that
where there is but little roof and even that tender, the coal will
prove mean and chargable working, by reason you can't drive
the *bords to any bredth, and the insett into a colliery is much
the same as the outburst off the seame, both being fagg ends and
of no intrinsick value. But I know you have the ablest off heads
to determine, to whose judgem[ent] I perfectly submitt, as also
to yours about building the *steath dyke with stone, and if you
gett that done for £15 a *keel birth itt will be a peny well
bestow'd. Cav[erley] has bin with me and inform'd me off some
of the particulars off that letter he last rec[eived] from the
honest Ald[erman]. You must know that on Saturday I gott Mr
P[oyen] to step with our rough draught to Tom B[ewick] who
had bin in a high wrath att us for keeping his fowl copy till
Wednesday; he said it was only tricking him and delaying of
time. Howe[ver] when I sent him ours last Saturday he was in
better temper, all which I attribute to the absence off Ut[recht]
who was gon into the countrey for a few days. He promised to
peruse and give notice when we should have a meeting, but not
the least as yet is come. I must not omitt acquainting you that
Tromantal called here on Tuesday as he went to visitt Tom. I
desired he would make this his way home and give an account if
any new discovery could be made. He accordingly came and told
me that all was broke off; that we had indeavor'd to foist in the

Riding and Kibblesw[orth] collierys which are neither p[art] or
parcell of Urp[eth] and that his bro[ther] Cav[erley] had nothing
to doe with either, and since we design'd to impose upon him we
should find our selvs mistaken. And further he added that he
did apprehend that J[ohn] Ord was imploy'd in drawing our
lease, and if that was [so] we should never have any thing to do
with the colliery. To this Tro[mantle] reply'd that he knew Mr
Gowland was our countrey attorny and that Cha[rles]
Sand[erson] did the family's business in town, and so forth.
This is the substance of what past, since which we have not had
the least summons. I communicated this to Cav[erley] who
seem'd surpriz'd and would be willing to serve us to the utmost,
but itt is not in his power att present. He thinks the damages
extravag[ant] but att the same time joins in opinion with mee
that his bro[ther] will never sign unless we first comply with that
and all other coven[ants] tho' never so unreasonable. In short I
apprehend he will raise new difficultys. 'Tis an easy matter to
find a stone to throw att a dogg. We must expect all the
hardships to be putt upon us, however we must dispence with
them as well as we can in hopes that Cav[erley] will be
after[wards] kind, and I would willingly part with Riding and
Kibblesw[orth] if Tom would sign our lease when those two are
scratch'd out. For Mr Ord assures me that the Riding is copy
hold and he thinks also that p[art] of Kibblesw[orth], and as our
landlord is extreemly touchy we must not give him the least
ground for itt. Another except[ion] he has, as Cav[erley] told
me, was that some body had wrote his bro[ther] word that you
were a party concern'd. To which I answer'd that considering
the difficultys we labor'd under, I thought we were much
obliged to you or any body that would embark along with the
Capt[ain] and me; that we needed the best off heads as well as
purses. I assured him that the Capt[ain] and I proposed to have
att least each ¼; that my father had not yet fix'd upon his
share; sometimes he talk'd of having the other ½ for him[self]
and the Esq[ire] but of what signification will itt be to the lessor
to know what p[ar]tners we admitted? I have read that part of
the Capt[ain]'s letter to my father ofter than once which related
to the settling his demands for *way leave, but never found him
in an humor disposed to talk off itt. You know itt must come
naturally and without force, therfore must wait a conven[ient]
season. Perhaps itt might not doe amiss if the Capt[ain] did

write a line or two to Dan[iel] and desire that he would put my
father in mind of adjusting that matter speedily. I am heartily
sorry to hear your complaints; hope that when Urp[eth] is once
a going coll[iery] itt will afford you some diverting exercise,
which may not a little contribute to the health of one of the
usefullest friends [in] the world. I wish itt may prove such, as
allso that this ensuing year may be successfull to you without
limitation. I am ....

[P.S.] I am farr from well, nay very farr, yet jogg on. My father
is rather better than when I wrote last to the poor Capt[ain].

60

Jan[uary] 6th 1712/13

I have just time to acquaint you that T[homas] B[ewick] has
sent back our lease with severall amendm[ents]. He will not lett
to farm any part of his lands to the lessees on any rent. As for
Ryding and Kibblesw[orth], he says the colliery of the former
does not belong to him, and the latter does not appertain to
Urpeth and consequently what he never did design to lett to us
nor ever would. I must desire therfore to know particularly if
the way we propose to lay our waggon way goes through any
p[art] off either Ryding or Kibblesworth; for J[ohn] Ord says if
itt be not off absolute necessity we had better not mention itt,
for there will be the utmost cavill about itt and perhaps we shall
not be able to obtain itt, and he does not know but our insisting
on itt may perhaps putt the old man into such a temper as that
may indanger the whole lease. You will likewise inform me of
any commons or wasts belonging to Urpeth, because they will
not allow those words in the lease since they say that they have
nothing to doe with them further than common [rights] off
pasture. J[ohn] Ord is of the same opinion. In the next place we
shall have a vast difficulty to obtain even the Ryding mill for
drawing off the water if necessary. They are so prejudiced
ag[ainst] honest Cav[erley] that they will obstruct, as far as in
them lyes, the going of the coll[iery] after T[om's] desease. It's a
hard game we have to play. For *way leavs we are to pay
according as assessed by 4 indiffer[ent] persons, 2 chose by them
and 2 by us. The making of brick [is] absolutely refused and

even [quarrying] stones unless we pay dammages yearly. As for way leavs Cav[erley] seems inclinable to make ½ allowances to us, which with what I formerly mention'd about the commencem[ent] will be referr'd to the honest Ald[erman]. I percieve that Mr Hedw[orth] has desired to meet the Capt[ain]; if the Capt[ain] does give him one, itt may not doe amiss to hear what he has to propose, but not to make any bargain positive till he has communicated to my father. I think I have touched on the most materiall points; must bid you adieu, being expected some hours agoe to take a farewell game att cards with some ladys. I am ....

61

Jan[uary] 24th 1712/13

Betwixt you and me, I have scarce ever bin more out of order than for these 3 weeks last past, which still hangs upon me. My complaint chiefly is off a pain between my stomach and bowells. It is constant without cease and from whence this should proceed I know not, unless itt be that the humor from my leggs be reverted to the stomack and so getts into my head. My appetite is so farr gon that an ounce will serve me more than a day. And my head is almost constantly dizzy; this redoubles my complaints to my d[octor] who has alter'd his medicines severall times without success. I leave you to judge of my circumstances, when a bottle off true and sound New[castle] clarett does not rellish in the least but every glass goes again[st] grain. I have bin vomited and purged times without number; nothing remains but patiently to submitt. Sure I am that every letter I recieve from you affords me more relief than the richest cordiall from the apothecary's shop.

But a word of business in the next place. I am fully convinced that H[edwor]th is endeavoring all he can to undermine us; which [is] after so many assurances that were not extorted from him, when last in town, that he would not be concern'd att present with her scarce on any terms since he had won his own [colliery] anew. Nay had he known that my father had any thoughts that way, he would never have interfer'd in the least and was sorry that by his means we were screw'd up to such high terms. But I find this is all Team talk, as Kitt Stockdale phrases

itt. He plays his game by Whit[field] who has gott the length of
old Tom's foot [*i.e.* his measure], who has wrought him up to
have a perfect aversion to us. I need not represent to you again
the violent passion he was in that we did not dispatch the lease
quicker. He said that was a plain indication that we did not
design to take her att all, but only to prolong a treaty so as to
exclude others. When we sent back his own lease with some few
amendm[ents] he had 3 or 4 days to consider, after which he
scratches out the most of ours and sends back word by
Whit[field] that if we did not comply, we should never have his
consent. Then we detatched Dan[iel] who talk'd a little to Tom
and told him there was very little difference 'tween us, that he
durst affirm that if we had a meeting for one hour, matters in
dispute would soon be adjusted. The next day I went to wait on
him to desire he would appoint a time and place. But that very
day he was taken ill and continued invisible ever since, save that
Cav[erley] had admitt[ance] once or twice and found him so ill
that he durst not mention a word of business, except that he
promised to send word to Cav[erley] and us when he found
himself fitt for discourse. Since that he has bin remov'd to
Kensington, and when my father very civilly sent his serv[ant] on
Tuesday last to inquire after his health, the answer was that he
was better but not a syllable of his hopes of seeing us shortly.
This morn[ing] Cav[erley] came here, brought no tydings from
Russell Street but that his bro[ther] did recover. He seems to be
very firm and steady to us. He told Mr P[oyen] this morn[ing]
that Jack H[edworth] should never have her as long as he liv'd,
tho' he should offer never so much; that he hoped in a short
time all would be concluded with us. Now my good friend time
spends apace and these delays off Tom's are purely to make a
hard bargain harden, thinking therby we shall grow sick off
waiting, and after all I durst venture a wager that he will not
receed in the least from his demands. As to Mrs Whitf[ield]'s
joining, I will be bold to say that she will never be prevail'd with
to doe [so]. If therfore there be no absolute occasion for her
doing, itt is better not to mention; itt will raise some new
scruples before the old ones are remov'd. For further particulars
referr you to Mr Ord who knows all the objections that were last
made by T[om] B[ewick] and amendm[ents]. I must own I can
but pitty the circumstances of that young gentleman [Robert
Bewick] which seem to tend apace to ruin. I did communicate to

Dan[iel] what you had bin doing for his service and to Mrs S[mith] what related to her; she wishes all lovers success. Sign[or] is in much wrath with the *fitters. Pray what steps are most advisable to be pursued in relation to Blackb[urn]; the Capt[ain] will inform you of a letter that my pappa L[iddell] wrote to Sir J[ohn] Middleton on that head. G[eorge] Vane will never lett his [*part] to any of the family. There is a share off Mrs Midford's, $^1/_{24}$; I should think that Jemmy Clav[ering] could be the best transacter there. For T[om] B[ewick] we shall find him as averse to treat as in any former [case]; could you think of any 3d person who might unsuspectedly treat with him? But can you think that any of these will be willing to part with any of their shares att a less price than they have att present? I fancy not till they have bitt upon the bridle [*i.e.* waited impatiently]. However your thoughts are allways very acceptable to ....

[P.S.] Pray what qu[antity] of gallons goe to a Newc[astle] *bowl: itt was inserted by T[om] B[ewick as] 35 and 3 pints, which I alterd to 35 ¾ with a reasonable *streak. I am heartily concern'd att your illness, which hangs long upon you. Poor Lord W[illiam Powlett] sent to inquire when I had heard from his friend W[illiam], if dead or alive, for he heard not from you above a fortnight since. Besides says my lord, does he write you ever a smotty story; yes I reply'd. Oh then he will doe well says my lord, but why does he never write me such? I made answer that I apprehended you were in mighty fav[our] with my lady att present and had no mind to be outed by a fatt [*i.e.* smutty] story. Oh says he, she likes itt as well as I.

62

Mar[ch] 10th [1]712/3

These continued n[orth] e[ast] winds have just given up my foot; I have not a place free from pain, which I must contentedly submitt to but the greatest of my grief is that I am so dispirited as scarce to be able to hold a correspondence with any friend. What I am now in hand with is a perfect farce; I have not the command off one free thought which when I have finish'd shall [not] be asham'd to peruse, but I presume of your candour in giving a kind reception. I have ingaged Dan[iel] to

answer p[art] of yours and to write to Mr Clav[ering] in relation
to severall matters when I could not doe itt my self, and
particularly to give him my thoughts in relation to your very
kind offer off supplying Chopw[ell] with a quant[ity] of rails att
the price yours mention'd. He had mine the last post about
J[ohn] O[rd's] account, which how unreasonable soever, yet on
consideration off the disservice he may doe to the generality of
the owners if we should break, I intimated my poor opinion
frankly. Itt is a great shame that yours, again[st] which not the
least exception can be taken, should be left unclear'd to this day;
but it is too frequent a practice in this age, when the business is
done, to lett the chief instrum[ent] pass unregarded. Before I
quitt this head, I must acquaint you that Peter has sent up a
copy off yours with particulars off the stock off wood expended
in the *way and wagg[ons] till [Chri]stmas last, to make which
compleat nothing is wanting but to sett down the prices of the
severall particulars, which may be the work of an hour and I
doubt not but you will allott that very speedily. In the next place
give me leave to return my wife's and own hearty thanks for
your noble present off charrs; a more acceptable present could
not have enter'd into any body's head. They were perfectly fresh
and good, nay had they had a little more seasoning it had not
don amiss. I am charged by Mr Freek and the honest d[octor] to
make their respective compliments. I believe your friend
Chapman has ofter than once tasted.

We hear nothing further off our lease since Daniell's account
off what passed att the last meeting. However I one day was
resolv'd to hear a little chitt chatt from that quarter if possible.
To this purpose I pinn'd my self upon bro[ther] E[llison] and
was an attendant of his to visitt old Tom. After smoaking a pipe
or two, I desired to know if he had had another interview with
Cav[erley], to which itt was reply'd by Ut[recht] that there had
not bin any since the last rude visitt and hoped there never
would be another. With that Tom fired furiously, saying he was
never so abused in his life by any man as by his bro[ther] after all
the signall services he had don and did design his family, etc. He
swore by his maker that he would never depart in the least from
what was express'd in the paper book, even tho' the coll[iery]
should never be wrought. He scorn'd to condescend to his
bro[ther's] importunities: to which I added, pray what will then
become of the poor lessees who are [undone] by the charges? Oh

says he, I pity them [and] am sorry they should be sufferers, but to think [to bring] me to submitt to my bro[ther] itt shall never be known; and so desired me to be silent on that subject. On the other hand Cav[erley] protests and vows solemly that he will never sign with his bro[ther] till the reasonable provision be made for his son in case Tom should survive and persists manfully to itt even att this day. What to doe further in this affair will need serious consideration. I must tell you Tom talks off going speedily for the north to take care off his concerns; I fancy itt is with a design to lett for his life. But 'ere I conclude, must give you to understand that after we had ended 5 bottles Ut[recht] lett me into the secrett of this affair. He lately had discover'd that one Mr W[illiam] C[otesworth] had about 2 years agoe prevail'd with Cav[erley] to grant him a lease off Urp[eth] coll[iery]; that over a bottle att a publick sessions that same W[illiam] C[otesworth] told a room full off company that he had secured such a concern to himself and that he hoped in a little time that he should be as considerable an owner as any in Weere or Tyne; that after finding that Tom could not be brought to join in with him on such terms, this same gentleman spirits up Cav[erley] to insist upon terms that could never be comply'd with on purpose to prevent the going of the colliery, etc. There is a piece of news for you sir, said he. To which I reply'd that I was convinced he was misinform'd, but had assurance it was so. I was weary and so the discourse drop'd but not without some sharp words. Nay att length he told me he had itt from your neighb[our] that offer'd 50 guin[eas]. Pray thee dear Will excuse me if I don't answer all particulars of yours. I keep them in my mind and take opportunitys off discoursing severall points with my father which you have recommended me. I am in all states and conditions ....

[P.S.] Yesterday the Justice and I drank your health in a bottle of Newc[astle] wine in Marlb[orough] Street.

63

May 8th 1713

I have bin under great tribulation for severall weeks by past, out off which I have no present prospect off deliverance or relief. My legs are more inflam'd than off late and the same humor has struck up into my body, stomack and head, which affects me not a little as you may imagine. My d[octor] has try'd severall new experim[ents] by altering off his prescriptions but without the least success. All which have weaken'd me extreemly; besides want off apetite and rest have perfectly confounded me. My wife would have the d[octor] sent for last night after 11 to take a perfect view off my legs, who gave me a dose off opium immediately, but alass I waked att one and never slept till 7 this morn[ing] after which I slumber'd till 9. Indeed my good friend I am in a bad condition, but conceal it as much as I can from my hands to avoid trouble. Your silence has a little added to my affliction, tho' I partly guess att the meaning. You have taken the right method off writing to my father directly upon business, and if you don't recieve an immediate and direct answer, yet now and then att some distance off time reminding him or getting Dan[iel] to doe itt will have the desired effect. I wrote to him by yesterday's post, with a desire to shew you the letter; itt was in the nature off a begging letter for a little off your assistance, if suited with your convenience. Must likewise desire the favor of you when att leisure to draw a short account off our partnership, that we may see how matters stand between us; and in the next place that you would lessen your stock as much as possible. I dare not venture to give you the reason att this distance, but it is what is practised by the most judicious and most substantiall people off this town, and you may depend you will find your advantage in so doing.[1] You see how I make free with my old friend, yet I have not don with my supplications. You must know that our friend Jemmy Cl[avering] was so kind as to send me up 4 doz[en] off extraord[inary] good clarett. I got itt but into my cellar on Saturday last. My father heard a character, came and tasted and highly approv'd, upon which could not doe less than make him a present of a doz[en]; and Lord C[owper] having some topp company, beg'd a bottle of north countrey bear which I readily supply'd him with as also half a doz[en] off the clarett, which was not ill bestow'd. In short I am reduced to my primitive half or therabouts, therfore if you could procure me 2 doz[en] off that which is right good I desire you would doe itt and send itt p[er] ship. Let itt be enter'd [on the bill of lading], otherwise we shall be putt to trouble. Sometimes perhaps you may meet with a tast of good Fr[ench] white; there is no such thing to be had here, none but ports. If such a thing should fall in your way, I would be very thankfull for a doz[en] or so. Be pleased to place to my account what you disburse.

There were two complaints a[gainst] one Allatson, master, who sold his coal as Bensh[am]: the people att Gate that had some off them make a demand off *praem[ium] off my father and no such ship was reported, whence I conclude they came from our Bensh[am]. However it would please my father much if we gave ours the name off Redhugh or any other, purely to prevent confusion at the latter end off the year. I had a letter from Dan[iel] last post, wherin he tells me that he has or will send up our coals from Chopwell that will prove good in nature, tho' will perhaps be small. Pray acquaint him that for a little quant[ity] they might be taken off, but he may depend that unless they doe come roundy we shall be dropt as heretofore. And when we were upon a project off retrieving the lost reputation off our coals, that the method is it not by sending up small coal tho' never so good in nature; no that will not doe. I requested him to give us a tast off the best att first that the dealers may experimentally find their amends, but now we loose time, which is very precious... [*Letter torn*] must first caution you not to shew this to any. Poor Lord W[illiam] has lost his only son by this lady, since which he has bin seized with a sort off an aguish fever [and] has bin vomited once or twice. I saw Tom Day yesterday who tells me his lordsh[ip] is better. I wish you joy off our peace with France; about middle of next week we expect another day of rejoicing for that with Spain. So I hope we shall be a happy people, and remain ....

[P.S.] I hear that the number Ten are publickly solliciting masters to load att the Grand Lease, with large assurances that they shall be del[ivered] within 6d off H[utton] and B[enwell] price. By this you may judge how naturall it is for some people to meet with favors. Pray my humble service to honest Ald[erman] Ramsay, whose *bill of £100 I have just now paid.

[P.]P.S. I have just now rec[eived] an account that Mons[ieur] Bern[ardeau] designs to import some good wine. If so itt will ease you off the commission, which I discharge, as also off the white wine; but must desire you to inform yourself of himself or

Dan[iel] and desire if they could gett a piece [*i.e.* cask] off good white that they would order itt accordingly. Adieu.

1. Peace with France was expected to cause considerable economic dislocation, particularly if the controversial Commerce bill was passed. The bill was defeated in the Commons in June by an alliance of Whigs and rebel Tories. See D.C. Coleman, 'Politics and Economics in the Age of Anne : the case of the Anglo-French trade treaty of 1713', in Coleman & A.J. John, *Trade, Government and Economy in Pre-Industrial England*, (London, 1976), pp.187-213.

64

May 12th 1713

You will be surpriz'd to find 2 letters in two posts from me. The occasion is this. The attorney in Chancery for my father was with him this afternoon, and in discourse happen'd to discover that Mr R[oge]rs did not design to make any answer [in the Bensham case] but design'd to join in with Clav[ering] against us; and particularly that they would file a bill against you and me to know the quantitys off coal you have wr[ought] out off the upper seams and by what authority. This affected my father not a little and me no less. I shall be very uneasy till I hear from my good friend on this head, and what answer I can make to my father as well as elsewhere. The order I sign'd was soly for your service and att your request. Excuse this fresh trouble but I can't be easy till I hear from you. Adieu, I am ....

[P.S.] The consideration of the wine bill is putt off for another week.[1]

1. The Wine bill proposed a temporary suspension of the duties on French wine imports.

65

June 13th 1713

I had yours some time agoe, for which fav[our] I am indebted to you. Your *bill was punctually paid and I have given you creditt in my account as I formerly hinted to Dan[iel]. This sort off imploy is very irksome to me on account off the bad circumst[ances] off health and indeed my complaints increase with the heat off the weather; however to hear off the wellfare off my friends (amongst which you will give me leave to style Mr May[or] none off the least) would be a cordiall and refreshm[ent] not inferior to any I recieve from my d[octor]. Lett me therfore have a line or two att a leisure minute, if such a one be to be had, for I know you have bin and I doubt are still upon double duty; I heartily wish that the same success as hitherto has attended you may accompany you to the end off the chapter. Pray lett me have your thoughts a little in relation to trade; itt is in great confusion beyond all dispute but as itt appears to me itt is not yet arrived to its full perfection. I draw my inference chiefly from the great number off large ships that are taken up by the Governm[ent] att this juncture for transporting our forces from Ostend to Ireland, att least 40 sail, some say 50, which one can't expect to return into the coal trade again before Sep[tember]. Again, I apprehend that our oversea trade is knockt on the head, if true what I heard this day, that the Fr[ench] have stopp'd 15 off our merch[ant] ships in Roan river; will not suffer them to unload nor return, itt is supposed till such time as they know the fate off the trade bill here in England. Besides I doubt a unanimity off the number 5, who were they actually all off a piece yet I don't see how they can preserve the trade from ruin. These are melancholly circumstances, off which I can't foresee any precaution that will effect a cure. 'Ere I conclude must acquaint my good friend that Mr R[oge]rs and [his] mother have both refused absolutely to join with my father in his bill off interpleader and answer unless you be brought in as well as Trumball, which if they persist in will occasion a great delay as well as charge. Further that my father is very unwilling to comply till he had first obtain'd your permission. He was pleased to ask my opinion: I told him without hesitation that since itt appear'd to be a point off consequence, I could paroll [*i.e.* swear] you would not oppose, nor entertain the worse thought off him for so doing. I desir'd he would write to the Capt[ain] to wait on you as soon as his came to hand, that you would lay your heads together, and if you had not leisure to write, that he would by the very return off the post, otherwise itt will be too late. He had the account off Mr R[ogers] from Hebdon by last post. Now my good friend I have finished my paper, and have left room only to assure you that I am ....

66

June 20th 1713

Tho' I have wrote 4 letters att least to you without any answer
to them, save a line or two about a month agoe, yet I can't
forbear you see giving the trouble of this and taking the
opportunity off lamenting my misfortune off having forfeited
the fav[our] of a friend whose correspondence I so much valued;
especially att a juncture when I stood most in need off his
assistance and advice. You don't know in what perplexity I have
bin in off late about my menagem[ent] or rather
mismenagem[ent] of B[ensham]. In short I have the following
account in relation to the upper seams as nicely as I could. That
during my uncle Tom's life, W[illiam] Johnson and Ned Carr
were the acting p[artners] for that concern, att which time those
upper seams were wrought by W. Watman, Trumball and
Donison, the first I was positive too; that the reserv'd rent was
10s per *ten to the Riddells, the 10 groats [*i.e.* 3s. 4d] to the
lessees, but off any paym[ent] to either I could say nothing.
That Trumb[all] continued work[ing] for severall years and does
to this day, but by what authority I knew not. That some years
agoe when the colliery drew near Gatesh[ead], Mr Johnson
thought itt for the interest off itt to remove the *way and lay itt
to the Rock *steath and gives warning off [the] £40 lease; att the
expirat[ion] off which we were disturb'd by the 24 [*i.e.* the
vestry]. But some time after Mr W[illiam] C[otesworth] took a
new one from the vestry off Gatesh[ead], gave us the liberty off
itt and have ever since bin protected by him in the peacable
enjoym[ent] without even so much as the least acknowledgment.
That about 1708 the said W[illiam] C[otesworth] being desirous
to try his fortune in the upper seams, apply'd himself to Mr
Rogers, one off the originall partners, who told him that he
should be assured off his consent but refused att first to sign his
consent, by reason that he was satisfied that H[enry] L[iddell]
and family would oppose him. Upon which the said W[illiam]
C[otesworth] made application to Ly[onel] V[ane] and the said
H[enry] L[iddell] and obtain'd their approbation that the said
W[illiam] C[otesworth] should work as Trumball had don, but
upon carrying the said writing to Mr R[ogers], he then recall'd
his promise and refus'd to sign. That the said W[illiam]
C[otesworth] promised to pay the like rent etc; that I did believe

he had discharged the same yearly. Now my good firiend I find that paper which we sign'd to you rises up in judgem[ent] against me. I should be glad off a copy; I don't remember perfectly, but as near as I can guess what we discoursed you about was an intimation to the Gatesh[ead] family that you were the person whom we approv'd off preferable to any, and whom we should not oppose if they lett itt to you, or to that effect. Now I must conjure you in the first place to secrecy, shew nobody this but committ itt to the flames; in the next must request off you to sett me to rights if in any p[art] I am wrong, and as speedily as you can, as also what rents you have paid, when and to whom. I again intreat you to lend me your assistance att this dead lift [*i.e.* burden too heavy to move]. I am sadly uneasy in mind, because I find itt gives a friend off ours [Sir Henry] great disturbance in Red Ly[on] Street and the rather since a good deal lyes att my door. I flatter my self with a speedy return to this, otherwise I shall look upon my self as forsaken by my old friend. Excuse this trouble att a time that I know your hands are full of business, and believe me to be ....

[P.S.] If you be a party in Cla[vering's] bill, in your answer would itt not be proper to own yourself ten[ant] to the Gatesh[ead] family, as those to whom you p[aid] rent, without mentioning the partners or any off them? Pray did you shew any body that piece off paper Ly[onel] and I sign'd and to whom?

67

20th Nov[ember] 1713

My kind friend's letter off the 15th inst came safe. I must own itt was an agreeable surprize to me to find (after so many months interruption) the correspondence with my old friend reviv'd: I read his letter over and over again, each line affording me fresh satisfaction save that which gives so sad an account of his own indisposition, which I hope att least heartily wish may be remov'd ere this arrive. In the mean time take a word off advice, that as this campaign has bin a long and toilsome one, those that have bin most exposed should solace themselves in their winter quarters and take care to recruit again[st] spring. Cha[rles] Sand[erson] has given you an account off what pass'd

in Chancery att the last motion, where your adversarys were
obliged, tho' with uttmost reluctancy, to comply to a tryall att
Y[or]k. Br[umell] is sadly mortified and it has bin spredd about
att Gate that the Ald[erman], dispairing off success in the
county, was resolv'd to try if he could prevail with the court to
remove the issue to Y[ork] where he expected to find more
friends in the jury; that Tom Shaftoe, being sensible off the
injury he had don Sir J[ohn Clavering] and B[rumell], was
resolv'd to drop his cause and give them no farther trouble; that
the Ald[erman's] aim was only to ruin poor B[rumell], however
that he did not dispair off succeeding att long run. This is the
language off the Gate, and just now one is come in who
happen'd to be in Brumm[ell's] company last night att
Billing[sgate] att the Tavern, where that gentlem[an] was pretty
full off liq[uor] and declared that Mr Pitts was to putt in
something into court that night which would be off singular use
to his cause and he hop'd would overthrow all his enemys.[1] He
entertain'd the dealers with a sight of a waggon way in frame, 3
y[ards] in length, and a little waggon carrying a bushell of coals.
He is att tavern all day with dealers in one room, the *crimps
and *undertakers in another, and the 3d for mast[ers]. These
leeches suck him dry and yet don't answer his ends: they
demand 18d a Newc[astle] *cha[ldron] for what they take off,
without being bound to a quantity. This perplexes him so
extreemly, he is weary off the town and talks off leaving itt in a
day or two. N.B. This minature off a waggon and the *way was
br[ought] up by sea in order to have shewn to the Committee (if
opportunity offerd) therby demonstrating att once the excessive
ch[arge] that attends coal owners, and therfore an inducem[ent]
to them to grant readily a bill for settling off *way leavs att a
reasonable rate. This notable machine has laid conceal'd in a
box att the Salutation ever since which is about a 12 month agoe
as I take itt. However I shall leave that gentleman where I found
him (viz.) att the Gate and proceed to the answer off yours.

What relates to Clav[ering] St[ella] concern is exactly
answerable to my notions. You have drawn itt into a very
narrow compass, into the 4 following heads: 1st either by
menaging the Gate, or 2dly give way to the *fitters, or 3dly goe
on as we have don this year, or 4thly *lye in for good and all.
Excuse iff I don't begin and say a word according to the division
off my text. I begin with the last first. By lying in our rents [on

the estate] must sink att least ⅓d, so that we must proceed while we can but even save our selvs or have but a fair prospect off so doing. The 3d point is in a great measure answer'd in the 4th. I doubt we have bin loosers and that considerably too; besides a constant fatigue to Mr Cl[avering] and other friends below, as well as to me above, I must needs say, such a one as I can't undergoe without hazard to my life. To the 2d, one had better fall into the hands off the D[evil] than those off the fitters; they have scrap'd all the flesh off and left us to pick the bare bones. Besides when we come into their clutches we never know the expence off the trade till the year ends, and then 'tis too late to redress. *Gift grows apace by their crafty and false representations, and still under a pretence off acting only as our neighbours doe. Which makes me call to mind when I went to school at Sir J[ohn] Kayes's, we used to attend upon the warren keeper to see the diversion off cony catching. He happen'd to catch a couple off poll catts in his trapps one night [and] summons us boys to be wittnesses to the execution, which was after this manner. He got a riddle, putt their tails thro', after gott a cloven stick and by that means pinched them cruelly; the poor creatures fell to fighting as long as they had breath, and after return'd till they scratch'd their eyes out and att last lost their lives. Don't you think that the man who had his hand on the other side [of] the riddle, with his 2 sticks, was nott something related to a certain generation off people who sport att the ruin off those they gett their dayly food by, besides what some of them hord up. Therfore I had rather throw my self into the hands off the Gate, which tho' they be nott off the same species, yet not unlike in qualifications; with this distinction only, that they pick your pockett but they tell you afore hand whereab[outs] the summ will be, whereas the other slides his hand into your purse, takes and takes again and yet will not bear a reprooff. I own that off 2 evills the least ought to be chose and therfore doe agree with my good friend that the first off the 4 is more preferable. But then how will this matter be compass'd; not so easily as one would imagine. We have so offt crackt our words with them in relation to the quality off our coals: any time these 3 years we promised that the coals should come roundier and better than for severall by past, and yet when deliv[ered] there they prove every year smaller than others, nay even to this very last voyage. Here were 9 or 10 off their ships all in a manner together; 4 or 5 are deliv[ered] but their bulks [are] proving so excessively small that they have intirely ruin'd the markett, for the other ships off that concern that had not sold are not offer'd a farthing. The masters run about the Gate like so many craz'd people; they bellow, swear and forswear every voyage that they will not be slaves to their fitters, that they will be damn'd before they will load again. Now you see in what a condition we are in. Dealers, masters and fitters are prejudiced to the utmost degree. As to the first, would you promise them 2s a ch[aldron] if they come as they did this last year, they will not take itt. Nay most off the midling [dealers] having burnt their fingers the begining off the year, shun them as if infected, which will appear by the account I writ to Mr Clav[ering] and Mons[ieur] P[oyen] off what each dealer has don, and shall send the rem[ainder] now att [Christ]mas when the whole *vend will be made up. There is scarce any that could vend a quantity but Dawson, Godfrey and the 2 Oldners, and all those went to the glass houses. Now suppose we were assured off all that vend itt would not am[ount] to 5000 Lond[on] c[haldrons] the yearly consumption, and I hear that Brummell has secured Godfrey by a *praem[ium] of no less than 12d, perhaps more, and [for] a good commodity which will vend itt self. How can we therfore propose to doe the same by our concern, which has had the worst reputation off any that comes to markett? Jack, Mr Clav[ering's] man, is come up to town. In case any off our ships happen to deliver this next week, I will prevail with his m[istress] to lett him goe aboard a day or more, that he may be satisfied how they work out. This boy tells me they have the roundest *ship coal in the river off Tine att Clav[ering] St[ella] pitts. To which I reply'd, Jack if you had such a stock off choice, itt had not bin amiss if you had sent up 3 or 4 off the last bulks for a specimen off what they might expect the next year, but instead off that we have the worst that has come this year. What can I say to them? Or doe you think they will believe me? No, were I to confirm itt even with an oath. Reputation may when once gain'd be easily preserv'd, but when that is sunk, itt is nothing but length off time that can retrieve. However I will try the dealers seperately (for they refuse to treat jointly with or for any concern); I will see what they say but dispair off success. I could wish that Mr Clav[ering's] (to whom I desire the contents of this may be communicated) affairs would give him leave to take a tripp up to town, that we might jointly transact what is to be done att the Gate: why might not he come and spend the holy days with us? He that is upon the spott and has seen the working off the coals, I say his words and assurances may perhaps have a greater influence on the dealers. I still continue off my old opinion, that unless the western people be not kept within bounds, that Cl[avering] St[ella] is blown up and many others not a little distress'd. I know itt has bin proposed by Mr Pitt's agent to Roberts, who was Shallett's partner and allways had his Tanfield Moor, to work 20000 cha[ldrons] to which reply was made, then that gentleman must advance his praem[ium] in proportion to the quant[ity]. Brummell att the same time proposed to work at least 20000 or 25000 Newc[astle] ch[aldrons]; this last was made to severall off the number ten, who were ready to ingage to doe their uttmost but then would have 1s 6d praem[ium] for what ever they helpt off with. In short they don't know how to ask enough. Severall had the assurance to ask 1s for M[ain] T[eam] but nothing was comply'd with by either side, nor any offer made by us save 3d as usuall. This is a secrett and must not be disclosed.[2] Besides they would not oblige themselves for any quantity.

My father received yours. He has had a return off his drowzyness within this week by past, which unfitts him to answer yours, therfore desires you will excuse him for a post or two and the first clear day he will sett about itt. We have had such continuall foggs as one could cutt with a knife, which has affected me not a little as you may guess by this confused letter, but a word to you is enough. You have a return off my best thanks for your kind remembrance off me. Pray make my humble service acceptable to the honest Ald[erman], his lady and your sist[er] Ramsay; to all I wish health and prosperity, and in a particular manner to you and yours being with all sincerity, honest Will[iam]....

1. Pitt and his employees were protected against legal proceedings by parliamentary privilege.

2. It should be emphasised that premium payments to the dealers were illegal.

68

Dec[ember] 29th 1713

Yours with the inclosed *bill for thirty pounds came safe to hand on Christmas day. Your kind and obliging remembrance shall not be forgott, and depend upon't your health is frequently drank by your friends here when you don't think off itt. Lord W[illiam] never fails of doing itt whenever and wherever we meet, not even excepting the Colledge. I am sorry you give no better an account of your [health]; should you drop or even [if] the infirmitys off body should render you uncapable of transacting business, from that very day should I date the declension off our trade. You are the only man that can keep the knott together, which has bin cracking a great while. 'Twixt us two, but lett not this goe any farther, I find a strong inclination in a certain gentleman [James Clavering] to dissolve the present union, as I may so call itt. I write to him this post and desired he would communicate it to you and take your advice. I likewise desired he would excuse me till the next post to you, but as I have ¼ of an hour to the good, I thought I could not employ my self better than by a short conversation with you. I find my successor [George Liddell] and he can't sett up there horses together [i.e. agree], neither has he any great opinion off Daniell's menagement; this is what I gather now and then from small and dark hints. I could heartily wish that you would lett me a little into those secretts, with your remark upon them. From Dan[iel] I have not had a line this month or more. I could freely part with 5 guineas for an evening or two with you hand to fist [i.e. intimately]; I dare say that itt would be off greater benefitt to bodyly health than all the d[octor's] physick for this 12 month by past, as well as an improvem[ent] to the mind. I acquainted Mr Sanderson with your commission, who said it was very well. He poor man was not so att that time having eat something the night afore that did not digest, but is better since. Now my good friend my time is near expired. I hope he will excuse me iff I remind him off putting the finishing stroke to his account off Cl[avering] St[ella] waggon way. The particulars off wood and workmansh[ip] as I take itt were formerly d[elivered] in; what then remains but fixing a gratification answerable to the trouble you were att and the services don the concern. Make your own demands; I dare ingage my word no body will gainsay

[them]. You can't imagin what a great sufferer I may be by the delay off our accounts not passing, and as I am inform'd, they can't close the year 1711 till they have that article off yours. Lett me intreat you therfore to finish that offhand, by which I shall be perfectly made easy and you will therby lay me under the greatest obligations. Adieu my good friend, lett no body see this and believe me to be....

69

Jan[uary] 15th [1]713/4

Kind friend, I justly call you such because I frequently partake off your purse, as well as other good things. The cargoe off French [wine] was safely laid into my cellar about a fortnight agoe. That very day Lord W[illiam] and Tom Day surpriz'd my father att dinner without giving the least intimation [and] in the afternoon sent to me to keep them company. They then discover'd the secrett, which was their intention off drinking an afternoon bottle with me, which I encouraged. Accordingly they came to my house and my lord who has his eyes about him spy'd my cargoe in the yard; began to examine what they were and whence they came, to which I gave direct answer. Oh says he, if they came from our friend Will[iam] I am intitled to a bottle and one I will have. Itt was sett upon the table and his lordsh[ip] began your health the first. The whole company brought in their verdict unanimously that itt was a wine off a good body and flavor but that itt was not in its full perfection, being almost chill'd with the cold weather, therfore advised to keep itt a month att least before I went farther. You can't imagin how fond my lord was off itt, insomuch that I had much adoe to skreen itt tho' I gave them the very choicest off Mons[ieur] Bern[ardeau's] last summer's importation. This lays me under very singular obligations and what adds to them still was the passing the wagg[on] way accounts, for it was want off that which putt a stop to our passing our accounts, at least [was] pretended to be such. Nay Johnson since yours wrote me word that the accounts were very backw[ard] and he did not see when yours and Mr Clav[ering's] would be deliverd in; therfore told me plainly that iff his were not pass'd in court, he neither could nor would serve the concern longer. But this I desire may goe no farther.

I have not been negligent in reminding my father frequently off U[rpeth] and the *wayleave; nay I fail not to press him. You know his slow way off acting and indeed having multiplicity off business upon his hands, one breaking in upon another, added to his state of health, all putt together perfectly distracts him. For instance, there is an unsettl'd account twixt him and my uncle [Robert] ever since my grandfather's death, which in case off either off their demise would involve my uncle's and our family in suits and controversys without number. Mr Freek foreseeing this had 2 or 3 meetings some months since and yet not quite brought a conclusion. However in this case of ours (for so I call U[rpeth] etc.) I have made him sensible that since your only design in making those troublesome stepps were for his and family's advantage, and how you had withstood very profitable offers which you could not well answer to your family, that he ought to declare himself openly if he would comply or att least that you should not loose the opportunity off making the best off your interest. To which he reply'd, you say right; I am under very great obligations to that true friend, I shall allways acknowledge his favors, pray remind me from time to time, you know my infirmitys, my head is selldom free an hour in a day. I have drawn out some short heads for the way leavs which I will shew to Mr Sand[erson] and gett him to digest into form. Now my good friend, since I have his leave I will pursue him close till we bring matters to a crisis. Would itt not be most proper do you think, that we gett the lease off the *way first executed or att least ready again[st] that off the coal lease? Depend upon't I will not be idle and from time to time you shall have an account off the success. Give me leave to rejoice with you on that this week before the Lord Chanc[ellor Harcourt] off which I doubt not you have heard by letter from Cha[rles], whom I have not seen since, he going out of town the day after but expected back this night. I long for that long letter you promised me, which will give me insight into matters as well as persons. I am a perfect stranger to what passes with you; be therfore so free with me as to explain what and who are the chief occasions off your greivances. You may rest assured that where you injoin a secrett, itt shall never be divulged to any living soul. What you think proper to be communicated to my father, lett itt be as itt were in a letter by itt self. What relates to Fenham he told me he had wrote to you about itt, and order'd me to do the like to the Capt[ain] which he leaves to yours and his transaction. I wish he would doe the like in the cases of the 2 leases to yourself and ....

[P.S.] My humble service to the Ald[erman] and Mrs R[amsay].

70

Feb[ruary] 16th 1713/4

The sudden alteration off weather from one extreem to another has had a strange effect upon me. All the last week was violently afflicted with a cold rhume which fell upon my gumms and gave a sharp tast off an infirmity to which I was all along a stranger, and that was the tooth wark [*i.e.* toothache]. I gott little or no rest for 4 nights successively, tho' made use off 2 doses off opium to procure itt. Att last ventur'd to pull a tooth last Fryday, and the day following was obliged to dine in Red Lyon Street. Gott back by 6 [and] found my self much out off order; 'twixt 9 and 10 grew very bad, my tongue fail'd me, had no strength in my limbs, my eyes were contorted, I could scare see any body. In short itt was a palsy or apoplectick fitt, tho' not to the degree off that I had last spring. The surgeon was sent for att 11 and took away 18 or 20 ounces off blood, after which I came to my self and have bin confin'd to the house ever since. This day the d[octor] order'd me some physick and to morrow hope to make my father the first visitt, tho' the pain and swelling in my mouth still continues. These frequent relapses prey upon my constitution much [and] disorders the whole fabrick; I find my self considerably weaken'd and not capable off undergoing many such shocks, and as for business worse than ever. However as opportunity offers I am still ready to exert my self for the service of my friend. Accordingly have wrote to bro[ther] B[right] to sollicitt 3 off his neighbors and acquaintance who are upon the speciall jury to attend the view [of the Bucksnook waggonway], and my father undertakes to confirm either by this or the next post. I told him that our friends had no fav[our] to request but that off a personall appearance, and trusted the issue to the justice off the cause.[1] All the agents off the adverse party look with a disponding countenance; nay even their former Billingsgate advocates alter their language, I mean the Dons. Major Loggin who has brought up a bulk off Mr Pitt's Tanfield had sold for 34s p[er] *ch[aldron] but they soon drop'd to 30, after to 29 and 28, nay I believe 27s. He has bin parcelling out near 3 weeks and was not d[elivered] quite last night. There is but one ship off Bucks Nook. Rob W[right] forced Blunkett to the tavern and ingaged him to take off the bulk, some say att 28s, others say 27s, but I believe she will not be expeditiously dispatch'd, for there is no demand and the lls [Newcastle] coals are fallen [here] to 25[s] 6[d] to 26, whereas had the ships forbore coming 3 weeks longer they would have met with a topping price and dispatch.

I thank you for the advice you gave in yours to Cha[rles] S[anderson]. I had a letter from the north the post afore I think, with an account that you had d[elivered] in your [waggonway account]; that the [charge per] *tenn amounted to above 20s, which was thought very high considering that itt was offer'd to be taken att l4s and that I had refused Jemmy Cl[avering] to lett him have itt att l6s, thinking the latter price extravag[ant]. Tho' this was not expressly mention'd yet itt was referr'd to my memory. Your reasons off the increase off charge were added; in my answer I added another you had omitted, which was the difficultys you struggled with att your entring upon the business by the old workmen, waggon men and agents, when they did what in them lay to destroy the foundations you had laid, besides loss off timber by pilferers etc. I advised my friend to discourse over the matter with you calmly, and withall I ventur'd to assure him that in case any article seem'd to bear hard upon us, I did not in the least doubt but you would rectifye itt. And further that as you were capable off serving the concern in other respects to the advantage off our pupill [John Clavering] we might depend upon your good offices and wholesome advice. The post after I had another with account that there was [£]l400 due to you as ball[ance] which I must own surpriz'd me, for according to your calculation you have not had pay[ment] for above 2 instead off 4 years. I am sure that in my hands there remains but about £700 att present, having fairly accounted to the latter end of the year 1713. Out off this I am dayly paying the maintenance of the 3 misses and our pupill, besides exp[ences] with the dealers and *praem[iums] as they become due. I have this satisfaction that we shall have in our accounts before the Master sometime next term to the year 1714.

And as my wife could not act as guardian since her marriage, our pupill has chose and prevail'd with Mr Freke to accept off that office, one who will not favor any party but push things on without delay. I must own I have not bin easy this 2 or 3 years but hope shortly shall be so. I am free and open with you. I disclose the secretts off my heart but itt is to a person in whom I can confide. Therfore desire you will not take the least notice off anything herin contain'd but committ to the flames. I wish you a good Yorksh[ire] journey and that it may be crown'd with the desired success. My humble service to Mrs Marg[aret]. Adieu ....

[P.S.] I hear the last year there has bin a great dem[and] for English salt abroad, wheroff I hope my friend has a share.[2] When the York assize is over and you a little recruited, should be glad to know how our joint tallent [*i.e.* investment] improves. If I can meet a favorable opportunity shall present you with a couple off Capt[ain] Steel's last Englishmen, wherin he takes a handsome leave off his readers.

1. The Liddells' influence in Yorkshire derived from Sir Henry's marriage to the heiresss of Sir John Bright of Badsworth, which brought them considerable property as well as political interest.

2. Salt exports from Newcastle were exceptionally high in the customs year 1713/4 because of a drastic shortfall in French and Polish production.

71

Feb[ruary] 23th 1713/4

I rec[eived] your long but obliging letter by C[harles] S[anderson] for which you have my best thanks. Itt found me in a sad way, as mine to you by the very same post would discover. I have gott quitt off the racking pain which had settled in my gumms for a fortnight, since which have had a constant feavor hanging upon me. I gett into the air every day but don't find my self refresh'd; this last night I lay in a dropping swett all night which has weaken'd me to a degree, my appetite is quite gon. Notwithstanding this indisposition I can't omitt troubling you with these few lines and I doubt not my friend's excuse, tho' I begin preposterously with answering the last part off your letter.

Considering my frequent relapses especially off late debarrs me off the greatest off satisfaction in the enjoym[ent] off your good company, which att this time seems so absolutely necessary, that makes me more ardently wish that some business off consequence should oblige you to come to town. I proceed in the next place to touch upon the antecedent paragraph relating to your quaery iff we shall continue in the Regulation this year. Now my good friend, pray what answer can I give? Were I sole menager I could then without hesitation offer my opinion, but as my partner [James Clavering] is the director below, what can I doe further than give my advice, which I have not bin remiss in doing; therfore consider that a breach with that gentleman att this time off day, with what consequences may such a rupture be attended! In my opinion itt would not doe amiss iff an offer were made him to this effect, that Mr M[ontagu's] *fitters undertake to vend us 50 *tenns, my father's 25 and Mr Wilkinson's 25, we paying for fittage 14 or 16d p[er] *ch[aldron]. I discoursed my father on this head, which he did not dislike. If you think itt worth while to communicate this to the severall partys, and in case they approve iff you with your usuall address should propose itt to my partner, and when once broached to him I shall back itt. I am heartily concern'd to hear off his misfortunes. I allways opposed his opening his Tanfield colliery when [I was] in the countrey; nay have ever since I came up repeated to him and inlarged upon the subject off his desisting even after she was open'd, and advised him to sitt down with the first loss. Affter this he wrote me word that he had taken Gells Field; my answer was that he would doe well to throw up all but my advice was not pursued. He has lost his son this morn[ing] so I can't att this time sollicitt the ball[ance] off your account but shortly shall.[1] Itt surpriz'd me to a degree to find such an arrear. Give me leave to returne my thanks in generall for the account you gave me off persons and things, to which I was till then a stranger. Be pleased to continue your usuall freedom; all shall be kept secrett, you may depend on't. I wrote 2 letters to brother B[right] to sollicit those off his acquaintance to attend the view. My father did the like and repeats itt again this post. The tryall comes on the 10th off next month. I hope that the justice off your cause will bring you off tryumphantly. Yesterday we had a meeting with honest Cav[erley] and C[harles] S[anderson] read over a new [Urpeth] lease, which is in effect the same as you sent up only much shorter. There are some little differences yet remaining undetermin'd. A close copy shall be sent you as Cav[erley] designs another to the honest Ald[erman] and the disputes will be left to the last gentleman. Sometime this week my father and I are to be closeted a whole morn[ing] (provided I be in a condition) to draw up the heads for the *way leave. I have gott farther than my head will admitt, therefore must conclude my self....

1. The boy had been staying with the Liddells in London in the hope of receiving a private 'touch' from the Queen. Clavering had bad luck with his children, losing four sons and two daughters before his eventual heir was born in 1718.

72

Mar[ch] 6th 1713/4

I venture to direct this to the Black Swan in hopes that itt will come safe to hand. Tho' I have nothing new to communicate, but my main business is to make inquiry after your health during this extreeme fatigue, which I do expect to hear off by the return off the post tho' itt be but a line, as allso off your success the following. Should be glad to hear what gentlemen attended the view. I find by the people off the Gate that they have not the least hopes left but that you will cutt all down before you, upon which the Bucks N[ook] stocks which wer £50 fell to £40 yesterday.[1] I can't omitt giving an account off what happen'd this morning att a house off our friends not farr from mine [*i.e.* the Powletts?]. Tom Y[orke] made him a visitt and just as he was moving off, turns about to the master off the house [and] with his shrill pipe ask'd iff he had a tryall att the assizes. The other answerd [he had] nott, why doe you ask? The other reply'd that he had a letter from his man last post, intimating that there was brybing (to make use off his own phrase) to gett people to attend the view and that his serv[ant] was a sollicitor. Our friend rebuk'd him sharply and told him that he could not believe a syllable of itt, since to his knowledge and as farr as he understood the case, there was not the least occasion. How strangely some people take matters. You know the nature off this gentleman. My brother [Bright] will be with you. I

recommended him to take your character off the school at
Newcastle as itt stands att present, he having some thoughts off
placing his 2d son there. For a polite education I dislike the
place intirely, and if I mistake not your friend Mr Jurin before I
left the countrey did not meet with the incouragem[ent] as a man
of his learning might have expected. I know you will give him
your thoughts freely on that head.[2] Adieu, wishing you the
disired success concludes all att present....

[P.S.] I hear Frank B[aker] will be in town about Easter as his
nephew says. If true, pray impart to him what matters of
mom[ent] you think not fitt to communicate by letter.

To Mr William Cotesworth, Merch[ant], to be left at the Black
Swan in Coney Street in York.

1. London dealers certainly invested indirectly in Bucksnook by lending
    money to individual partners in the colliery but this is the only suggestion
    that Bucksnook was floated as a joint-stock company. It is more likely
    that Liddell is referring to the discount at which the colliery's *bills and
    *notes were circulating : see letter 8, note 2.

2. Local grammar schools were falling out of favour among gentry families,
    a trend accelerated in the Liddells' case by their distaste for the politics of
    Newcastle's school governors. Young John Bright and Cotesworth's own
    sons were transferred to Sedbergh on Jurin's resignation.

73

Mar[ch] 12th 1713/4
past 10 att night

By the date off this, so late, you will conclude I have but
barely time to acknowledge the fav[our] off yours from York, as
also another from brother B[right] the day off battle, after
examination off 12 off the barr[onet, Sir John Clavering's]
wittnesses with a fair prospect off desired success. And this
morning we heard off Mus[grave] Davison's arrivall post after
the tryall was over with account that the verdict was brought in
fav[our] of our friend the Alderman after 12 hours' sessions; off
which I heartily congratulate you and the rest off our friends. I
expect to hear particulars from you, which will be most
acceptable. I must further add the conjectures off friends here

upon this post hast off Davison's; itt is generally believed that he is indeavouring to promote a *way leave bill in the House [of Commons]. Now my good friend, I must recommend to your consideration and serious thoughts some well digested heads to inform Members off, and the sooner the better. I foresaw something off this, therefore wrote to Mr Poyen for his thoughts on this subject a little before or about the time off your Yorksh[ire] journey, with a request that he would consult you; but as you were busy att that time, I suppose he has not had an opportunity off discoursing you and so expect a prolix account from him, which makes me the more pressing to have your well digested thoughts on this subject, as short and concise as usuall. My father, honest Charles your attorney general, Matt[hew] Hutton and Mr Gen[uini] are all present and congratulate you heartily upon your extraordinary success. The same is heartily don by....

74

Mar[ch] 23th 1713/4

I am much obliged to my good friend for the favour off his last dated the 16th after so tedious and troublesome an expedition as that off York was. I can't but stand in admiration how itt is that you are able to withstand the vigorous efforts off your enemys, who spare no cost nor pains, and have boldness enough to putt any thing in execution. They make slight off decrees, injunctions; they look upon such as buggbears only to affright the dastardly, but they being men off spiritt drive on Jehu-like. However give me leave to tell you the opinion off some off our learned, which is that a day off reckning was approaching, when itt will be found that the Lord Ch[ancellor] is not a person to be dealt with after the manner they now treat him; all these contempts off the court will fall shortly on their heads and great will be the fall. Their creditt here is att a low ebb as I formerly hinted, and iff the blow be but follow'd and improved rightly you will have them in a cloven stick. To talk off a *mount, 'tis a jest; that will not answer the end. For as their coals come att present they don't escape complaints att Gate, I mean off smallness, which is owing to the finess [*i.e.* friability] off the mettle, and iff ever they be obliged to load, unload att a mount, load again in cart *carriage and after into waggons this will crush any coal to dust; I was going to say excepting such a one as our Chowden stone coal was. These things being allowed, as matters stand now I am in amaze to hear by yours that any owner who has any interest in colliery should be backward in standing to their lift [*i.e.* making an effort]. Itt must be an infatuation, when people will not see what so evidently tends to their interest. Don't you apprehend that some have a fellow feeling with the adverse party? I heard since the tryall that Ald[erman] W[hite] and J[ohn] W[ilkinson] were both att Y[ork], but the occasion of their being there I can't guess. My father is mighty hott off a northern journey this spring. I incourage itt all I can. He has not yett fixed a time but I believe itt will be the beginning off May, but this is a secrett that he has not I believe communicated to any one off the family save my self, therfore lett itt remain with you. I should hope that his presence would animate more than one off the principalls concern'd, wherfore I wish him well down. In the mean time we are assuring ag[ainst] the worst that may happen here. Mr Lowther is perfectly possess'd off the matter and right sett, tho' such a bill would not affect him in the least; therefore what he says will have more weight. We are advised to act cautiously and appear as little as possible, till we see what course the advers party steers. We shall have a watchfull eye upon their motions here.

I admire att Dan[iel's] coolness towards you. If I mistake not, the contents off my letter to him which was about a month since was to have his thoughts and reasons well digested against such a bill; that I knew none so capable as you and he, but att that time I knew your time was so taken up that itt would be barbarous in me to ask itt off you till after the assizes. I have but had one letter from him since, complaining off ill health which would not allow him one serious thought, therfore desired I would excuse him till his head was clearer. In the mean time must begg off you whose head is always free, to sett down in a clear light and few words some choice heads for instruction off a great man but particular friend [Sir Peter King?]. Itt is the hardest case in the world that while you are thrashing out a benefitt for the use off 4 or 5, not without hazard off life, that you should suffer in your own concern. Sure they must take these services into consideration, tho' I am sensible what or when ever they doe such a thing, itt will be farr short off your desert. What would itt be iff each concern patroniz'd your coals so much as to help off with a proportionable quantity, when they dayly see that the avertion off the *fitters below and the dealers here to your commodity has its source from no other head than that off a furious spiritt off revenge, for your espousing some people's interest and cause so cordially and zealously as you have on many occasions shewn. I promised you in one off my former to remind my partner to take care off the ballance off your account and as he designs for Lond[on] speedily, I requested that iff he could not provide before he left the contrey, that he would leave orders with Dan[iel] to see itt don. I told him I thought part money and part *bills would answer your ends. Pray when you see him I desire that you will remind him off itt. I shall not fail off spurring up Dan[iel] and Peter when that gentleman has given directions. After all I hear that Jemmy brings but up with him our accounts for 1710, 1711 and that off 1712 will follow, but that off 1713 will not be ready till Michaelm[as] term. J[ohn] J[ohnson] has not brought in his last year's accounts. What can be the meaning? I am strangely perplex'd but don't take the least notice. You know C[harles] S[anderson] is a man so full off business that we can never see him but off a Sunday, and but then for ½ hour. I fell upon him about U[rpeth] : had he made 2 close copys, had he added a coven[ant] which Cav[erley] insisted? He cry'd *peccavi*, assured me upon the word off an honest man he would have them ready for Thursday's post and that Cav[erley] had appointed I think to morrow to compare the copys; adding he was sure you would pardon this his failure and he hop'd to lend my father a day for his *way leave. Now my dear friend I must begg yours for this confused and long account. Lett me hear from you as oft as suits with your convenience and believe me to be semper idem....

75

Apr[il] 1st 1714

I am this minute return'd from the Gate, consequently you may judge not very fitt for this employ, however can't omitt adding a word. Cha[rles] shew'd me your letter off particulars what had already and what you apprehended would occurr since the tryall. I had an account from honest Ch[arles] Wait's mouth

off what passed 'tween the judge [Robert Dormer] and Sir
Edw[ard Blackett?] he being then present, and his opinion was
that the judge lent an ear to the barr[onet] but could not say that
he made any impression. We advised with Mr F[reke] on this
subject (tho' not in time to impart for the affair would be over
before a letter could reach your hand); his opinion was that
none off you should appear att the sitting, so that you might
avoid therby giving the Chancellor any opportunity off
solliciting a reference. However in my poor sense of matters, the
course you have pursued is the best; as also ingaging Berrisford
and the favourite in your interest was a prudent forecast. What
they are procuring by numbers off hands at Newc[astle, *i.e.* a
petition] will make a noise, but from the Gate I hear not a
syllable, neither doe we think itt advisable to touch upon't;
when we hear off their motions we must watch them narrowly.
As to C[oltman], he is a cunning crafty k[nave]; I don't say that
he would not recieve a summ, but att the same time underhand
he would be as active as any off them in promoting any thing
that had a seeming tendency off advantage to the new concern. I
have ofter than [once] heard from good hands that he, Sir
Rich[ard], G[eorge] Oldner and Blunkett were the people who
have all along supply'd your neighbours (tho' not friends) with
considerable summs, with a prodigious interest; nay and that
some off the above named had actually advanced them some
hundreds even after the last defeat. At this rate to support the
extravagancys, that myne ought to have bin a silver one instead
off coal. Itt is absolutely carried against feeing Sir Peter, for
says the Phylosopher, he will not take one, but thinks itt
reasonable that he should be thoroughly appriz'd off the matter
and then he will ingage he will doe what service he can. And my
proposall is that if we find the great Dons stirring att the Gate,
we must try iff we can't gett the reverse with the hands off the
midling ones, who are greater in numbers tho' not in bulk. This
last is my own project. I think I have touch'd upon the most
materiall points off yours. I am certain your pains are
indefatigable, your judgem[ent] and menagem[ent] superior to
any that I ever knew, and I doubt not but will be in due time
crowned with success. Company is come in to see me which is
not a little perplexing. Give me leave to add a word more. I
design shortly to inclose for your perusall the new copy off
U[rpeth's] lease. Suppose the Ald[erman] has or will shortly

have the like from honest Cav[erley]: we leave any amendm[ents] to you and the Ald[erman]. This morn[ing] my father told me that the next month he design'd for the north [and] that the *way leave should be made easy; making use off this expression, that itt was for the use and benefitt off his own family chiefly and one particular friend more, by name Mr W[illiam] C[otesworth] which he reckon'd next to his own; that itt was necessary to satisfye my sister L[iddell] on that point, which he would effect the very first thing after his arrivall. Adieu, Signor waits impatiently to take this to the post. I have not time to peruse what I have writt; am sure I am to my good friend W[illiam] ....

76

Apr[il] 8th 1714

Yesterday's post brought your narrative off the proceedings since the Chancery sitting, as C[harles] S[anderson's] did what passed att Durham during the sitting, which he shew'd me and the same time desired that I would not fail supplying him with what intelligence I should have from you. Accordingly, after I had perused your last and read itt over to my father, I seal'd and sent itt by an express messenger, who deliverd itt that even[ing] to his own hand where itt lyes att this juncture, with a request from my father and self that he would be expeditious in performing what you recommended therin. Thus you see I am like to answer yours without book [*i.e.* from memory], therfore if there be any omissions you must charge them to the treachery off my memory, which is and has bin for severall years last past a very sorry one. These things praemised I proceed by begining with the close off yours, which I must own affects me not a little. What C[harles] S[anderson] has wrote to you I know not. I design to call him to account; for him to tell you that we made a laughing stock off your letters is a scandalous, false and unjust reflexion and what I thought that a man off his principle would not have bin guilty off. But I won't trouble you with more in my own justification, till I have inquired more particularly off the gentlem[an] himself what he has laid to my charge.

The copy of your inclosed [letter] seems to be an originall; iff not such I think however I may be allow'd to compare the stile to that off the Grand Monarch's [Louis XIV], hectoring, bouncing and threatning all his neighb[ours] with fire and sword, even immediately after he himself had rec[eived] a defeat. By this letter, one would think that they would try what bullying will doe. If so I can tell them they mistake their man; they have a person to deal with much superior in genius, courage and better manners than all their party putt together, meaning Mr Mayor, a particular acquaintance off yours. But I shall proceed. What I hinted to you about a contre petition from the midling dealers was what I hoped might be compass'd, tho' we must not attempt such a thing till we hear that the others are moving: we have a watchfull eye over them and are endeavoring to procure to have a spye in their cabinett. My father and self have bin almost every day abroad informing some Members off this design'd petition, but we move warily and secrettly that the other party may not suspect. All those [who] have seen itt both Whigg and Tory, exclaim ag[ainst] itt horridly, and if itt be brought into the House in those very terms as itt now stands, without alteration, itt will I doubt not gett a kick in the very cradle. Sir Peter is just now returned from the circuit; my father and I are not without hopes of prevailing with Mr F[reke] to accompany us to that gentleman. As for C[hapma]n, itt was in vain to trouble him with itt till such times as his own election be decided, the meritts whereoff were to be try'd either yesterday or this day if not postpon'd by the House. By this you will readily acquiesce that itt would be to no manner off purpose to speak to him till that affair be first ended; as soon as that is, I have secured a friend to apprize him fairly off the matters.[1] I heard by the by that Lord S[carborough] and J[ohn] H[edworth] had a meeting last Monday with Tubman on this subject and both resolv'd to oppose with all their might and main. Jemmy C[lavering] who is expected in town next Wednesday will be off service in solliciting, for he coming direct from those parts will be able to explain and his words will have weight, besides his body will bear a brush now and then att the tavern, which is necessary to be don sometimes. I percieve by what he writes me word in his last that he had rec[eived] mine, for therein he tells me that he had paid you £7[00] or 900 since you gave in your account and that more would follow. Nay to use his own words he hoped in a little time to clear all, or to that effect. Pray when you write hereafter during that gentleman's stay in town and have any thing to communicate not fitt for him to see, direct with another hand and seal. Att the Gate I find that the *notes upon Bucks Nook grow every day to a greater disc[ount]; people are now suspicious how they will come by their moneys. One is p[aid] to John Loadsman for £90 att which he is not easy. But what surprizes me most is to find that Ch[arles] Atk[inson] is concern'd in the circulating off these notes, or some way or other ingaged in that interest, and so is Ch[arles] Horton by the latter's means. This last his circumstances are but very low and this damp [*i.e.* discouragement] makes him hang his head strangely. Some apprehend he is next door to ruin'd.

Last Monday's work in the H[ouse] off Lords has raised stocks and this day they are gon upon a further consideration off the state off the nation. The Commons the next week are to be upon the same head. The Torys them selvs begin to open their eyes, and if creditt may be given to common fame, the Treasurer [Harley's] white wand shakes. These are the notions that the factious Whiggs sett about.[2] Mr Freeman off Hartfordshire and Sir W[illiam] Pool off Devonsh[ire], both Members, have had a sight off the Newc[astle] petition and I believe will be our friends. If you want £100 to be paid in town to C[harles] S[anderson] I will doe itt, and if another off the like value another friend off yours is ready upon the first intimation. I think I have answer'd yours fully, especially considering that I read itt but twice over; must referr what is matter of business to C[harles] S[anderson] and I remain ....

1. A petition objecting to Thomas Chapman's election for Buckingham was rejected in the Commons on 27 April.

2. Both Houses defeated Whig attacks on the Government on the succession issue, but the margin in the Lords was extremely narrow thanks to the defection of the Hanoverian Tories. There were persistent rumours of changes in the ministry and of Harley's impending dimissal.

77

Apr[il] 15th 1714

I was ingaged abroad att supper last Monday and just as we were sitting down to table, came a messenger from my father and Ch[arles] S[anderson] summoning me to attend upon

extraord[inary] business. As I came to his door was not a little
surpriz'd to find Jemmy Clav[ering] knocking for admittance.
This disturbed us for a short space, but the complim[ents] were
soon over and Ch[arles] read over Mr Rudd's, and yours by way
off p[ost] s[cript] to the other, as also mine. He was strangely
puzzl'd what resolution to take, as you would percieve by his
last to you and for the same reasons therin mention'd to which I
referr. He had early the next morn[ing] an opportunity off
discoursing Mr F[reke] upon the subject, who told him he had
acted as he himself would have don. C[harles] S[anderson] was
wonderfully sowr'd att Mr Rudd's which seem'd to tye up his
hands, but as the cause could not suffer (iff Sir J[ohn] continued
in the land off the living) for a week's delay we all though itt [the
offer of a settlement] would take off all odium or aspersion
what ever from you in the eye off the world. In one respect itt
was advantagious to you for Mr Vernon and Sir Joseph [Jekyll]
came but to town Tuesday night. The former did not come to his
chambers till 8 att night and the other not till next morn[ing] so
that they could not be rightly appriz'd. Cha[rles] expects by the
return his last instructions, which I hope will arrive by Monday's
post which will be time enough to give the other party notice off
a motion.
P.S. Past 8. I was interrupted by uncle Liddell and son, uncle
Allanson, Matt Hutton, Jemmy Clav[ering] and Mr Genuini,
who all together laid a plott to sink my cellar. They have bin
with me since 4 and have lessen'd my stock something more than
a half dozen off clarett, besides some French white. This
incapacitates me from inlarging; can only add that my father
and self attended Ch[arles] att his chambers yesterday evening,
where we found him uneasy. He desires but a liberty to proceed
but would not interfeer with any ingagem[ents] you were under
to Sir J[ohn] etc. When he has itt positively under your hand he
doubts not making havock off your adversarys. We could not
gett a smile from poor disconsolate Cha[rles] but I att last
produced him an Excheq[uer] bill for £100 which I make you
deb[tor] for in account off exec[utorship], in further part off
clearing the arrear due to you for repairs off Chopwell *way.
While on this subject, I can't but put a friendly question to you.
We are likely to have but a very sorry *vend from the concern
this year, perhaps not exceeding 800 *t[ens], which consequently
must inhance the [unit] charges off *keeping the way. I desire

your thoughts freely if itt were not better to have itt in the owner's hands. I could give some very good reasons for what I offer and what am certain you would agree to be such; and I have a fair handle off getting you honourably quitt off itt, since if in our own hands I am satisfy'd will amount to much more than when you had itt. Consider and give me your speedy thoughts on this head, and I shall accordingly proceed or forbear. I presume Cav[erley] B[ewick] has sent down to Ald[erman] R[amsay] the rough copy off the lease for his advice; if it be with him doubtless you have seen itt, iff not shall send you our copy. There are somethings which you will find hard on the *undertakers, tho' in the main points we agree. I don't particularize since they will be obvious to your eye. My father and I are doing (tho' in a clandestin manner) what is in our power to apprize proper persons off the petition, so as to confound itt in the Commons if possible. We hope for success from our undertakings, tho' no dependance can be had on people till the work is over. We may form scheems which promise fairly but the end crowns all. We shall not fail to ply, tho' with the less outward appearance the better. When you relye on the M[ontagus'] interest you have but a broken reed; it is exactly what you found when here. I could give you a fresh instance off itt no longer than yesterday but it is not worth relating. We are busy adjusting our accounts so that from Monday morn[ing] till Saturday night I have not a free thought. My good friend will excuse me for I am not my self, but in all respects and att all times to my good friend ever ....

78

Apr[il] 17th 1714

You see I can't forbear scribling, tho' to little purpose since itt is generally my misfortune to answer yours off book, for when there is anything of publick business in them they are directly dispatched away to Ch[arles] and there they remain till he has finished what is contain'd. Last night att my return from Billinsgate and the City, where we dined with Jemmy Clav[ering] and father York, I mett with yours to C[harles] S[anderson] and the inclosed copy of the *keelmen's petition. This morning early my father and I went a visiting some

Members about rejecting that [petition] for the *way leaves. First went to Sir W[illiam] St Quintin, whom we thoroughly appriz'd off the state off the case; thence to Mr Hedw[orth] where we found Cuddy Fenwick and another stranger, which prevented any discourse save what had passed in their House 2 days before, but as we took leave mett with an opportunity off discoursing upon the stair head. He frankly declared that he would oppose itt with might and main [and] that Ch[ief] Justice [Wright] had like to have quarell'd him because he would not come into his measures, adding that had he [Wright] known before he left the countrey that he was a man off that principle, he would have pull'd up his *way cross Chester Street. The other reply'd that he would have patiently laid itt again; after this high words on both sides. Mr H[edworth] added that Lord Sc[arborough] was off his mind when he saw him last and Lord L[umley] zealous; that R[obert] W[right] had bin with Sir W[illiam] B[lackett] to have come in with him but he absolutely refused, telling him itt was not his interest and he wonder'd what could make him expect his favor in this case. Thence we went to a Tory Member near Golden Sq[uare], where we were disappointed as we had bin 4 times before, since the gentleman happen'd to be allways abroad. So we proceeded to the court off Requests: the first person that presented was James M[ontagu] who told us that his uncle Wortl[ey] had already ingaged all his friends and even Sir P[eter] K[ing], but that we must not rely on. I thence proceeded to the Lobby, where the company was very thin, the House being upon business and scarce a Member to be seen. There I mett with R[obert] W[right] who had no mind to take notice off me but att last was pleased to inquire after my father's health. I remov'd thence back to a coffee house where I drop't my father. I sent for a friend or two who is acquainted with some Tory M[embers] for itt is among them that we must carry our point. I gave him a copy off the petition, with some few remarks off my own to refresh his memory; had his promise that he would make use off them and hop'd to meet with success. So we return'd to dinner att 3 a clock. We have severall emmissarys abroad who work heartily for us. Att our coming away we mett with a gentleman who will prove the best sollicitor against the keelmen's petition off any in England. We hope to ingage him. But friend off mine, the case ought to be stated, the chief grievances and inconveniencys display'd; this in a few lines

would be very useful and as speedily as may be. I am heartily
concern'd att the melancholly account you give off your own
state of health. Lett me advise you as to your hoarseness, send
to Mr Ord for a few off the St John's wort red drops; take att
going to bed 50 or 60 drops in a little ale warm'd and well
scumm'd first, then add the drops. Itt is an admirable medicin
for this distemper as well as the gravell or stone. Jemmy
Clav[ering] is by, salutes you heartily, as also does ....

P.S. Jemmy is angry att his chief's sparage [*i.e.* Sir John
Clavering's wrangling?] this week.

79

Apr[il] 27th 1714

This comes to congratulate you and the honest Ald[erman]
off yesterday's success under the auspicious conduct off your
general C[harles] S[anderson], who had but to ask and itt was
granted. Mr C[lavering], he and I went in the afternoon to wait
on our Master with our accounts in Lincoln's Inn; as we passed
thro' the square, who should come up but Mus[grave] Davison.
Immediately began to talk off the defeat they had rec[eived] and
what next to be don; why nothing but proceed to the removall
off nusances to highways in both rivers. Cha[rles] told him that
he had gott att least £500 by the cause. The other reply'd not
above half but hoped to compleat that summ 'ere itt was ended;
adding withall that he found by discourse among some Members
off his acquaint[ance] that the petition could not be carried and
that Sir John must now give up the cudgells to Mr Pitt to battle.
There is no relying upon what he says; perhaps in his opinion
this would make us slacken our sollicitations but he will not find
us so very credulous neither. We goe on (tho' with a seeming
unconcernedness) which I believe will have a better effect. My
father and Mr C[lavering] were att Westm[inster] till 3 a clock,
where I should have bin had I not bin much disorderd by a
violent pain in my kidneys for 3 days by past. I [pass] urine very
little tho' take daily provocatives; am very feavorish withall,
which dispirits much. However am a little revived with my
friends' victory and every thing that contributes to their
advantage is to me the same as if itt were my own. The report

off Denzill Onslow's election was made to the House this
morn[ing] when he was confirm'd without a division, tho' his
opponent was confident itt would have gon for him.[1] I heartily
wish you could putt us into a method this year off supplying
Waters' *vend att Chopwell. Our coal is in good repute att Gate,
therfore the difficulty will be the less. The Capt[ain] should take
itt into consideration and so should the rest off our friends.
Believe me, dear Will ....

[P.S.] Some were in expectat[ion] that the petition would have
bin brought into the Commons this day, but as it was not believe
they will attempt the House off Lords first. Mr Cl[avering]
desires what would have him doe in the relation to a lease with
Lord B[arnard].

1. Onslow's election for Guildford in March had been contested by the
    defeated candidate, John Walter.

80

[May 1714]

  [*Damaged text*] As to Mr P[itt] he is an impracticable man.
Those that are most intimately convers[ant] with him give him
the character off strange, positive temper, and when he has once
imbibed a notion the world can't beat him off itt; however in
regard to his serv[ant] C[olepitts], as soon as the House is up
you may proceed with safety. W[right] and Davison attend the
House almost daily, which obliges us to have an eye upon them.
Yours of the 28th ult. is come to hand. Am sorry you should
putt your self to such a needless trouble to justifye your
proceedings in relation [to] the pacifick treaty. All that was in
the matter was [that] att Mr Clav[ering's] arrivall, when
C[harles] S[anderson] came in with Mr Rudd's letter and yours,
[he] was att a loss what to doe, considering Sir J[ohn's] bad state
off health; was wishing that he had not rec[eived] any that post
and then he should have proceeded the first day off motion. But
att the same time we could not but justifye you as having acted
the most prudent part that could be, for by that means you
shew'd to the world (who were not much in your interest,
meaning the countrey) that after such a victory yet you were as

forward to hearken to peace on hon[ourable] and secure terms
as the vanquished party could [be] att that time, whose business
itt was to sue for itt. Depend upon't there was not the least
censure nor reflection on your conduct than as above, which I
look upon to be quite the reverse. The 2nd complaint as you call
itt was that C[harles] S[anderson] should say that he had wrote
to you to gett in the bill of charg[es] that he might gett them
taxed and so secure them before Sir J[ohn] drop'd. I
immediately reply'd that if they were in a certain person's hands
[*i.e.* John Ord], I doubted they would not be so quickly
expedited, but that he might depend he did not want the best
quickner in England to spurr him up. Indeed I thought itt had
bin the father not the son that was concern'd [as your lawyer].
But Frank [Baker] explain'd in some measure and since that
yours does fully. But no more off this. You can bear me wittness
that I told the Capt[ain] att a meeting att Percivall's, you and
others present, that I would putt her [Brainslope] into condition
for work[ing], viz. my share, and then he should enter on his
own account and recieve what proffitt she cast. Now had there
bin any, doubtless there would have bin an early claim; as itt is
the reverse, not the least notice. I read my father that p[art] of
your letter [and] told him itt was matter of fact what you
represented, as I had don some years agoe. I likewise gave him
to understand some other usage you had rec[eived] from that
gentleman. Att which he lift[ed] up his hands and [was]
perfectly amaz'd. When he comes into the countrey he will not
take notice directly (for that I made him first promise), but as
things fell in naturally he would take an opportunity. As you
state in your letter, I take itt to be that you buy *pan coal from
my father's Bensh[am]; neither he nor I see any reason why you
should not be intitled to att least an equall favor with any person
whatever. I design to see honest Frank once before he goes and
shall referr to him for some particulars, in the mean time rest ....

[P.S.] Whatever treaty you enter into, I can tell you will be to
the intire satisfaction off your friends here.

81

May 13th [1]714

I am gott abroad again after a fatiguing illness, the effects off
which I find hangs upon me still, that is to say the feavor has not
quite left me. I have yours to Jemmy last post, itt lyes before
me. Don't take itt amiss if I pretend to answer part off itt,
because that gentleman is busy taking leave off his friends. I
fancy he will decamp about Monday and comes down by sea,
but not a syllable must be mention'd on pain off excom-
unication. I have perused along with C[harles] S[anderson] your
exploits. He approves what you have don, as must all your
friends; he says you and he will lay them flatt upon their backs.
He wants mightily the bill off costs from below that he may gett
them taxed without loss of time. I can assure you our friends
high and low in the H[ouse] of Comm[ons] are pretty numerous,
insomuch that Mr W[rightson] and his party have not thought
fitt to make any motion as yett. As matters stand att present we
don't apprehend their succeeding, tho' they may give us trouble
enough. What you mention about certifying the stocks off coals
resting att each *steath att [Chri]stmas would be very usefull to
know. Itt was what I wrote to the Capt[ain] to gett don above a
week since, that is for T[eam] and Bensh[am]; have spoke to Mr
Cl[avering] to write to Weatherly and Lowry about that of
Cl[avering] St[ella]. Must leave to your procuring those off
H[utton] and B[enwell], Scotchw[ood] and Fell[on], Jesmond,
that off the Grand Lease iff to be had, as also the prices each
concern sold for, which must be return'd up with convenient
speed. Itt would be no difficult matter to prevail with the
masters to certify, if occasion, that the occasion off scarcity off
coals last year was soly to be attributed to the lowness of price
that commodity gave att this markett the beginning off the year,
which occasion'd numbers off the greatest ships [to] seek out
foreign fraights. But I believe there will be no necessity for such
a certificate, att least till we see farther.

Coltman, Bennett and Blunkett are the only furious advocates
against the Ald[erman's] proceedings. I believe they have most
reason, being as I am informed deeply soused; the latter would
not speak a word to any body att the Gate this day [and] is
morose to a degree. But was inquiring very lately what estate Mr
W[right] had, where itt lay and so forth, but recieved no

satisfactory answer. The 2 Oldners are tollerably easy and for
ought I know have slipt their neck out off the halter, which
perhaps was owing to a hint a friend off yours gave them 2 or 3
months since. Will Robinson be able to shew his head [*i.e.* get to
work] speedily? Iff he did not and iff the [Bucksnook] wagg[on]
*carr[iage] be in a manner excluded, then I must advise all our
friends to slip no opportunity off *leading down to the steaths
what quantitys they can possibly, so that there be no clamour
for want off coals to supply the ships. J[ohn] H[edworth] seems
apprehensive that his *way will be pull'd up and several others,
but I propose that those which are not should contribute to the
charge equally, being for a publick advantage; and I do imagin
that iff this [offer] was made to him, itt would remove his
apprehensions and induce him to continue firm in the
opposition. Nevill Ridly was att the Lobby the morn[ing] the
petition was to be presented, but what interest he had made or
who were his friends he did not impart to any off our friends. I
can tell you who exerts himself against us, that is Tom Gibson,
and were itt not for his interest they would be able to make but
an indiffer[ent] figure. I need to tell you no more off our interest
with the Torys than that Lord Lansdown told an acquaintance
off mine last [week] he was assured that iff any Member in the
county off Cornwall should be for the petition, he was certain
they must never think [of] being chose again, for there they were
as choice off their propertys and made as much by *way leaves
as any people whatever. Chopwell coal is in great demand here,
notwithstanding I can but join with your notion about letting if
feasible, att a moderate *quantity. I must leave to Jemmy to
transact that matter with the gentlemen here. I long to see Frank
B[aker]; he was the other day to pay a visitt to Red Ly[on]
Street. Last night we melted down yours, the Capt[ain's] and
Rob[ert] Ellison's tokens att Jenny Man's, where was Lord
W[illiam Powlett], Ch[arles] W[aite], Ch[arles] Allinson with
many friends. We drank all your healths; [I] retired soon after
ten, tho' some did not part till itt smote little ones [*i.e.* the early
hours]. Adieu. Take care off your own health, which I am sorry
to find so very fickle and uncertain....

[P.S.] I design when I see Fr[ank] B[aker] to read over U[rpeth]
lease with him if he can spare so much time and after trust itt to
his conveyance to you. My father salutes you.

82

May 20th 1714

I begin with that part off my kind friend's letter which affects
me most and putts me into the deepest concern, to have from his
own hand such a melancholly account off his health. I could not
rest till I had hunted out the d[octor]; read him your complaints
off the cough and hoarseness that stuck so close by you. To have
enabled him to have made a compleat prescription, he was
wishing you had bin more particular in your account, but as he
is no stranger to your habitt off body he has promised to send
me his thoughts by this post. I spoke to the d[octor] about you
last night in the presence off Mr Freeke who has bin troubled
with a cough as violent as ever I knew for severall years; we
thought it would have carryed him off about a fortnight agoe.
You must know he is no friend to the apothecary's shop but
leavs nature to work its own way, but att last was prevaild with
to take some pills off Barbadoes tarr, or where that is not to be
had [of] common tarr, made up after the following manner with
the following powders. Take powders off orris and alicampane
[*i.e.* elecampane] a like quantity, powders off liquorish double
quantity. Mix them together and after rowl the tarr till itt comes
to the substance that it will make a pill. Take 10 or 12 in a day or
more. Itt is extreemly balsamick and has recoverd Mr Freeke to
a miracle in less than a fortnight's time. He has known many
others recovered by the same without any other application. He
recommends itt to you from his own experience. I will gett some
off the Barbadoes tarr and send itt you down by the first
opportunity. My father had the 3 packetts from Lord W[illiam]
with the 6 inclosed papers; no more are since come to hand. By
what I can learn we shall hear no more off the petition this
sessions. 'Tis the generally rec[eived] opinion off both high and
low. However itt is our business not to lye dormant but be upon
the guard. C[harles] S[anderson] has attempted I believe severall
times to wait on Sir W[illiam Blackett?] especially att the House,
yet has never had the good luck to meet with him. And he must
not pretend to itt now because that gentleman is gon to the races
att Guilford and Bansted Downs, but will do itt the begining off
the week and itt must be my business to remind him. I have not
seen him since Monday night when he took leave off Jemmy
Clav[ering] att my father's, where were abundance off your

friends att supper, among the rest canny Frank who not
knowing off this invitation came to pass the evening att my
house. He and I had half an hour's discourse before we went to
Red Ly[on] Street and are to fix an afternoon this week, when
he will be free from Lord B[arnard's] business, when we are to
solace ourselvs. Jemmy went on board Mark Noble the next day
but that is to be kept secrett. My father sends you 6 p[ounds] off
his best chocolate by Jemmy. Your servant's which came to
hand a post or two before that which lyes before me now, was
communicated to none but my father. The objections you made
are just and would bide a strict eye to survey them. My father
longs to be with you [and] had bin ere this had itt not bin for the
petition, which he can't forbear attending. We are this
morn[ing] going to wait on Lord Sc[arborough]; if anything new
occurr you shall have a line.

P.S. The lord was not in towne. I took that opportunity off
visiting F[rank] Baker; had him to my self during a pipe. We
discoursed on severall things and he has promised to come to
morrow evening to compleat our conversation. Att our return
we found Sir Rob[ert] Haslerigg, uncle Allanson and 2 more
gentlemen that were come to dine with my father. They staid till
near 8 and putt about the glass briskly. I was obliged to skreen
my father, so that the labouring oar fell heavy on me. I wonder
Mr Poyen does not send me up the stocks att Clav[ering] St[ella]:
pray desire him to doe itt. The 3 persons yours mention att
Gate are hansomly dipt. They begin now to say that they were
drawn in and exclaim against the [Bucksnook] projectors. We
are all sensible that the western concerns would cutt out the
whole river, I mean the old standers att least, but very few off
them would be able to carry on any trade to advantage. If itt
would not be too much trouble to you to sett T[homas]
G[ibson's] case in a true light and send itt to my father, he might
find means to communicate itt when opportunity offers. Pray
excuse this imperfect answer and consider itt is after a bottle and
half for my share, for which I shall doe penance to morrow. I
heartily wish success to the 2 doctors' prescriptions and remain
....

[P.S.] My father when I left him charged me to assure you off
his best wishes and had not I writt, he would; but in truth he is
distracted by this afternoon's expedition.

83

May 31th 1714

You would percieve by my father's last that yours came safe
to hand. He in effect answerd itt fully save what C[harles]
S[anderson] undertook, who would likewise give you an account
off the baffle he mett with in his last motion. As this was the
first he mett with during the whole series off the cause, he does
not know how to bear the disappointm[ent]; he lays itt to heart
as much as if itt had bin a concern that was his own. This will
doubtless affect us all. Rob[ert] W[right] was elevated beyond
measure. But if their coals come not after another manner than
they have don for these two last fleets, they will have no great
reason to boast. M[ain] Team kept pace with them or very near
itt in price and dispatch. The Bucksnook came very small and ill
colour'd by which one may conclude them to work wett. Fr[ank]
B[aker] and I melted down your token att the King's Head last
Wednesday, hand to hand. My father hearing the occasion off
our meeting told us that he would venture himself for an half
hour, and accordingly came to us about 8 a clock, smoaked half
a pipe, drank to your good health, the honest Alderm[an's] and
some others off the like stamp and then went to Colledge, a
frollick I have not known him guilty off for a 12 month by past.
Frank and I had a lobster to supper [and] each off us a flask off
morgew [i.e. Margaux]; we chatted over the particulars you gave
him, which we finished soon after eleven. He dined with my
father on Fryday and talks off getting away ab[out] latter end
off this week. I don't hear that he has drove a new bargain with
the noble peer. Last Saturday even[ing] Sir Rob[ert] Haslerigg
invited himself to drink a bottle off wine att my house [and] my
uncle Allanson accompany'd him; the watch went twelve ere we
parted. I found an opportunity after some previous introduction
to try his thoughts off his colliery. He told me freely he had but
little experience off [mining]. Sir, said I, you that live att such a
distance and never come above once a year upon the spott and
are in some measure a stranger to those matters, I admire you
have not lett her all this time; and I recommended Mr
Wilkins[on] as a ten[ant] who could afford a better rent than
any body else by reason that he had a *way ready laid, *steaths,
*drifts etc. ready for *wining her att hand, water courses etc. I
had no sooner named the man but he fell into a passion. Sir,

says he, I have bin ill used by that person, as also by Sir W[illiam Blackett]. He shall never have an inch off her as long as I breath, no rather than that she should fall into his hands, I would sink both land and colliery. He thank'd me for my advice and withall added that iff Sir H[enry] L[iddell] or I had a mind to have her, he would be glad off such ten[ants]. Snowden *fitts his coals. I shall acquaint Fr[ank] with the reasons off this outfall, and what other remarks I have made in my conversation with him on the severall heads you intrusted him with, he will inform you. I am sorry you should have mett with such usage from a person that I had the like from as soon as I was Jack out off office [George Liddell?]. But no more off this at present.

On board off John Charleton off Yarm[outh] I have put a small gally pott off Barbadoes tarr; the ship loads with Tom Dodds. [It is] recommended to the master's particular care, directed for you. It is extraord[inarily] good and the fame off itt spreads apace. The ladys make no difficulty to make use and with success. Frank desired me to procure him a small quantity for one off Robin Bowes' nieces that lives in town. I believe she began with the same prescription last Saturday, therfore be not affraid to venture where you have the fair sex for a pattern. By the same ship is a p[ound] off excell[ent] bohea and the like quant[ity] off green [tea] for your particular use, sent by my father in a box directed to the Capt[ain] and recommended to his carefull delivery off them. I can't but be off your opinion that there seems to be a sort off an understanding twixt some off our grandees with Bucksnook, which made me sometime agoe inquisitive why Ch[arles] Horton and Ch[arles] A[tkinson] did bestirr themselves about that concern. I am affraid we have one or more snakes in our bosom. I wrote to Mr Clav[ering on] Saturday was 7-night to take cognizance off Peter's man. I grounded my complaint upon a secrett which was revealed and could no otherwise come to light but by Peter or some body that had the custody off our books. I recommended to him a strict and sharp inquiry into itt, so that a stop may be putt to such proceedings without loss off time. Steph[en] Dryden suffers deservedly. Had he not bin forwarn'd then there would have bin room left for compassion, but where people will run upon a sand where a buoy is sett up to prevent their misfortune, who can help or who can be blam'd but themselvs for self sufficiency? I am just come to Red Ly[on] Street where I found

my father in his slippers, occasiond by cutting a toe nail which
has occasiond his sending for the surgeon, who has apply'd
some sharp powder which gives him pain. He desires your
acceptance off his best services ....

84

June 10th 1714

I was favor'd with my kind friend's letter bearing date the 4th
inst in its due course. Itt afforded me a double satisfaction, first
because your complaints off bad health are not so loud as
formerly and [from] which I am perswaded, when you have
taken the Philosopher's prescription half a doz[en] times, you
will find sensible relief and by a perseverance will intirely
remove the cause. What makes me so confident in this point is
that I see dayly the good effects. My father began with itt this
week, taking 2 pills in the morning, as many after noon and the
like number before he goe to bed. Has found much relief as to
his cough and shortness off breath. Mrs Frances Shaftoe began
much about the same time, takes but half the number and yet
she owns her self better by them; tho' I doubt she is too farr
gon, being inclinable to a consumption and in a manner given
over by the great Rattcliff. I mention to you only these 2
instances, as an incouragem[ent] to you to proceed. The other
cause off my joy [is] that you have so good and substantiall a
body off reserve in petto [*i.e.* in secret], wherewithall you will
effectually humble the extravagant insolence off your
antagonists. I can assure you they don't in the least suspect any
aftergame. They sleep secure without either watch or ward. This
I could discover by Blunkett and some other the great Dons,
who with a smiling countenance ask'd me yesterday att the Gate
iff Bucks N[ook] *ledd any coals. I reply'd, iff they consulted
their own letters they were able to answer the question
themselvs; that I did never correspond with any off the
proprietors or agents off that concern. Oh, says Bl[unkett], but
we hear that they are still pulling up the *way which lyes in a
lane, a known reputed high way; that these practices were
executed by a Lady Hutton [*i.e.* Bowes] as they were inform'd.
However to prevent that they were forced to keep an arm'd
patroll by night for 3 miles together etc., a vast charge and what

poor Brummell could never bear. No, I answer'd, without he calls in aid some off their body, who were always ready to assist the distressed and so forth; thus we banter'd till after one a clock.

But I must now proceed by taking leave off those master pieces off impudence, and acquaint you that you mistook a great toe for a least. My father is well off that ailm[ent] but has had a strange hoarseness or sinking off his voice ever since Saturday, and even off that he is much better and hopes to compleat by lying in the air for a fortnight; to that end has secured a lodging att Kensington, where I fancy he designs to morrow. He would not divulge a syllable off what our trusty friend communicated till I had obtained his leave for so doing and for the reasons which he will communicate. I was assured and can depend that itt will be kept a secrett. Perhaps some things may fall in naturally in way off discourse which may give an insight, tho' but a short one, and may give a handle to an enquiry. If I find my self out off order I complain, but to whom should I? Why to my friend. But as it is not in his power to relieve, ought not he goe to the best off advice [and] give some hints off my distemper that may lead the d[octor] to a distant knowledge off my symptoms; who without making any discovery may point out something that may be off present service and prevent for the future. A word to the wise. Trusty F[rank] left us last Monday noon, taking his rout by Oxford so that when he can reach Mr May[or] I know not. After my prescriptions for your health, my father recommends to your particular care not to travell late att night and never without some person; and sent you by our friend his own pair off pockett pistolls, which he presents you with but at the same time injoins you never to travell without them. They are clever, well made and lye in little room. I just long to hear how you will mumble [*i.e.* maul] poor B[il]ly. When I mention that name [it] puts me in mind off our accounts. I wrote to Jemmy as formerly hinted : he took Peter to task, who has promised a care more than ordinary but that shall not doe. I will attack him likewise, for if he keeps him he shall not entrust him with a sight off our books, but twixt you and me Jemmy is more suspicious off another under his roof viz. D[aniel] P[oyen]. Don't take the least notice. That concern is under most unhappy circumstances considering the present situation. The differences twixt poor

Jemmy and J[ohn] J[ohnson] grow dayly to a greater height, which must undoubtedly be a vast prejudice to that concern, which without them is under the greatest difficultys. This makes me frequently think off resigning and I believe shall speedily doe itt. The Bish[op] of Durham was to goe out off town this day. He generally talks off giving my father the trouble of a tryall about the eastern fell but I dont hear he took notice off itt yesterday when my father took leave off him.[1] If you hear off any stirridge off that sort, you will be so kind as to impart to ....

1. The bishop brought an action against Sir Henry on this question but was defeated when it came to trial two years' later.

85

June 19th 1714

I have but time to acknowledge my good friend's last favor. Have bin with Tom Shafto all this afternoon att Kensington, Hyde Park, nay att the very Ring among the throng off the ladys, so can't answer any part off yours save that I have yours to Jemmy inclosed to father York, which came to hand late last night. I am not without hopes off seeing you sooner than you expect and then shall endeavor to sett all to rights. According to your directions, have communicated your last to Cha[rles] Sanderson; he told me he must have itt along with him for 2 or 3 days to consider well off matters in hand. Promised to return itt this evening, but hearing nothing from him conclude he will send you his refin'd thoughts. Pray don't fail off giving the Capt[ain] your advice how to behave himself in this troublesome business twixt the b[ishop of Durham] and my father. Have but time to assure you that Tom Sh[afto] and I drank Mr May[or's] health no less than half a doz[en] times this afternoon. Adieu I am ....

[P.S.] Last night I had a cruell pain in the thick part off my foot which disturb'd my rest. This morn[ing] itt appear'd fiery and much swell'd, which increases; some wish me joy off a troublesome companion, comonly call'd the gout. I shall write to Jemmy next post. The franker off this [Thomas Chapman] joins with my father in joint services and are now drinking your health.

86

Midsummer day 1714

As I told you in my last, Cha[rles] S[anderson] desired to have yours to me to consider off and [I] hope he has given you his thoughts. He has bin so busy off late, and especially this week about an appeal to the H[ouse] off L[ords] wherin Mr Freeke was a defend[or] and carry'd his point yesterday, that one could not exchange a word with him. However I wrote by Tuesday's post to Jemmy to acquaint him that itt was my opinion that he should let you have money upon account off last year's ball[ance]. My good friend, under favor I think you were wrong in making up your account as you did. You ought to have brought in first off all only what related to the *way and waggon *keeping and in a distinct article the charges you were att in laying new *branches, repairs off ongate [*i.e.* ramp onto steath], *steath and steath dyke, which are not mention'd in your proposall [and] consequently not in your bargain. Had they bin don after this manner and the stock resting brought to account, I don't know that the least exception could be taken by any person whatever. In mine to Jemmy I in short sett that matter in its true light and more in one to Peter by the same post, more at large and consequently I hope more intelligible. I doe assure you that my chief end off coming into the countrey this year is to settle matters relating to that concern to mutuall satisfaction, to see the accounts forwarded so that when they are passing to obtain my quietus from further acting. Believe that concern has all along created me more trouble and anxiety off mind than I am willing to express. I have sacrificed my health, I have expended out of my own purse since I had a share in the menagem[ent] many hundreds, and yet perhaps when I resign shall not be overburthen'd with thanks. I hope to see you sometime next month but begg off you to conceal what I write on that subject. You shall know farther when we meet. As I understand, Mr Ord etc. is to shew cause yesterday fortnight why he should not stand committed [for breach of privilege], so that should the cause prove insuffic[ient] yet there must an order be made and a messenger be dispatched; but in my opinion itt will never come to that, the House will be up. However his sollicitor will be better able to inform him. My father has not bin able to gett on a wastcoat all this day, so full off a pain in his

back and side [that] was obliged to lett blood this afternoon. I
doubt itt is the stone in the kidneys ....

[P.S.] Sign[or] yesterday att Westm[inster] mett Jack
H[edworth] who told him that Mr Wright had desired his
mediation; that he would wait on my father with very
advantageous proposals as he calls them. But my father will not
concern himself.

87

July 8th 1714

    The ship I propose to adventure my person in came up the
river last Monday even, sold [its coal] the next day and I had
advice to be ready to imbark as to morrow; and expected itt
would have bin so, but last night att 8 a clock had an express
with account off a reprieve till Monday, occasion'd by the
labourers insisting on a double price for delivering. This induced
Jacob Hudson, the master off the Liddell, to deferr working till
this afternoon, when he hopes those people will be brought to
reason. Every body is for putting off the evill day to the last and
that is my case. I could not think off packing up or preparing
for the voyage till yesterday morning. Soon after I had begun,
came a summons to Westm[inster] to try what could be don in
Burrell's case; away my father, uncle, Mr Allanson and self
posted to the Lobby, not that we had bin negligent in solliciting
our friends 2 days before but to remind the few off our
acquaintance that were left in town. There we all waited till near
3 a clock [and] did all that lay in our power, nay prevail'd with
uncle Rob[ert] to return att 6 in the even[ing], which both my
father and self should have don but we were both spent with the
morning service. I leave you to the 2 Charles' [Sanderson and
Waite] for an account of what passed, which tho' itt may make
a noise in the countrey and perhaps may occasion the burning
off another *chald[ron] in Swallwell town gate, yet itt will all
end in smoak since the House will be up by Saturday next. So
that from that day's work you need not apprehend any
disturbance but may proceed in your tryalls, obtain a verdict
and depend you will never after that hear off Mr Pitt's
complaint in the House, but he must be a petitioner to you for

what he can't be without.[1] I am just return'd from diner att Red
Ly[on] Street where I left the old gentleman much out off order;
he setts forward on Saturday if want off health don't retard,
which I hope will not. But this is a secrett, as also that Cha[rles]
S[anderson] accompanys him. But if you mention the least
syllable off his coming till you see him, I shall be gregg'd [*i.e.*
rebuked]. I believe must take up my first quarters att Hebb[urn]
for a night or two. I need not tell you that iff you be an early
guest, itt will not be unacceptable to ....

[P.S.] Lord Will[iam] is just come in; desires me to acquaint you
that by his means att the report he gott your name left out, tho'
Mr Pitts was very hott and mighty intent upon having Mr
May[or] in the list.

1.   Pitt was again using parliamentary privilege to defend the passage of his
     coal through Whickham. On this occasion he obtained orders for Ramsay
     and several of his agents (though not Cotesworth) to be taken into custody
     but the prorogation on 9 July frustrated his efforts.

88

[Durham] Fryday morn[ing]

   As Peter Bernard[eau] goes home after dinner, itt gives me an
opportunity off informing you that I have not bin unmindfull
off what you recommended to my care when see you last att
Hebburn. He will pay you one hundred pound on demand on
account off the waggon way, and as soon as this busy time off
the assise is over I hope to gett over to your parts and adjust
matters. In the mean time I have a project in my head, which if
practicable might be off service to the concern and perhaps no
prejudice to you. Itt relates to the supplying you with a quantity
off *pan coal. Peter will explain itt to you. In the next place
must acquaint you that yesterday morn[ing] my father and I
waited on both the judges att their chambers before 9 a clock;
after satt in court and heard Judge Tracy give an admirable
charge [to the jury]. My father dined att the Castle [and] staid in
town till near 6. This extraord[inary] fatigue has brought his
pains afresh upon him and disorder'd him extreemly; itt has
incapacitated him for business and in reality I am not free from
complaints neither. We had the saddest wine att Nicol's that

ever was drank. We can't yet learn the certainty when our cause comes on or iff att all. All manner off tricking imaginable must be suspected from the Castle, which we are endeavoring to fence against as much as possible; all heads are att work on our side but we want one of the best when we want Mr May[or] off Gateshead. Could you therefore contrive your matters so as to gett over to Durham this even[ing] and could dispence with your markett day to morrow, you might be off singular use to us even tho' you did not appear with us. To have your opinion off our method of proceeding would contribute much to the ease off my father's mind and consequently would be the most effectuall means off removing his complaints. That you hasten over without loss of time is his earnest request, join'd to that off ....

[P.S.] Our services to good Mrs Marg[aret Ramsay] who we hope will excuse us if we robb her off your company.

89

Aug[ust] 1st 1714
5 a clock

Yours with the inclosed came to hand this minute. Am much concern'd att your complaints, being apprehensive that I might have bin inocently the cause therof by tempting you from home such a stormy evening. We are not certain but doe believe our cause does not come on this assize. Jemmy Clav[ering] and your town's people have agreed to deferr theirs to another year, since there was no prospect of the judges having leisure. Your maugh [Ramsay] and Dr Finny's comes on to morrow the first and your friend Nixon's the next, which will detain the judge till itt be time to sett out for Newcastle. The 2 actions against Raw and the overseers were both quash'd by reason off the 2 certiorarii which were wrong, for which the judge did rate Stonehewer and he laid the blame on his deputy Blenkiship. This is the substance off what I can learn. I shall goe to Stow house to morrow or Tuesday, design for Rav[ensworth] on Thursday and thence the first visitt shall be to Mr May[or], whose indisposition is much lamented by all this family and company, who present their best services and well wishes. I design to spend half a day with you when I come, in the mean time excuse the shortness off this and believe me ....

[P.S.] I like yours to Mowbray very well; it speaks plain English. I have seal'd itt and del[ivered] to the bearer of mine.

90

R[avensworth] C[astle] Wednesday

Some business detains us all here till to morrow, when we propose getting over to Durham early in the afternoon. Could not Mr May[or] contrive to quarter here this night, itt being the last we shall spend this year? If you can't possibly answer this request off your friends, I hope you will lett them see you to morrow morning att breakfast. We long to hear the issue off your two Durh[am] conferences [about Bucksnook]. Your last still confirms me that we are harbouring a dangerous snake in our breast. Have you gott Peter Dent to draw up the charges off Chopwell *way for the present year? Last post brings advice that Blunkett should extoll those coal[s] beyond any Team what ever, which he told uncle Rob[ert] to his face and offended him much thereby. I must remind you off drawing out a rough sketch off an account twixt you and me; if itt be but 2 lines itt will doe. Adieu. Pray tell Rob[ert] Bowes that we shall see him to morrow. I am ....

91

Saturday 12 a clock

Yours rec[eived] which came att an unlucky time, just as bro[ther] E[llison's] business was transacting about amending sis[ter's] jointure, and being limited to an hour's time to answer puts us to a non plus. My father had but barely heard itt read when the Justice came in post hast from Ra[lph] Gowland and pressed to be admitted; this could not be denied without the utmost offence to that gentleman and to his attorney so I was obliged to withdraw. What remains then for me to answer is only my own thoughts in short. First as the Cap[tain] is att Ravensw[orth], we want his opinion; you know full well that 2

heads are better than one, therfore desire you will send to J.
Hull's and if he be in town, gett half hour's discourse with him
before he come here on the severall points. 2dly should not you
have Ald[erman] Wh[ite's] sense of matters, Mr O[rd's] and Mr
Wilk[inson's]; for as they are partys concern'd [in the
Regulation], if they be not appriz'd in some measure may think
themselvs not well used, and consequently may take handle off
flying off from us and treating with them seperately, giving for
reason that we had privately endeavor'd to make terms for our
selvs. I mean particularly Mr O[rd]. 3d. I don't see what I can
recommend to you further than that you would not ingage
absolutely, but adjourn the further consideration till middle off
the week or any time after our decamping, by pinning them
down to 1600 or 1700 *tens, as also costs (which you have a
good plea why you can't make a demand certain, having not got
in your agents' bills) and severall other heads to keep them in
play. And lastly I earnestly recommend your coming over here
this even[ing] if possible, if not to morrow, when upon a full
hearing off all partys you will be able to have a finall resolution.
A fortnight hence will serve for the account off Chopwell *way.
I mention'd only the account from hopes that this year's
produce would make some small amends towards the defraying
off the damages you suffer'd in former, I mean after [i.e.
because of] the ten tail rate [for *keeping]. Excuse these short
and undigested thoughts, and believe me to be with all sincerity
....

92

Lond[on October] 26th 1714

After having been passed from constable to constable for
about a fortnight, without much fatigue, we arrived att this
place off Saturday night, where we design to take up our winter
quarters.[1] I find that as the town off Whickam in situation is
much exalted above the rest off itts neighborhood, so does its
zeal for the present establishm[ent] exceed in lustre. Pray
remember me kindly to those true patriots, Canny [Frank] and
the honest greeve [Shafto], and that jolly blade who threw the
priest's wife's mugg into the fire (tho' unknown) should not be
forgott. It is a pitty there were not more off such publick spiritts

dispersed over your diocess.[2] Mr W[right] gott to town 2 or 3 days before us; was att the Gate on Fryday or Saturday [and] assured the dealers that Bucksnook would after all revive, seemingly intimating as if the Ald[erman] and he had come to terms and he hoped this next year to clear all their old demands. In short I am still off the same opinion, that itt is better to end this dispute upon reasonable terms than run the hazard off a tedious contest, the determination off which must be own'd incertain. Especially considering the unsettl'd situation off publick affairs att present and a medly itt will be att best. His Maj[esty] is off an admirable disposition, willing to doe every thing for the best. Here are great numbers off loaden ships come into the river, I believe the whole fleet that was loading att Newc[astle] when I was there. No demand, so that the price is very low, which must occasion complaints both by masters and dealers where there is no just occasion. My uncle is just come thence; he tells me off some against our Stella and they needs will have itt that your coals are *mix'd with them, which makes the alteration. I ridicul'd that wild notion as I shall doe itt in person att the Gate on Thursday next. I know not but that I must trouble you with an inclosed list off the justices for our county as they stood this present year; if you know any that are fitt to be added, lett me know. The method this Chancell[or Cowper] takes in adding new ones is if they be qualify'd with a [landed income of a] brace off hundreds a year; I do believe there are many in the present list that will fall short. Pray how does our Farnacres *drift goe on? You will make an offer of my best services acceptable to our worthy landlord off Westgate [Ramsay], to Mrs Marg[aret] and all friends. Adieu, I wish you all health and happiness, and rest ....

[P.S.] I am sorry that Jackson should have come as a deputy to the controllers. I can assure you my friends have not bin awanting in their application, not for that post but some other off consequence; no success as yet but not without hopes.[3] I charge you not to mention a syllable. I must have a speedy answer to the inclosed. My father salutes you. Just now I hear the K[ing], who has bin mightily press'd by a very great man who sollicited for his friend a military preferm[ent], took courage and told him, my lord, I have gratify'd you in all your

demands but am resolv'd in this to oblige another. If you will
not, I will make my self easy. Upon which the lord retired into
the countrey.

1. This is a jocular reference to the way in which paupers were moved around
    the country under the Settlement Laws.

2. The accession of George I in August and his coronation on 20 October
    gave the beleaguered north-eastern Whigs a long-awaited opportunity for
    asserting themselves.

3. The purge of Tory supporters from all ranks of the administration which
    began in 1714 created a greater appetite for preferment than it was possible
    to satisfy. Liddell's letters reflect this struggle and the growing disillusion
    which it bred.

93

[November] 9th 1714

I have your two with politicall reflections on the present state
off the publick, as also your last upon business. I have but little
time to spare att present; what occasions itt, you shall have
when more att leisure. I shall begin with the last first, being what
chiefly and immediately affects you, therefore I choose to make
you easy. You might very well have assured your self that had
the new scheme of taking out off your hands the repairs off the
*way mett with any countenance here, you should have heard itt
from me the earliest, but as there is not the least likelyhood off
itt I thought itt needless to disturb your thoughts. Mr
C[lavering] wrote me a letter about ten days agoe intimating that
he had found out one that would undertake to *keep all for 15s
a *ten and sent up the proposall under Stephen Coulson's hand.
Immediately I address'd to Mr Freke as guardien [and] askt his
opinion. His answer was, if the present *undertaker made up his
accounts by the tenn as proposed by him and kept all in good
repair, he did not see how in justice another should be allowed
to come in upon the first contractor; and desired me to acquaint
Mr C[lavering] therwith, that if you had failed in either off those
articles, then he might petition the court and take their opinion
upon the matter, and that the court would allow you to make a
defence. But as the matter appeared to him, the court would
never give way to itt. This I wrote down by the return off the

post, since which have not had a syllable from Mr C[lavering]
and I fancy you will scarce hear more off itt. If any further stir
should be made, you may depend you shall have the earliest
notice. I find Mr Fr[eke] well disposed in your favor and to be
sure he must not be disobliged. Therefore my friend rest easy;
don't take notice off this. You know itt, that is enough. As to
publick, his Maj[esty] begins to see who are his friends and in a
little time he will stick to the old maxim off his family. You will
hear shortly that the Bi[sho]pp off St Asaph is translated to that
off Ely; there has bin a strong contest with him and Mr Hill,
formerly an envoy abroad. D[uke] M[arlborough] and Lord
N[orthampto]n espoused the latter strenuously, the latter [*sic*]
was supported by Arch[bishop] Thomas [Tenison]. These
contests made our gracious [sovereign] very uneasy but 'tis to be
hoped that for the future he will exert himself. I write to the
Capt[ain] by this night's post. I presume you mean by the close
*drift, where they sett into the coal; when that is once done, the
next thing will be to turn thoughts on sinking [the pit]. I referr
you to the Capt[ain's] letter, being in hast but always, honest
Will, with my service to the honest Alderman and Mrs
Marg[aret Ramsay] ....

[P.S.] Matt[hew] Hutton is dead £120 in my debt, the greatest
part lent 3 years agoe, a terrible stroke to one under my
circumstances. 'Tis too late to retrieve so must submitt.

94

Nov[ember]

I thought I was so farr out off your fav[our] as that I should
never have had a line from you again. 'Tis now I believe near six
weeks since I answer'd your former by the return off the post
after the reciet theroff, to which had no reply, neither in yours
by yesterday's post is the least notice taken. I doe think that
considering the ebbness off our pitts and the small quantitys
that are gott out off the old wrought ones, that what [new track]
is above 200 yards [long] by your proposall seems to fall upon us
to be att the charge off, that is to say all new laid *branches.
This my dame agrees with me and therfore ought to be adjusted
accordingly in the countrey. The next article that lyes heavy on

you is Lowry's old stock, which his wife told me no longer than when I was att *steath this summer that her husband charged no more than 3½d p[er] yard for the rails he bought in, and doubtless what was first used in the *way were not the worst; consequently what stock remain'd could not in my opinion be valued att the stretch above 4d. And as to the wheels lett them be viewed over again by two indifer[ent] persons and what they doe value them att accordingly they must be charged. This is the most equitable method of proceeding in our judgem[ents], the readiest way off adjusting and I think what will be off the best advantage to our pupill [John Clavering]. All which you will communicate to Mr Bernardeau and lett him order accordingly. In the last place I can't think reasonable that money paid on account off the Regulation can be brought to any other account than that for which itt was originally paid, even supposing that the Regulation had not had the desired and expected success, which still I can't be off another opinion that had there never bin one, our Stella had bin long since bett out off the trade. Mons[ieur] Poyen (who was much better appriz'd than I off the advantage itt was to trade in generall as well as to every particular) no longer than this sumer in Peter's counting house, Mr Clav[ering] and I present, did make itt appear, therefore press'd Mr Clav[ering] not to desert the Contract. Had he bin in your town he would have bin off singular service att this time in adjusting many differences, but since he is not Peter is capable if his business would permitt. Poor Mr Cl[avering] has involv'd himself in difficultys which I wish for his sake he were ever able to extricate himself, besides the terrible afflictions by the loss off 2 sons and the other like to be attended with the same fate ....

[P.S.] Lett Peter sett each article distinctly. When once our long accounts are passed, itt will be an easy method for the future to adjust them, for the accounts must be yearly brought into court so that every body's account must be ballanced att [Christ]mas. I had a letter 2 posts ago from Dick Allen who writes word that he has 100 boats att steath off *pan coal, ⅓ Leadgate, ⅓ Bucknook and ⅓ Coalburns, which *mixture I hope will please, being ⅔ good to ⅓ indifferent. He writes likewise that the *carriage have don and I could wish the ships would likewise cease running, for they spoil the trade and make nothing to themselvs. I long to hear Farnacres' close *drift were finish'd, for then one might form some judgem[ent] how matters stand there.

95

Dec[ember] 2nd 1714

Yours off the 28th ultimo lyes now before me. Am much concern'd for your confinem[ent] and that itt should be on account off want off health. I percieve by what pass'd in the company you fell in with att the H[igh] Sheriff's [Johnson] that the spiritt off untruth reigns as much as ever in that corporation [Newcastle]. I could wish that the report off changes in the commission were as they represented. Lord Scarb[orough] told me not long since that he design'd shortly to wait on the Ch[ancellor], that he design'd to have 4 off the 5 yours mention'd left out as also Stevenson off Byerside, that he would take care to add the Capt[ain] for one and a few others to be inserted. Itt is his business to transact so that if you don't find itt answer exactly to your scheme, you may guess att whose door itt lyes. The adjusting these commissions gives our friend more disturbance and uneasiness than the most intricate causes that come before him. I wish you were to hear no more off medlys [in government]. I can't say as yet we are freer than when I wrote before, yet I may venture to tell you that his Maj[esty] who hitherto has bin passive will exert himself shortly. He is a man off few words but a nice observer off persons and off a very profound judgem[ent], and I doubt not in time will make us a happy people.

Guard again[st] large quantitys from the west hand and they can't doe their neighb[ours] much harm. I was drinking a bottle the other night with 11 off the top dealers; they exclaim'd highly against Byermore, seem'd not thoroughly pleased with H[utton] and B[enwell]. Bucksnook is their darling, provided they would send them rounder and were assured off punctuall performances, which they doubt much tho' has had honest Gil[bert Spearman's] as well as the Ch[ief] Justice's [Wright] words and honour. You desire to know what company Pitts herds with : I can't resolve you but I fancy rather with the low than otherwise. As to the Stella *way I answer'd what relates to itt the last post so need not repeat. What you desire as to the brace off hundreds should be readily comply'd with could we but come att itt; but I doe assure you in Mr Clav[ering's] hands there is a round summ but not a peny to be had to pay the works, which I believe have not had a farthing these 2 months. Peter is out off pockett £40. The H[igh] Sher[iff] perhaps has about £700 in hand; he offers *crimp notes which I am sure will not be paid, some till Candlemas. I desired Peter to tell him from me that if he would advance what would carry on our works, I would gratifye him tho' out of my own pockett; what success he will have I know not. I am to pay into the [Chancery] Master's hands on Saturday the ball[ance] that is in my hands by order of court, insomuch that I shall not have left what will supply our pupill and his sisters with bare necessarys till trade putts in, so that if never so fain I am not in a condition. However if you could gett us some *pan coal disposed off and turn'd into moneys, you should be wellcome to whatever arises from thence. I don't mean what you take for your own use but [what] you can prevail with others to take off. Poor Mr Cl[avering] is to be compassion'd. A miserable case God knows. His whole stock of children swept away in few months, his wife like to follow speedily, such an arrear due from him, poor man, must certainly break his heart. In respect to the latter he lent a deaf ear to the advices of those that wish'd him well, [so] for the misfortunes in circumstances he may blame himself. Elswick will be a thorn and a sharp one in our sides; she will gaul us confoundedly. Now honest Will that I draw towards the conclusion of the paper, must spare so much as acknowledge all your favors, especially for the last in furnishing my cellar with 3 months' provision, but pray take care itt be sent with a [customs] cockett, which will save us a deal of trouble. My service to Madam Marg[aret] and the honest Ald[erman]. I remain ....

96

Dec[ember] 16th 1714

Yours by yesterdays post came safe. I shall begin to answer each article as farr as I can. This frosty weather I find does not suit your constitution; I wish itt did because itt is most agreable to mine. I made a shift to walk as farr as the Temple last night and this morning perform'd the like backwards and forwards, without any inconveniency or complaint save a weekness in my ankles, which I hope by frequent use may wear off. Brumm[ell] always was and ever will be a trifler, and so are some off those concern'd with him. This day 7 night I think it was that Spearm[an] and Wright gave a meeting to number ten. The first passes for a man off [£]2000 a year. They proposed to the dealers the taking off 2000 *t[ens] Newc[astle] measure, for which they would give 12s *praem[ium]; that they had gott better hold off the colliery by which means the coals would work roundier and consequently more acceptable att this markett; that they had fix'd all matters amicably with Ald[erman] R[amsay]; that if even that were not don they had made the *way so firm cross the common that the surcharge [for *wayleave] would not be above ½ a waggon; that if the dealers would stand by them in taking off the above quant[ity], they would be enabled to pay them the 12d [and] in a little time to clear the old arrears, besides an extraord[inary] profitt to themselvs. But notwithstanding all that was proposed, nothing was accepted unless in the first place the old arrears were discharg'd and then they would talk off the rest. They broke up dissatisfied and you may assure yourself that Mr Pitts will have nothing to doe with them, I mean the 2 gentlem[en], for he does not like to have any conversation with them; to this effect he declared his mind to James Roberts the dealer and refused to see them. By this you see their is no faith nor dependance can be had on what some people say or doe. You mention taking Lady Clav[ering's] concern into your hand and the menaging off her to your self. Give me leave to tell you you were never so yoak'd; I wish you a happy deliverance. Keeping the western way within reasonable limitts off quant[ity] and conjuring down Elsw[ick] upon easy terms would lay the surest foundation for a flourishing trade.[1] This is my own opinion. But before you proceed further, do apprehend my friend off Westgate [James Clavering] has some design in his head that may prove off bad consequence to the above project. Itt is only my own bare suspicion and what I apprehended as I told you and the Capt[ain] before I left the countrey, but not a word off this to any body. But what you doe must be strictly private and amongst your selvs, otherwise you all may hear on't. I would fence again[st] the worst. Consider but that poor man's unhappy circumstances : itt is too naturall for people that are plunged in misery, on any rate to gett in others for company. Tho' I own I should not suspect him to be guilty off [anything], yet as he has quarrell'd with severall off our agents and none more than your self, who knows how far the spirit off revenge may carry? Therfore I again caution to act circumspectly. I can't but apprehend that since his own accounts probably will be objected too, that he will cavill att yours and the High Sheriff's; therfore I recommend to you the making off yours plain, easy and unexceptionable, and as soon as don deliver them to honest Peter who can't by any means please that gentleman. But all this is to yourself, I conjure you. As to politicks you must have patience; things we hope will doe well. I told you some time agoe that the spirit off the d[evil] reign'd among you. Your neighbourhood send people to the Tower without a warr[ant] : whatever that great man might have merited, I never heard the least hint nor was any such thing design'd. The Lord Presid[ent, Nottingham] is not in that extraor[dinary] fav[our] and as to the Co[....?], he keeps his post att present but how long he will doe so is not known.[2] You will find Bowman's assignm[ent for debt] in the Capt[ain's] hands. I heartily wish well to Farnacres; had a particular account from him of their proceedings and hopes that by or before midle off February to gett all the *drifts finish'd and secur'd. Mr Freke is come in which obliges me to conclude abruptly, only with assurance that I am ....

1. Cotesworth and the Liddells hoped to nip potential competition from Elswick in the bud by paying *dead rent for the colliery. This was the natural reaction of any cartel striving to maintain prices in a crowded industry.

2. Whig supporters were unsettled by the persistence of Tories like Nottingham in the ministry and feared that the political balance could swing against them once more. They also feared that the 'medley' would allow the leading Tories who were responsible for the peace settlement to escape without impeachment.

97

Jan[uary] 8th 1714/5

This kisses your hands with sincere wishes to your self and family that this ensuing year may be a happy one and many more. Att the same time give me leave to return my thanks for the handsome cargoe off wine you were so kind as to send me; itt is in my cellar, though not without a misfortune, being packed up in a countrey where white fodder is very scarce in so much that a few bottles happning to lye bare off straw were demollish'd. I have but tasted one bottle and find itt extraordinary good, and design wetting my commission with itt shortly, being the choicest in my opinion that my cellar affords though have att the same time severall parcells off Peter's importation in stock by me.[1] You know that the sex are always ambitious off claiming and appropriating the choicest for their own use, and upon that score Madam has seized mine, calls itt hers and I must be obliged to petition for a bottle. You see how you sow dissentions and differences twixt man and wife, however there is one way off removing them; since I am master off the key that opens her lock, I shall have liberty to partake off your bounty. Pray acquaint Mr Bernardeau that since my last I have p[aid] the article which he must insert in my account 'ere he closes itt: by Mr Bragg p[er] a year's board and schooling etc. att Eaton for Jacky Clavering, [£]43 11[s] 6[d]. You would remark what I wrote last about secrecy in transacting your affairs. Itt is certain that number ten have agreed with Spearman to vend 16000 *ch[aldrons] Lond[on] certain, they obliging them selvs to raise a considerable summ towards carrying on that concern. I can't learn upon what terms further than 6d [a] Lond[on] ch[aldron] *praem[ium] and doubtless that for advancing ready moneys will be very considerable. I must add that I hear Mr Pitts is not very anxious iff he work his colliery or not since itt will fall sometime or other to his family. This is hearsay so must not be depended on. However this I mention that you may regulate yourself in treating with Brummell, for if this should be and you leave them to adjust their proportions [of licensed coal], Br[umell] will gain an advantage. There is a greater medly than ever. Differences among the great men increase. Lord Sc[arborough] has the regulation off the justices. I wish you find the alteration to your mind; if any itt is but small as I hear. Don't ask the reason, I can give you none for itt. Some say the ministry are apprehensive that the Parl[iament] should be too much whigg, which party would be for prosecuting the last ministery. How things are I know not. But charge you not to mention a syllable to any living soul; if you doe itt may prejudice me. Adieu, I am always the same to you ....

1.   In December 1714, Henry Liddell had been appointed receiver-general of stamp duties, with an annual salary of £300.

98

Jan[uary] 18th 1714/5

Your 3 letters otherwise called *double coal came safe to hand and requires the like measure of thanks in return. I am heartily sorry for your confinem[ent] but att the same time considering the multiplicity off business you goe thorough and with that clearness off expression, who can imagin that you had the least subject off a bodily complaint. For my part when I lye under a burthen nothing near so heavy as yours, my spirits flagg to that degree that I am render'd therby utterly incapable off business off any sort. Itt is about ten days agoe that I began to find the return off my old complaints; the humor is gott into my body, which affects both head and stomack. This obliges me to be short and must tell you that my father intirely approves off your bargain. He writes this night att large to the Capt[ain] wherin he repeats his notion about Elsw[ick], as also recommends to him the care off so good an advocate as you have bin for the trade in generall as well as a friend, and that a summ should be fixed by him and his brethren [in the Regulation] for your extraordinary care, pains and diligence when they make up their books, exclusive off the sallary. I think £500 for Els[wick] a suffic[ient] recomp[ense] and so does my father, but if you find that that summ will not doe you may adventure 50 more rather [than] fail, but this is only my own notion. Robinson has one shipp off the 3 safely arrived; the other two I hear are in Harw[ich]. I hear not one off number ten will buy a coal off them, however she is att work among the Wappineers [*i.e.* small dealers of Wapping], pedling out to none more than 5 *ch[aldrons] and without making any price certain. If they fetch 26[s] 6[d] I believe that will be the outside and under 28[s] Robinson's bro[ther] and

menager says they will be loosers. As to your new serjeant [at
law Cuthbert], depend he is att the topp off his preferm[ent]. He
will not be barron'd in this reign. There is a call off serj[eants]
shortly to be [made] and it is always customary to call up those
off the ancientest standing. I know a friend off ours who made
interest not to be made and had much ado to be excused this
time; the charge is [£]400 or 500. Pardon me if I putt you to a
great charge extr[aordinary]. Read the [enclosed] proclamations
and the representations, by all which you will find his Maj[esty]
has not his eyes shutt. That scurrilous pamphlett intitled 'Advice
to the English Freeholders', wheroff great numbers were lately
seized att Exeter, has rouz'd our most gracious, who was not
asleep before but with a judicious eye made his remarks. They
talk off military removes as certain: the Duke off
Northb[erland], North and Grey, Strafford, Ross, Withers,
Steward, Primrose and 3 or 4 more generall officers; Lord
Cobham formerly Sir Rich[ard] Temple, is to have Strafford's
draggoons. By this you will judge that the medly mayn't be long
lived.[1] Adieu, I am interrupted by company and have but time to
subscribe my self ....

1. George I required a number of senior army officers whose loyalty was
    suspect to sell their commissions to more reliable commanders.

99

25th Jan[uary] 1714/5

Yours by yesterdays post lyes before me. I am gott into Red
Lyon Street, where I wait the coming off the Philosopher before
I can pretend to give you an answer to the main article off your
letter, therefore shall proceed to the other parts off itt that are
less essentiall. I percieve that the people in your neighbourhood
continue still infected; what is itt that will open their eyes?
Would the black coats [*i.e.* clergy] but shew an example,
doubtless the populace would be fond off copying after. I must
own what you write concerning the reverend's [Thomlinson?]
behavior was more than I expected on that occasion, while we
had the bell weather [the bishop of Durham] as fierce and
violent as ever. Should be glad to know the person suspected for
dispersing the most scandalous pamphlet that ever was wrote by
any party. I presume your magistracy don't think itt worth their

while to take notice off the dispersers or publishers. Tho' the
design off itt be off the most pernicious consequence, yet I may
venture to say itt will not answer the end proposed by the
compilers so fully as they expected. His Maj[esty] has now his
eyes open'd and perhaps by nothing so clearly and effectually as
by this paper, the effect wheroff, tho' not so readily discover'd,
yet in a little time by actions you will be able to judge. I presume
your chief intent off pulling up the *way is to lett Mr P[itt] see
that the Ald[erman] is for asserting his right and by that means
to bring him to a reasonably complyance. Upon this supposition
I goe, and as at first promised you shall have the opinion off the
learned as soon as he arrives. Shall goe on with what offers sure
in relation to elections. That off Southwark is over, 2 Whigs
without opposition; that off Rochester, 2 off the same stamp in
lieu off 2 Torys. Ned Wortley is a new Member for
Westm[inster] in Medlicote's room. The City off Lond[on]
began theirs yesterday. The 4 merch[ants] are computed by most
will be the representatives.[1] If I hear off more shall add before I
seal, therefore I hasten now to give you joy, good Mr May[or],
off your new office [as justice]. I know not any one person in
the county fitter and more capable off a due execution but how
you came there I am a pure stranger. I believe you are beholden
to our Lord Lieuten[ant]; I must own my satisfaction that he
had you in his thoughts and should not have bin less so had his
lordship succeeded in the alteration design'd. All I can say on
this head is that had he prevail'd, there would still have bin a
superior number [of Tories]; therfore patience. Pray salute the
honest Ald[erman] and sis[ter] Peggy from him who is att all
times to Mr Justice ....

P.S. [Parliamentary] privilege takes place 39 days before 17th
March. Our friend's opinion is that since you had an order off
court for pulling up, which he takes to be in force yet, that you
should without loss off time pull up; you can't suffer in
Westm[inster] Hall by this account. Charles S[anderson] is gon
to Rygate election which puts us to a loss off explaining to Mr
F[reke] how that matter stood last, but you will be able to guess
by what I have express'd, therfore you will determine as appears
to you. Just now I hear the merch[ants] are near 400 [votes]
above Sir [William] Withers etc.

1. The 1715 elections replaced a Tory majority of 158 with a Whig majority of 124. See W.A. Speck, 'The General Election of 1715', *English Historical Review* xc (1975), 507-22.

100

29th [January] 1714/5

By yours rec[eived] last post am sorry to find that our friend Jemmy is not yet come to himself; all I can say on that subject is that you will inform Dan[iel] and he will settle any difference as well as any person whatever. Itt appears to me that there is a sort off a design by that gentleman off bringing the C[ontract] upon the table. If he should scruple that the concern should pay itts proportion off charges, sure in such a case that same concern can't lay claim to any share off reimbursem[ent] as otherwise itt might by the last agreem[ent] with B[rumell] when ever itt takes effect. I wish we were in a condition to discharge the ball[ance] off your account. I p[aid] £1046 into the Master's hand six weeks ago by order off court and am to pay in the like summ beginning off Feb[ruary], att which time the *bills I have will become due. In the mean time there does not remain in my custody above £100, out of which our pupill and his 3 sis[ters] must be maintained till the trade putts in; so that iff money does not come from the countrey, I mean if our friend does not raise a considerable summ, we shall be att a loss. I wish they be able to keep the works a foot. The price off our *pan coal you will adjust with Dan[iel]; may they not deserve 5[s] 3[d]? All we desire is to make both ends meet and I doubt att that price we can't. I have consulted our friend about what you desired, who tells me there is no apprehension off a confirmation [of Bucksnook wayleave?] more than for a year. That same gentleman meaning Mr F[reke] and Pappa are both off opinion that you should be swore into the commission and act.[1] The Middlesex election was shamefully lost by mismanagem[ent]. The City poll closes this day; the 4 merch[ants] double distance the old candidates. The town off Bedford have chose Mr Farrer and another off his kidney against the great Gower and Jefferys, who had distributed 20 guineas for a vote. In short the elections go hitherto as wel as you could wish and that is saying much in a little. If any information were made against the publishers off the traiterous pamphlett doubtless examples would be made.

You will hear something off this nature from Canterbury shortly. The high party are outrageous more than ever, which is not unpleasing to me; did yŏu never see the gamesters when they dispair'd off success, toss about their box and dice? I leave to friend W[illiam] the application. Sure there will be demanded the qualification att your neighbouring election.[2] Att Westbury in Wiltshire honest Cha[rles] Allinson and General Evans's bro[ther] had a majority off 5 votes; notwithstanding the may[or] being high return'd Frank Annesly and Bruce [*i.e.* Willoughby Bertie], upon which a petition will ensue and perhaps the returning officer may be trounc'd. The like att Hartford city. I have bin much out off sorts for ten days past and under my d[octor's] directions; rather better att present. If any thing remarkable happen ere I seal, shall be added by ....

[P.S.] The lowest off the 4 merch[ants] carry'd by a majority off 553 above the highest off the others.

1.   Cotesworth was reluctant to take up his place on the commission of the peace, being conscious of his humble background and current trading activities. The Jacobite rising therefore plunged him into forceful exercise of an authority which he did not technically possess, an omission which was used against him once the danger was past.

2.   The Whigs maintained that William Wrightson did not possess the real estate worth £300 p.a. which was necessary to qualify him as an M.P. and that his Newcastle seat should therefore be turned over to the defeated candidate, James Clavering.

101

15th Feb[ruary] 1714/5

I am indebted to yours off the 8th and another of the 11th inst; shall begin with the first. I hope 'ere long to see Laidler rewarded according to his meritts; iff he be not, there be no looking out for an honest man. Now that the term is over Cha[rles] Sanders[on] will be att leisure to study and advise about your business, and I will incourage him to exert by acquainting that in a few weeks I expect an order from you for payment off £100 to him. In the mean time Muss[grave Davison] exclaims much ag[ainst] the breach off the treaty and says that one off your men has almost chopp'd off a man's head with his

ax, and many more complaints; which I take notice off,
knowing itt to be their own party that were guilty off those very
crimes they industriously charge others with, but truth and
honesty will shew their heads att last. I am infinitely obliged to
you for the extraordinary care you take off my health.
½ h[ogshead] will be a suffic[ient] quantity for my use, and I
can afford out off that a bottle or 2 a day for evenings'
conversation during your stay in town and there will remain a
handsome stock, enough to keep me till next vintage. Therfore
don't streighten yourself. I am very sensible that malt liq[uors]
have shortned the Esq[ire, Thomas Liddell's] days considerably;
the late post brought an account that he was something livelier
and more sensible off his infirmitys, but I doubt those hopes are
but flattering. Charles Sanderson is confirm'd in his post off
distributor off the stamps [though it] was not fitt for me to
appear. Besides whatever of that nature is don comes from the
Treas[ury] commiss[ioners]. Lord Sc[arborough] has bin
promised this month or 5 weeks that Ra[lph] Gowland's son
have the Durham distribution; nay Ned Wortley assured him
that their board had fixed [on him] and had his name enter'd,
but is not sent down to the comm[issioners]. Since I began this
[Gowland] came to visit me [and] told me he had bin att Lord
Scarb[orough's] this morn[ing]; that lord told him that Mr
[Wortley] assured him that his deputation would be ready by
Monday next and bid him write his father .... I durst venture an
even wager that he does not gett itt then, nay I almost question if
the other [will be put] out. You must know the b[ishop of
Durham] and Tom Conyers sollicit Wortley strenuously. Our
Lord Lieut[enant] ... swears heartily. He wonders what can be
the occasion off such delays. Itt will be no easy matter to gett the
12 p[er] *cha[ldron duty taken] off. That duke [of Richmond] is
very zealous and active .... My father and I design to shew a
friend that part off the [Newcastle] charter which relates to the
Hostmen ... and have advice; in the mean time itt might not doe
amiss when ever you have half an hour [if you] drew up the
advantages and disadvantages that belong to that company and
inclose them to my father ....[1] [Calverley] Bewick came last
week to my father's in quest off a copy off the settlem[ent]
which he had left with [us], to advise with Attorney Gen[eral
Northey] if his bro[ther] could work the coll[iery] without him
.... [*Damaged text.*[2]]

[I must] add a word to yours off the 11th. You have don a
work off great charity and Christian [duty in settling] the
differences 'tween the two familys, which I dare pronounce no
other body would ... and what will or may prove of vast
advantage to our poor unfortunate friend. Pray in the [articles]
Dan and you are preparing lett care be taken not to sett an
overvalue, for if such should be the court [will expect] what is
proposed to be made good; if not either the menagers or
projectors will be censur'd. The *makings out should not be sett
down too high. Tis better that the concern bring into court more
than [was proposed at the] end off a year than less. As to the
*pan coal [in] 1714, we ... have a nice game to play and you
[may] depend that a certain gentlem[an] off your town will
endeavor to [trip us] iff occasion off any sort be given; but this
to your self. I own since that we recieve our money [promptly]
for our coals [with] a large quantity taken off, such a customer
were he a stranger ought [to be better] used than one that takes
but off a small parcell, late pay and perhaps not without hazard,
and a [nuisa]nce in getting in the money. I think there ought to
be some consideration on these [points; you I am] sure know by
experience that is the daily practise and was in my time such
through out [the river. You] will acquaint Mr Poyen with this
who knows that the new bride groom Coulson, buying quantitys
[and pay]ing good, buys much cheaper than any other; and I
dare say he and you will adjust this to m[utual satisfacti]on, as
also what you are to pay for the year to come, which must be
regulated considering the price [of coal of] like goodness and
distance off *steath. You need not move for a confirmation off
the article till ..., perhaps not then neither. I percieve by Dan
that he proposed to you an abatem[ent] off 2d p[er] wagg[on]
for [way *keeping], which you seemed to acquiess in provided
you had the coals att 3d less than others paid. [There] is not
much in that but then you must insist on working out the
Moorgate [coal] as fast as they can [and] then you will be free
off a large half mile *branch. I desire you, Peter and he will
adjust these [points] among your selfs. It is a certain indication
that the patient is in desperate circumstances [when] d[octors]
are call'd in. Good God, where could they pick up 23 *viewers?
Tis plain Hutton ... has bin a grateful concern to both landlord
and ten[ant]. Your *bill on me shall be punctually [hon]er'd, as
also that to Cha[rles] when you draw. Pray satisfy Dan how that

article of [£]260 disputed by ... was paid. In the next place must tell you that Peter writes that the works begin to murmur [for a] little subsistence; that had he but a brace off £100 would putt off till April. What to doe I know not, and [I am bound to pay] for classis [lottery] orders [£]1050 being the 2nd paym[ent] I have made into court, to make up which I am [out of] pockett, yet must obey the orders. I spoke last night to Mr Fr[eke] how he would advise in this case. I [proposed tak]ing upp att interest £200 till May day; he agreed to itt.[3] Now iff Peter or you could procure that summ I [would be bound] to see itt repaid with the interest when due. Send to Peter and acquaint him forthwith. Ere I conclude must [turn my thoughts] higher. I have itt from good authority, I think, that you will hear off impeachm[ents] very shortly ....

1. This is the first reference to the north-eastern Whigs' attempts to use the favourable political situation to reduce Newcastle's restrictive privileges, if necessary by amending the town's charter.

2. The text of this letter is particulary difficult to piece together because the edges of the paper are badly eroded.

3. Freke had considerable financial expertise and is known to have published a price list of securities. In addition his brother-in-law, Charles Blunt, was a financial dealer involved in administering the second 1711 lottery.

102

Feb[ruary] 17th 1714/5

Doubtless after my last which carry'd Sunderland *measure, you will admire att my impertinence in troubling you so soon again. The principall reason is that you would gett the inclosed convey'd safe as directed and speedily, and the next is to salute you with a paper called the Citizens' Advice to their Representatives in Parl[iament] iff I can gett one; if I should fail you will see them att large in this day's Flying Post. They will please Mr May[or's] tast to a nicety, tho' not your bro[ther] on the north off your river [the mayor of Newcastle]. Perhaps you may hear that Ross, Ecklin and Hill are to keep their regim[ents]; they have made their submission, 'tis probable, and his Maj[esty] as he is wondrous good is pleased to continue them. I designd a visit to Lady B[owes] and son yesterday with an intention to touch a little upon the borders off her ladysh[ip's] concern att Hutton but both off them were so ill off colds that I had no admittance. Try'd again this day but they were gon down to Westm[inster], I suppose to see Capt[ain] Byron. Indeed the young gentleman I am affraid is in a very bad way; he has had a violent cough accompanied with an hoarseness that has hung upon him ever since he came to town. Would not listen to any advice, trusting to the strenght of his constitution that nature would work itt off, but within a week he found himself obliged to send for a doctor; I wish he may not have future cause off repenting the delay. Last night I paid Mr Freke within a very few pounds off the second thousand, so that he has had in all off me upwards off £2030 which he has laid out in classis [lottery] orders for the benefitt off the Infant. I have a *bill on Tom York for [£]49 1[s] which I expect to recieve on Monday next out off which I shall pay your bill to Mr Cay's order, and you may draw on me att sight any time next week for [£]100 to Ch[arles] Sanderson. Att the same time if you give another on the account off ball[ance] off my own account, I can give my self creditt for itt and then I can give in a clear account to the Master; I call itt clear, because I shall not have a five penny piece in my hands off the exec[utorship] money, and that I would willingly doe that the court may see I have given a full account of what I was intrusted with. Indeed my good friend iff Dan charges more than 5s for the *pan coal, I think he bears hard on you. If have time shall write to him this post on that subject and answer his last. He has to my thinking strange notions off the Lond[on] trade; has given his opinion to lay aside the dealers intirely, to allow the masters 2s [per] Newc[astle] *chalder and lett them fight their way, by which means he proposes cutting off all charges off menagem[ent] here. I question much iff that be complied with, iff itt obtain the desired end. Sure I am itt will be the worst off presidents that ever was brought on the trade. Will make all concerns very touchy and uneasy; this makes me remind you to see if she [Clavering Stella] could be lett and then the *undertaker or undertakers may menage as they think fitt. I frankly declare to you that those coals as they came up the 2 last voyages were as much sought after as any att Gate, always fetch'd within 3d off M[ain] T[eam] and frequently equall price. I could say more on this head but will only mention this: that Blunkett, Watts,

Coltman, Bennett, when I paid them the *praem[ium] at Christmas which was 6d [per] Lond[on] ch[aldron], told me that if they had suspected I would have paid them as I did, that concern instead off vending 17000 Lond[on] ch[aldrons] should have sold 40000, and upbraided the 2 Oldners and Godfrey for not letting them into the secrett. This is enough to say so I shall close all with assuring that I am ....

103

19th Feb[ruary] 1714/5

Did not I tell you in my last that I should prove a troublesome chap? The humor off writing has taken me in the head but where will itt end? However I must be short in this, the occasion wheroff is my conversation with Lady B[owes] on the subject of your last. She told me her *viewer had given an account of the 16 but she had none off number six [the viewers at Hutton?], which gave her great offence, tho' her positive orders to Willson were to give her notice as soon as possible of all their steps and designs as farr as he could sound them. Her ladysh[ip] threatens them with bell, book and candle: she will gett an injunction to stopp their proceedings forthwith. I told her she ought first to take advice off the learned by shewing them the originall lease or a well attested copy. If acted without itt, perhaps might draw herself into a praemunire. She return'd me many thanks for the information and told me by this post she would send down the key off her closett (where there is 600 good pounds worth of plate) to her son Challenor and he should send her up the originall. To which she added that never a M[onta]gue in Christendome should confound her m[ain] coal, which the late J. Emerson always esteem'd as a jewell not inferior to the topp. She kept me by the ear for a good hour 'ere I could gett away.[1] By the by poor Will Bowes' cough and horseness kept very close to him; his d[octor] advises him to countrey air and accordingly Capt[ain] Byram does accompany him this afternoon to Hamsted, where they design to stay a week. Att my return to my father's I found our agent Gilroy come from the Gate, where the top price is from 24[s] 6[d] to 25s. Poor doings, and when the fleet comes in from the northward they will scarce be able to fetch 24s. The last off Robinson's freighted coals were

d[elivered] yesterday or the day before. There is one Taylor
bro[ther] in law to Robinson, who menaged these bulks for him.
He vows and protests that his bro[ther] can't clear above £20,
nay he says £17 for every ship, which must goe towards the price
off the coals att Newc[astle] and charges, laying on board etc.
He is positive that Robinson is incapacitated from proceeding
and that he designs disposing off his concerns. This is the chief
occasion off this letter, to give early advice so that if thought
conven[ient] that friends should take Burnopfield or the
Contract in generall [should], the Capt[ain] and you will consult
and act accordingly. I am a perfect stranger to the place, prices
off *leading and working [etc]. I heard last night likewise that
B[rumell] was return'd from Hampshire and thrown himself
into the Mint [*i.e.* taken refuge from his creditors]. I don't say
that it's true to my own knowledge but 'tis very probable,
therefore be cautious how you impart save to friends, but this is
a needless precaution given by ....

[P.S.] Coll[onel] Blakiston call'd here this morn[ing] when I was
att my office; left word that last post brought him an account
that Cullercotes [colliery] was drown'd. It's given out that
Brummell is gon to the north but that is but a blind.

1.   Lady Bowes' hostility to the Wortley-Montagus and accusations that they
     had robbed her colliery during their tenancy met with little sympathy since
     she was known to be tight-fisted as well as belligerent.

104

Mar[ch] 19th 1714/5

I am not neither have I bin these ten days in tollerable plight
off health, which made me answer yours by peacemeal;
sometimes I recomended half a doz[en] lines to the Coll[onel] to
communicate to you, att other[s] to Dan[iel] or Peter, as
opportunity offer'd.[1] I don't remember to have omitted any
thing materiall; iff I have you must attribute itt to bodily
infirmitys. Pray what are your thoughts off my amendm[ents] to
[the] Chopwell scheme formerly sent up signed by Dan, Peter
and Weatherly? I must own I wish that concern were lett for the
term off 3 or 4 years and then I should be eased of a perplexing
and daily trouble. Ever since Wedensday we have bin alarm'd

with the loss of the new ship called the Clavering and yesterday itt came confirm'd both by land and sea. What I mention this [for] is upon the account off the 3 misses off that name who are great sufferers therby, having all the household goods etc. that were left to them by their mother in that bottom, besides all the family pictures, which can never be retriev'd. Poor Dick Bellassis is computed to have lost near upon £1000, he having ⅛ off the ship, all his house furniture and some say a good deal off plate and some jewels on board. I am now preparing to goe along with our pupill to the Master in Chancery with our books off accounts for the year 1713, as also to gett his reciet in form for the last thousand pound I paid into court, which probably a certain gentlem[an, James Clavering] now on the road may be so curious as to desire a sight off. Poor man, I dread his coming up for his own sake; if he be not provided with a very considerable summ towards the discharging a good part off his ballance, I don't know the consequence that will ensue unavoidably. The court has had hitherto a more than ordinary complaisance upon his account, but if there be but a weak performance off what has bin so long promised, I doubt his reception will not [be] what he expects. But don't lett this go further. The church has lost the greatest pillar and ornam[ent] in the person off the much respected Bi[shop] off Salisb[ury] who I hear is to be succeeded by the honest Bi[shop] off Oxford and his post to be supply'd by Dr Potter, Arch[bishop] Thom [Tenison]'s chaplain, to the great mortification off high ch[urch]. I inclose you the Dutch ambass[ador's] speech to his Maj[esty] which you will not grudge reading, and lett Mrs Marg[aret] have the perusall of itt. I can't but apprehend a very bad coal trade this year. Our joint adventure in Farnacres I wish may answer our expectation; hitherto we have had but a sour and expensive prospect.

P.S. The inclosed from Denzill [Onslow] came to hand this afternoon and he himself follow'd a few hours after. Has promised to lett me have a particular off the last contract on Monday next, which shall be sent you, as also will befriend you as much as in the power off a commis[sioner].[2] As to your adventure off dails [*i.e.* timber], I have inform'd my self particularly off one who has bin on the same foot with you but happen'd to be in 3 or 4 cargoes. His advice is by sad experience to sitt down with the first loss.[3] The Coll[onel] has a discretionary power for both parties here concern'd to act what he thinks most beneficiall in relation to E[lswick]. I must add no more than that I am on all occasions ....

1. Whig ascendancy had brought George Liddell's promotion from captain to colonel in the county militia.

2. Cotesworth hoped to use Onslow's influence to win contracts to supply salt to the Navy Victualling Board in the teeth of fierce opposition from established contractors.

3. Cotesworth's first attempt to import timber from the Baltic in 1713 had ended with the bulk of his consignment shipwrecked and a considerable financial loss.

105

Mar[ch] 22th 1714/5

I have nothing to add to my last save performing my promise by sending you the inclosed salt contract, which was punctually transmitted by honest Denzill, on whose friendship you may depend as farr as in him lyes; which is thus farr only that in case another should bid as low as you, he perhaps may contrive that your proposall shall be preferr'd. In the next place you will find his Maj[esty's] most glorious speech to his Parl[iament], which after reading must desire you will give Pow a groat and send itt with my humble service to Tom [Shafto] off Whickham, honest Frank [Baker], Carr and Barras, and place the 4d to my account without further advice. As you had in my last the Dutch ambass[ador's] speech to his Maj[esty], if that to the Prince and Princcss [of Wales] come out this even[ing] you shall have itt likewise. Mr C[lavering] came to town Sunday noon [and] has bin much among the Members since his arrivall. By what I learn, he has discover'd by Lord Wharton that iff W[rightso]n should not be able to prove his qualification, he doubts the House will not goe further than declaring the election void and order out a new writt. In drawing the Lord's address there happen'd a dispute and a division upon the following clause: 'And to recover our reputation in foreign parts, the loss off which we hope to convince the world by our actions can by no means be imputed to the nation in generall'. Contents 66 : not contents

33. Communicate this to the Capt[ain] and where you think fitt.
I remain ....

106

[March] 24th 1714/5

I wrote to you last [post] and inclosed his Maj[esty's] speech;
this serves for a cover to the address of the L[ords] as also the
resolutions of the Commons on that head. This day there was
flaming work in the latter House. Gen[eral] Stanhop open'd
very powerfully that before we had stipulated any thing for our
selvs or allys, the Duke off O[rmon]d had instructions to obey
the orders off Villars and Mons[ieur] Torcy, att which every
body stood amaz'd; but 'Gentlemen you seem to be in
admiration but this is but a trifle to what will be laid before
you'. He added that we had lost creditt with all our old allies
and that with our new allies made with Fr[ance] and Spain by
that infamous peace, not any one article that was beneficiall was
perform'd. That the differences 'twixt the Emp[eror] and the
Dutch were referr'd to his Maj[esty's] determination, not as an
Englishman but out off respect to his personall creditt and
reputation.[1] That not withstanding by the last treaty Spain was
given up to France, yet this Grand Monarch thinks itt necessary
to enter into new alliances with Sweden, Hesse, etc. and what
are we? Can any body suppose this i[s]land capable off
subsisting without alliances? No. But none will trust you as
English but by his Maj[esty's] influence and interest, such a one
he hoped might be form'd as might make our enemys affraid
off ingaging or attempting any thing against us; or to that effect.
Sir Gilb[ert] Heathcote he fell fowl upon the S[outh] Sea trade
and exposed itt terribly. Many others [spoke] but my head is
turn'd, therefore make out these short hints as well as you can.
Don't shew nor talk off the person from whom I had the list I
sent you last post relating to the salt; it may be off bad
consequence. Adieu honest Will; communicate what you think
fitt off this to friends or others. It is in substance what pass'd,
though not clearly expressed by ....

[P.S.] Earl Oxford last Saturday or Tuesday transferr'd £5000
... stock, all he had in S[outh] Sea Company.[2] The Prince was in
the gallery during the debates.

1. This dispute was settled by the Barrier treaty of 15 November, whereby the
    Dutch acknowledged the Emperor's authority over the Spanish
    Netherlands in exchange for the right to garrison eight forts on the French
    border.

2. Despite this rumour, it was St John and not Harley who fled the country
    on 27 March rather than face impeachment for his conduct of foreign
    affairs.

107

26th Mar[ch] 1715

Though I have not heard from you this age, yet when I meet
with any thing that I fancy will make you an inch or two higher I
can't fail letting you have itt with the earliest [post], which is the
reason off inclosing the address off the Commons. Pray remark
the words, 'We hope to bring the authors [of the peace] to
condign punishm[ent]'. Can you guess the meaning? Itt is what
your heart hath long lusted after and what I hope you and I shall
see shortly put in execution. The City is wonderfully delighted;
they are for having the suspected persons arraign'd on Monday
next but I believe itt will rather be that day [sen]night. However
I can positively confirm that Ox[ford] has disposed of all his
S[outh] Sea stock and this day am credibly inform'd
Bull[ingbroke] has don the like. If diligence in solliciting would
entitle a person to be a sitting Member, am sure our friend
would prevail for he spares no pains, though wish he meet with
the desired success. I have scarce smoak'd a pipe with him, save
one evening in Red Ly[on] Street, since he came to town; he
keeps his office att Westminster. I was near Billingsgate this
morn[ing] but durst not appear there. Coals are gott to 22[s]
6[d] to 23[s 6d], about 300 sail in the river and very little
demand. I heard of complaints made by one off the dealers that
a master loaded att Bensh[am] and offerd to sell them for my
father's Bens[ham]. The master will not tell what *fitter laid
them aboard and we have no report off any. Yesterday I visited
the lady [Bowes] off Gibside. She told me she had wrote to a
friend off hers in Gateside some time since but was not so happy
as to have any answer. Now my friend if you know a person that
has recieved such a favor from the lady, pray tell him that such
things ought not to be slighted. If I meet with any remarkable

occurrences shall add them 'ere I close; if otherwise you may conclude there is none. Adieu ....

[P.S. The King's Speech:] I thank you for the many kind assurances you have given me in your dutifull and loyall address. No endeavors shall be wanting on my part to promote your interest and endear my self to all my people, and I will depend on your zeal and affections and defeat all evill designs that may tend to disquiet the minds off my people and disturb the tranquility off my governm[ent].

108

The eve of the great eclipse [21 April 1715]

Yours came to hand last night, upon which I left orders with Mr Roper to goe early this morn[ing] in quest off Mr Sleigh, but before he gott to the Bank that person was att my bedside. Upon 2nd thoughts I must correct the day off delivering in the proposalls, which as Ben Sl[eigh] assures me is not till Monday the 25th. He has bin with Mr Hodgshon and I referr to his [letter] what occur'd. They both insist on an order from you to them as a security to indemnifye them; as that can't be had twixt this and Monday, I proposed to give them a coven[ant] in form, which was to be redeliver'd me upon your giving them such a one as they desire. Sligh has agreed itt shall be in his name (though not without some hesitation) and as such must be made privy to the contracting price before itt be given into the com[missioners], as also Hodgshon, otherwise they stand bound for they know not what. The former is to meet me on Saturday even[ing], when we are to draw up the proposall in form and insert the price, after which I will seal itt and deliver itt to his further care. Though my friend promised you the preference, yet on second thoughts my father and I thought itt would be a straining the point that a stranger offering the same rate should be preferr'd to one that has dealt and perform'd punctually severall bargains with the board. I say this might raise a clam[our] on our friend which might be prejudiciall. To remove this objection, I have thoughts off offering att [£]7 19[s] 9[d], which is but 25 in the hundred tunn less. I do for you what I should for my self. My friend is but one off 5 or six so that itt might not be in his power to preferr you if on even terms off offering. But suppose that Nicollson should make his [£]8 2[s] it would vex me to abate the odd 3d beyond your commission. However before I doe itt shall advise further, as also about Walker, which I wish you had explain'd a little more att large. Have they purchased the land or only the shore? Or can't they build a key upon the new purchase without license from the Crown?[1] My friend to whom I shew'd itt desired to have fully explain'd before he would give an opinion. Mr F[reke] is the man. I am not sorry that E[lswick] proves so leaky: if people don't know when they are well offer'd, they may suffer unjustifyed. I thank you for your kind offer; I should like to be concern'd in a small share off the Park or Fellon colliery along with you etc. but want a fund to advance proportionably. Are the water drawers to *win the colliery from day[light]? Who is to be att charges off sinking the water shafts? Capt[ain] Savory (off whom the men have liberty off his engine) came to my father's the other day but he could not resolve the particulars off their terms, only they were to allow him for the use off every large engine ... and proportionably for less.[2] I shall detach an express this afternoon to Ch[arles] Sand[erson]; can tell you that last week he was very busy in drawing out what you desired off him [and] was examining a large bundle off papers, I suppose comparing with what had formerly passed in the same case. I have no less than 5 letters to write this post, some will fall short off measure. I can tell you that where a corporat[ion] is limited as to purchasing [land] by their charter, which if exceeded it is not only a forfeiture to the Crown off the purchase but also of their charter. Jemmy insists on [£]320 5[s] paid to you as on account off wagg[on] way. I wish you could satisfye Dan on what account itt was paid as also about the price off *pan coal and charges off the way for those coal[s], which he represents that you agreed to with him. These will be necessary to be don early to prevent disputes. 'Tis time to conclude, my head is turn'd. Therfore lett me according to custom abruptly subscribe my self ....

[P.S.] The Archb[ishop of] Cant[erbury] lyes a dying and probably will be succeeded by Lincoln.

1. Newcastle corporation's unauthorized purchase of the strategically important Walker estate on the north bank of the Tyne intensified the campaign to restrict the corporation's powers. However the Walker issue did not come to a head until 1717, when Newcastle applied to the Crown for a pardon.

2. Cotesworth and five partners leased Gateshead Park colliery from Ramsay in 1715 in the hope of draining it with Newcomen 'fire engines'. His partners included Stonier Parrot and George Sparrow, who had experience of these engines in Staffordshire.

109

26th Apr[il] 1715

My last would surprize you, as indeed the transacting that matter with Sleigh vexed me heartily. For besides his peremptory insisting on security from me, I found he had gott but little information, which doubtless he might have bin more exactly appriz'd off by the clerks. I have not seen nor heard off him since, but by another hand [hear] that att £8 you have gott a bargain (but a very hard one) as most people call itt. You have to furnish 400 tunn and have 4 or 5 months to doe itt in. By what I can discover the old contractors offer'd at [£]8 10[s], other att £9 [0s] 6d and some att £9 thinking that none would bid again[st] them. But when Sligh's proposall appeared they were struck, saying you could not gett a farthing by itt; they blame you for lowering the markett. How they knew you were concern'd, I can't imagin. They were assured the commissioners would have accepted [£]8 5[s]. I am heartily concern'd that this odium should be cast on you, which may partly be laid to the charge off your menagers here. I could not pretend to any step in this matter further than what I procured you by the means off my friend the commissioner; for the rest Sligh should have taken more pains in getting informat[ion] off the used methods off proceeding. Be that as itt will, you must expect all the disservice from those people that used to contract formerly. Pray send as much [goo]d salt as you can so that there will be the least loss [in transit]. I percieve by one this day that you are to be att the charges off delivering itt into their ware house. I hope Sligh appriz'd you off this, if itt is so. I heartily wish you may make both ends meet. If the ships from the Isle off May happen to miscarry any of them, then salt will bear a handsome price, if

they don't, I don't know but that the bargain may prove
tollerable. It was given out that att Sheilds the price of salt was
risen a crown a weigh [*i.e.* a ton]. The Sweeds have lost 7 men
off warr and about 2500 soldiers and sailers.[1] Don't take notice
to Sligh off what I write to you. Give him no hard language. I
could wish you had a better and more active man for your
purpose. I remain ....

1.   Sweden had been fighting an alliance of Baltic states since April. The
     campaign inevitably attracted interest in Hanoverian England, even before
     Hanover declared war on Sweden in October, since the English fleet was
     used to further the electorate's interests.

110

2 June 1715

I know your zeal for the publick raises in you a curiosity more
than what is common; shall therefore as well as I am able give
you a short account off something that passed yesterday in the
House. You must know that Mr Sh[ippe]n happen'd in a debate
relating to an amendm[ent] made by the L[ords] to the mutiny
bill I think it was, to ask with a pleasant air when they should
have any tydings from the secret committee. This fired some off
the partys concerned; among the rest stood up Mr Boscowen,
told that [hasty?] Memb[er] iff he had but had patience till the
business off the day was over, he should have heard a motion
made to know the pleasure off the House when would be ready
to recieve the report. That they had sufficient articles for
impeaching not only some lords but also commons, nay even
some that have the hon[our] off sitting within those walls. We
are ready to make our charges good and I desire that the door
may be lockt and a message be sent to the L[ords] to continue
sitting for an hour or two longer; they shall have papers laid
before them, and that he was ready to carry up one against a
noble peer. I flatter my self that what is laid to their charge,
which is treasonable, vile and basest off practices, will be made
out as clear as the sun att noon day. If they be not I will forfeit
my head, my estate and my reputation which is dearer to me
than silver. He was seconded and thirded by Walpoole and
Stanhope. The offer he made being unprecedented itt dropp'd,
and then the H[ouse] went on Cha[rles] Allanson's report and

the House squared with the committee.[1] You will find the scene open next week, att latest. Pray read this to the honest Ald[erman] R[amsay]. True 'tis our friend the Record[er] has I doubt lost himself beyond retrive. I could but observe yesterday att my uncle's report, [he] left the House; this is look'd upon as an affront don to my Lord Ch[ancellor] but I charge you don't take the least notice. By this you will find that he must not expect the least fav[our] in any court off Westminster having before fallen fowl upon the Ch[ief] Justice off Common Pleas [King] and Judge Eyres at the King's Bench. I am heartily concern'd att itt for he is a very valuable [man]. Now my good friend, notwithstanding this I think itt would not be improper to give him half of what formerly was thought necessary if you [took] a *part. I see young Ja[mes] M[ontagu] att the House yesterday; he never mention'd a syllable of any letter from the north. I had old Wortley by the [hand] in the lobby, would not vouchsafe a word. Pray is the purchase off Walker in trust for the Corporation or no, and to what value, as also their forme ... [*text damaged*].

1. In the Westbury election, the two Tory candidates had been returned by the mayor and the two Whigs by the constable. The Commons first seated the Tories but on 1 June decided in favour of Allanson and Evans.

111

10th June 1715

The death off Signor Esq[uire, Thomas Liddell] was [unexpected] to my mind as being in a manner the eve off his taking journey and after repeated advices off his improving daily, off gaining strength, seems beyond what could be expected. You remark very well he has left as he ... [*text damaged*]. Thus farr I wrote in the office this morn[ing] till the clock struck ... and then we shutt up shopp. Matt[hew] Prior was taken into custody last night and this day I hear Tom Harley is so likewise; severall others are also order'd the same. The report which was redd by Rob[ert] Walpole yesterday att the barr took him up 6 hours, after which it was to be redd by the clerk off Parl[iament] but being so prolix they could not gett through above half and are return'd to itt this morn[ing]; perhaps this day and to morrow may give some insight where the thunderbolts will fall. Near midnight, the Members are just return'd from the House, quite spent. They impeached Bull[ingbroke] of h[igh] treas[on], and after that Oxford of the same; though not without some difficulty because what did appear by the papers would not quite am[ount] to h[igh] t[reason], yet the Soll[icitor] Gen[eral, Lechmere] was off opinion he should be impeached because he did not know but that upon examining several [witnesses] he hoped the charge would be made out. There is a warr[ant] out against Admirall Wishart, another they say against Canada Walker, and severall others. The House has adj[ourned] their proceedings on the above points [until] Thursday or Fryday 'ere they goe farther, since itt will take up a good deal off time to sett their articles into form. This is the substance off what I hear. Gibson is inflexible. [In the] paragr[aph] which you do not ... is meant one Cooper off Peterhouse, on whose [behalf] Ald[erman] White, P.Foster, the Capt[ain], Justice, S[ir] W[illiam] Williamson and I thought you had signed the certificate.[1] Could we but reach to a living off £100 a year we should think our selvs happy but so few there are off that value in the Chan[cellor's] gift that they are always bespoke by some nobleman or other. So that I in a manner despair off success, att least att a great distance. As to that you had your eye upon for your relation, it is not in our friend's disposall though I believe itt may be in the Crown['s], consequently I take itt to be in that of the Governm[ent] and how they are to be dealt with I know not. I percieve Cha[rles] Atkinson is in town; was inquiring after me att the Gate, told our agent that old Wortley was very sorry he was stirring when I was att his house, that he would be very glad to see me [should I] visit him on Monday or beginning off next week. G[eorge] V[ane] setts out on Thursday for the north. I presume I have wearied you as well as my self; it seems therfore reasonable to release you by subscribing myself ....

1. The Hanoverian regime was very cautious in distributing ecclesiastical patronage and restricted preferment to clergy whose political and religious principles were guaranteed by an array of oaths and certificates.

112

22th Sept[ember] 1715
Near 10

I have but one word to add. 'Tis to acquaint you that a
particular friend off yours was spoke to by 2 great men, to know
if he could recommend any notable person in your parts who
could be trusted and on whose intelligence one might depend; I
was spoke to on this head, told them I knew none so capable in
every respect as your self. He desired when you had any that it
might be directed to Mr Edward Curll att Baker's coffee house
in Exchange Alley or to our friend [Thomas Liddell] the corner
off Bedford Rowe where you eat venison. He was the man that
spoke to me. You need not putt any name and depend whatever
is wrote will be kept secrett. This will intitle you to a fav[our]
more than ordinary. By this post you will see that T[om]
Fos[ter] is orderd into custody and 5 other Members; could you
not dive into some off their projects? Pray consider of this well,
[it] would be an extraordinary service to your k[ing] and
countrey. Can you have any intelligence from Scot[land], even
that would be kindly taken.[1] Adieu ....

1.   This sudden concern to obtain accurate information from the north
     reflects the opening moves of the first Jacobite rebellion as well as a
     certain lack of confidence in more official channels of communication.

113

27th Sep[tember] 1715

Though I am jaded with writing yet can't but acknowledge the
fav[our] off yours by yesterdays post; but before I begin to
frame an answer, must acquaint you that cos[in] L[iddell] has
bin upon the hunt after Mr Poultney Secretary off Warr severall
times but at length discoverd he was gon into the countrey,
where most off the [Members] are now gon for the benefitt off
the air or sent by order off the Governm[ent]. He does not know
yet if any forces will be sent from abroad, but he is assured that
if they be that they will be orderd directly for Leith. He desires
to serve you in any thing within his reach and you would do well
to write him a line now and then; he will take itt kindly and itt
will spurr up his zeal.[1] You may direct mine to him. You have

putt your wooden man [Cooper]'s case upon the best footing possible; sure S[ir] W[illiam] W[illiamson] and brother Ellison will not refuse tendring him an oath which ought to be transmitted here. As soon as a certain great friend off ours [Cowper] returns out off Hartf[ord]shire, I shall take the liberty off reading him yours without asking your leave. W[right] and Sp[earman] told all the masters that they had accommodated the matter of the [Bucksnook] *way; this I heard att Gate last Saturday by masters who had it from themselvs. I told them I knew nothing off itt.

We long to hear what is become of your next county['s] Member. You find that young Crowley is taken up and offerd £100,000 bail, but would not be accepted. Mr Harvey off Combe who was in custody off a messenger, stabb'd himself yesterday about noon. 'Tis reported one cause to have bin because they would not hear his discovery, for they knew more off the secrett than that unfortunate gentleman could inform them. He is not dead as yet. One Fairo a Jew was taken up for conveying letters undersigned over to the Pr[etender's] friends who is still at B[ar le] D[uc]. Just now your friend Sig[nor] is come from the coffee house; tells that the scheme used was that this Harvey was to have seiz'd St James's, Wyndham Bristoll, Packington was to have rais'd his men att Worcester and join'd Kynaston in Shropshire, your neighber was to have secured the town [Newcastle] and Tinmo[uth] castle. Some others were to have attempted the Tower and Bank. The plott was certainly as deep a one as ever was laid and was to be executed as yesterday. The Governm[ent] knows the very bottom off the whole; in a little time you will hear off abundance who have absconded from their usual places off abode. Some will have it that Sh[ippe]n made the first discovery, others that a young man, Catholic [did] but all this is but guess'd work. Oh Will had you bin in town this very day, you should absolutely have mett me att the K[ing's] Head, where I have never bin since [you left] nor att any other taverne save att Billingsgate; we would talk this whole business over. You have your Lord Lieut[enant] 'ere this, sure among you the Northumb[erland] expedition will be hammerd out. If you hear any thing remarkable that may be depended on pray don't fail imparting and that freely; you may do itt with safety, I pass my word.[2] I inclose you 2 speeches off the Speaker's, which are admirable. One is for Mr May[or] to be transmitted to Park House, the other for the High Sheriff [Johnson]'s and Geo[rge] Iley's use. Pray what character has parson Geo[rge *sic*. Cuthbert] Fenwick, who is recommended by Morpeth to the Earl Carl[isle] for Long Horseley and solicited by your friend Nevill [Ridley]? If I knew but the names off some of our gown men [*i.e.* clergy] who diserve something else better than preferm[ent], I might perhaps sometime have an opportunity off preventing [it], for occasionally I have bin askt a character [by Cowper]. I must trouble you with the inclosed to honest Peter. My best service attends always my good Ald[erman] and sister Peggy, and am ....

[P.S.] Our friend Bart[holomew] Scott having lent Rob[ert] Wright, Spear[man] and Snowden one hundred pounds last Dec[ember], Spear[man] gave him this *note in part, which has bin return'd back. You are earnestly requested to putt the *bill into any honest attorney's hand that will in your opinion be able to deal with Snowden, as he desires no quarter to be given. What charges attends this shall be deducted out off the money rec[eived], or in case itt be not to be had whoever is employ'd will be thankfully rep[aid] by the said Barth[olomew] Scott.

1. Cotesworth hoped to combine politics and profit by securing a contract to victual the troops sent north to defeat the rebellion.

2. As Liddell reports, the projected rising in the south-west was dealt with while still in the planning phase. The relative lack of planning for the Northumberland rising paradoxically made effective counter-measures more difficult.

114

6th Oct[ober] 1715

Your two last came safe and bring a most particular account off transactions in your parts. I do assure you they were very kindly rec[eived] and laid before the Secretaries by your friend [Thomas Liddell] off Bedford Rowe. They are much obliged to you for their intelligence and never see him but are inquisitive what news he has from your countrey, for as much as I can gather they depend more upon you than all the rest. Before I proceed must take notice that I have (pursuant to your orders) bin att the Grecian [coffee-house?] to see Mr Gibson. Itt was as rainy an even[ing] as any we had this year. Not one off the family was there; which gave me an opportunity off transcribing that part off yours and sending itt the next morning by express. This afternoon your above friend came to see me almost half drown'd; tells me he has severall commissions from the two Secretarys. 1st. They desire you will inform them iff T.F[orste]r be gon over to Lord M[a]r. Also that there are some English gentlemen gon lately northwards in their way to that lord as is supposed; if possible to learn their names. Pray who is the reciever generall of your customs? 2ndly. They will have from you the state off North[umberland] with your opinion what force would be necessary to prevent any disturbance in that or your county, as also what would be requisite to secure the peace off your corporation. 3dly. You are further requested to send your thoughts freely, and that what relates to publick business might be in a paper by itt self that itt may be kept by them to refresh their memory. And lastly I am order'd to assure you from the above mention'd partys that iff any thing be to be don in relation to the troops, send word in time by making any offer and itt will be comply'd with. I am charged not to read yours to any one body. The[y] caution you to take what care you can that your letters be not open'd to the northwards [*i.e.* in Newcastle]. I have no reason to suspect as yet any practice off that sort; therefore you will direct as usuall. I could wish to have a further account off parson Cuth[bert] Fenwick off Morpeth I think; the Capt[ain] writes word that Sir J[ohn] Delav[al] gives him the character off a Tory. This should be sent by the first post (though I doubt itt will be too late). The Duke Som[erset] and Lord Castlecomer espouses him strenuously for Long Horseley. I doe what I can for parson Cowper [*i.e.* Cooper], but am not so sanguine off success as formerly because his grace is not to be putt out off humor att this time off day. There will be 6000 men from Flanders speedily. Exert yourselvs and all will goe well, and no incouragem[ent] will be awanting. This is the last push off the desperate faction, which I hope when once over will settle us upon a sollid foundation. Now dear friend excuse hast and believe me to be ....

115

10th [October] 1715

Yours off the 4th and 7th lye before me. Your accounts have
bin communicated as I formerly wrote you, within an hour after
came to hand. The two great men told my cosen they were the
best intelligence and clearly stated, beyond what they had from
any other hand. They desired him to assure you that your
extraordinary zeal on this occasion should not goe unrewarded;
I will not say further. As to the choice off your [militia] officers,
I find 'tis in the same strain; the other part shall be examin'd as
soon as my father returns. I could wish you could gett me (iff
time will allow) a fuller account off parson Cuth[bert]
Fenw[ick]: his grace persists strongly in his sollicitation. How
does he vote in the county elections, is he very high [church] in
principle? You may depend no name shall be made use off.
However a few particulars off his conduct seems necessary. I
come now to your last but most dismall letter. I pity with the
utmost degree off compassion the deplorable condition both
you and our other friends find yourselvs involved in by the very
quintessence off the faction. If you could but be true to each
other within the gates, there would be the less apprehension.
Pray take care that they don't convey either men, arms or both
into the town, under loads off hay and straw: I mean if att this
time itt be in the hands off friends. I doubt not your
watchfullness. It behoves every one to be strictly upon their
guard. They don't divulge the sending any speedy succors, they
will lett them shew themselvs; but you may depend there will be
and sooner that you expect a hansom reinforcem[ent] off
dragoons. No sollicitation is awanting. Remember the accounts
off the soldiers att Oxf[ord] and Bath; since the first it's said
that the county off Sommersett, though the highest in principle
off any, have begun to cry *peccavi*. The zeal off the magistrates
iff unfeign'd is beyond what could ever have bin expected. Your
early dispatch was wonderfully well rec[eived] and will be kept
secrett; the other came after, about the time yours mention'd. I
am surpriz'd that your Lord Lieuten[ant] did not send you down
armes. Pray how stand your keelmen affected? This afternoon I
see a letter which says that tis suspected a certain bar[onet,
Blackett] was amongst them, but I can't imagin a man off his
noble fortune would run a risque more than probable off

loosing all.[1] From the Secr[etaries'] office I hear that the Duke
of Ar[gyll] writes more sanguinly than he ever did. I long with
utmost impatience [for] the arrivall off next post to have a
certain account off matters; am in no less pain for our friends
than iff I were actually with them. I scarce slept a wink last
night. You may assure yourself, after my cosen had your[s]
d[elivered] him, I did not sitt idle; left Lord Will[iam Powlett]
(who din'd with me) att home and other company, went into the
Fields and imparted the substance to our friends there. Nay
madam [Ann] took coach and away to Kensington, where to the
good lady [Cowper] she sett matters out in their lively colours;
upon this the lady wrote a pathetick letter to Mons[ieur]
Bernsdorf, which I believe his Maj[esty] see last night. Pray
oblige me with a line as offt as you can and rest assured that I
shall not fail doing what is necessary within my poor sphere,
which is by spurring up others. God have you all in his keeping
is the sincere prayer of ....

[P.S.] You will hear from Tom Gibson this night. 8 att night.
This minute Mr Fr[eke] is landed from the west; says there has
bin a desperate design on Bristoll but by the help off the militia
they are out off any apprehension. There is likewise another in
Devonshire, but as the Governm[ent] are perfectly appriz'd 'tis
odds will never come to light.

1. Liddell's judgement was sound: Blackett was soon on the road to London
    to protest his loyalty. In the event, the other Newcastle Tories were equally
    unwilling to court disaster and the town gates remained closed to the
    rebels.

116

13th Oct[ober] 1715

I was in perplexity not hearing from you last post, but att 9 att
night, 4 hours after my cosen L[iddell] had sent to the posthouse
for his letters, I had one from the High Sheriff which gave us
some ease off mind. Pray lett us have a line, if itt be but one itt
will please us. You will have 3 or 4 regim[ents] off dragoons and
a battalion off foot with all expedition. I doe assure you a good
Kensington lady has sollicited for speedy succors and press'd
harder than any whatever for the relief off her own countrey,

but this to yourself. She will not leave them till she has effected and succeeds very well in her sollicitations. This day I gave you a letter by a young officer who is going northwards to his regim[ent]; he desires only your advise which way to steer. My father came to town from Bath last night pretty hearty. Mr Fr[eke] came the day before; both present their services. Adding my best wishes, remain ....

[P.S.] Mr F[reke] will not lett me add nor read what is wrote. Adieu.

117

15th Oct[ober] 1715

Yours by last post came safe and am much obliged for the particular account you give off the present state off affairs in yours and the neighbouring parts. I can't keep any thing from you, therfore will tell you that I rec[eived] itt in Red Ly[on] St[reet]. My father and I retir'd into the parl[our] and read itt to our selvs. My cos[in's] man who brought the letter waited impatiently to carry itt to his master, who he said was going to tother end off town. My father told me I was to blame in not going my self because that gentlem[an] would have all the creditt off itt, and press'd me to goe; upon which I sent word to the serv[ant] that I would wait on his master presently and accompany him to Mr Stanh[ope]. Away I went, first read my dame the substance and dispatch'd her to my lady att Kensington (by the by as I said before that lady is the most effectual sollicitress). After this I went to my cos[in's]; when I came, he told me with a serious face he should be glad off my company but withall said it was ten to one if we found the gentleman att home; in short I plainly discover'd his averseness that I should appear. He desired to see my letter, which I read. He told me that Mr Stan[hope] did not care to read any part off a letter but what related to his business, so he fix'd upon 2 or 3 paragraphs that he could intrust his memory with and would communicate. Upon this my father and I went to Lord Ch[ancellor and] read itt to him. He approv'd off your proposall off mounting with 20 gentlem[en], Hotham's regim[ent] as you proposed, Cobham's dragoons (which he hop'd would be with you 'ere this arrive) and with what force the country can raise, and endeav[ouring] to dislodge and disperse them. For, says my lord, while they lye undisturb'd in the open countrey, itt gives incouragem[ent] to people to join them dayly and is a president for other countyes to rise in hopes off the like success. You can't imagin how he came in with this project off yours; said itt was the best concerted off any he had heard off and would be off the most effectual service to the Gov[ernment]. He desired the country might be incouraged, assuring express orders were sent to the 3 regim[ents] off dragoons to march without stopping on any account. What was most materiall in your letter was putt this morning into my lady's hands who applyes to the fountain head [Bernsdorff?]. Goe on and prosper. Now my good friend I don't know any reason why my cos[in] should take ill what my father recommended so earnestly to me. Had it not bin for that I should have bin glad to have bin excused. What I wrote to you in relation to the troops that may be landed in your parts, probably a part off them, was that iff it were necessary to make a proposall on what terms you would supply them (iff that be the practise) that you would doe itt early; I know not how the custome is in those cases. You may depend upon't that whatever encouragem[ent] can be given from hence, your friends will not grudge their sollicitation. My advise to you is not to take the least notice off this little distast my cos[in] has taken to my offer to any person whatever. But write a line to him self, what you think conven[ient] upon account off the victualling, and itt will be don. This will be the readiest way to succeed, take my word. If you hear any thing from Scotland, send him word. But att the same time I expect from you an account off neighbouring affairs, which will be a continuation off obligations already conferr'd on ....

[P.S.] In answer to this take not the least notice of what has pass'd because my cos[in] must see itt.

118

18th Oct[ober] 1715

Your last lyes now before me. Excuse me if ... I ended my last, which was with recommending to you not to take the least notice off what I caution'd you in in any off yours. I doe as formerly send or carry yours into Bedford Rowe, where 'tis perused and the most remarkable pieces off itt he [Thomas Liddell] setts down in a piece off paper, iff too long for his memory, and away he goes to the proper officer. I was desired to come to Kensington yesterday after the rec[eit] off my letters, which I readyly obey'd; found the good lady all alone, staid till after 8. You must know that I read yours off the 11th to my lord, which after[wards] was convey'd by a safe hand to the above place with a strict charge not to lett any person see itt. On Sunday my lord came over and read itt twice over again; told my lady it was the cleverest account he had seen, very full and well express'd. I can tell you that you will be the topp favorite off the family. I can't omitt acquainting that the lady told me that what ever Lord Sc[arborough] should propose for your particular [reward], that her lord would second itt and she would exert her self in your fav[our]. And added that the Gov[ernment] seem'd resolv'd when this hurly burly was a little over to make a large reform in the port [of Newcastle] and elsewhere; desired to have an account off some honest names that might be ready when an opportunity offerd. I had in my thoughts honest John [Bowes] of Cleadon. Att leisure you will consider off this subject and my sollicitation shall not be awanting. While my lady and I were head to head in came a letter from Mons[ieur] B[ernsdorff] with an account that 10000 armes were coming from Holland, and that itt should be in his care to secure what was [necessary] for our parts; but then lett us consider into whose hands they should be putt for distributing. I should think that your good neighbours [Newcastle corporation] should not have that left in the least to their disposall. But itt seems principally to appertain to the Lord Lieuten[ant]. The lady has taken minutes off the number off troops you think necessary for the future security of yours and the adjac[ent county] to be ready when that subject comes under consideration. Be sure don't mention her upon any score. I do believe you will have a couple or more cruisers to be off your coast, to Berwick or further as occasion may require.

Yours names the 2 lords [Derwentwater and Widdrington] and Mr Clav[ering] who was att [the] proclam[ation] att Morpeth. I fancy you meant T[om] F[orster]; if not, was it Callily or Barrington? I percieve they were marching westward; if so then you will be able to establish again your correspondence with N[orth] Brittain, which is much wanted ever since yours was interrupted, therfore you will bend your thoughts that way. I can't think as yet you are perfectly safe till Cobham's dragoons be got with you and another regim[ent]. I hope the former is [there] 'ere this and hastening orders are dispatch'd for the others. I look upon't as a strategem, their march to Morpeth, to try iff you would be tempted to part with Hotham's regim[ent] in order to attack them, and then when the town was clear off them to shut the gates upon them, etc. It is my notion only. You may rest satisfy'd that any solicitation for a gen[eral] pardon will be in vain. I find by parson S[hafto] to his cosens in town, that either an amnesty or some speedy execution seem'd off absolute necessity for the publick safety and repose.[1] My father has this mom[ent] call'd in his coach and robb'd me off yours; he is very hearty, sister E[llison] no better by her Bath journey, Mr Fr[eke] wonderfully recruited and very pert, as Hugh used to call itt. Adieu, with a tender off my father's service I rest ....

---

1.   Liddell and his friends were convinced that the Jacobites should be treated with the full rigour of the law. The letters follow their efforts to ensure that those named in informations should be prosecuted and that Parliament should be summoned to impeach the rebel lords, as well as their frustration when many escaped retribution.

119

20th Oct[ober] 1715

Kind and never failing friend. Yours by yesterday['s post] came to hand. But before itt did I had a message from Lincoln's Inn Fields desiring the fav[our] off a sight off it. While I was reading, another messenger waited impatiently and away he carrys itt. I gave a strict charge to bring itt back as soon as perused, which was done accordingly, safely sealed up. Soon after came my cos[in] L[iddell] who likewise had itt. He promised this day (when the Parl[iament] mett) to acquaint Mr Stanh[ope] and Walp[ole] with the contents. Pursuant to your orders, I had itt to the Colledge, but iff I had not had them must however have imparted [it], for that gentlem[an, Freke] gives me a summons every post night and no express he relyes on but what comes from Mr Mayor. Last [night] Sir Jos[eph] Jek[yll] was there and was not a little taken with your intelligence; they made me read itt twice over. They all agree with you, that the best pollicy is not to press the oaths [of allegiance] at this unsettl'd juncture. You talk off a few Highlanders being gott over to No[rth] Berwick; I doe assure you, that has given a much greater disturbance to the great men that itt seems to give you. They are upon the watch, and readily take an allarum so as to provide ag[ainst] itt, which I don't dislike. I should think 2 or 3 more small frigates to cruise in the Firth would be off singular service. During the time the rebells lay on the sea coast in Northumb[erland] my lady [Cowper] press'd hard for that number to ply off that coast and itt was agreed too, so perhaps they may be order'd directly to Leith. Am glad to hear the dragoons were so near you and hope 'ere this they may be in pursuit off the new generall [Forster], whose aunt the Lady Crew dy'd on Sunday morning last att my lord's seat in Northamptonsh[ire]. Your Collect[or] Is[aacson] pretends a mighty zeal; writes up to the Board off Customs that the magistrates notwithstanding that representation had bin formerly made off them had exerted them selvs heartily in the cause, and by that means would insinuate, etc. I always took him to be according to the company he was in but now is a profess'd W[hig]. I shall take an opportunity off discoursing G[ibso]n. The 6000 men from Holl[and] are expediting as fast as possible. I can't but think that the Hexham camp will now think off traversing the country in order to join the N[orth] Berw[ick] Highlanders, if they be not assured that their friends in Lancash[ire] be ready to recieve them.[1] Oh Will, the holy men [*i.e.* clergy] have damnably poyson'd by much the greatest part off the nation. However, if we gett over this decisive stroke (which I don't much doubt), the throne will be thoroughly establish'd. The H[igh] Sh[eriff] wrote to me last post that Rob[ert] Lawson off Chirton refus'd to appear or so much as send a horse to the posse comm[itatus] upon his summons, and desired I would take Lord Ch[ancellor's] opinion.[2] I sent the letter last night; have no answer as yet, for I heard he was gon into Hartfordsh[ire] for a few days. This you will inform the

H[igh] Sh[eriff] off that he may see I don't neglect him; but happening to discourse this point att Mr Fr[eke's] last night, told me if he were in that post [he] would send and seize his horses for his Maj[esty's] service, leaving him only what was not fitt for use, and after[wards] he should be prosecuted for neglect. But says he since another's opinion is desir'd, pray wait for itt. This non attendance off many off the half pay [officers] is by no means warrantable and will not escape attention. Lord Will[iam] is provided [as] to your mind. Now my good friend I know you will readily excuse my imperfect answers, which are not methodicall as you write, but as things come to my thoughts I down with them, though without form. When I sett up a coffee house, shall desire no other letter than yours, which alone would bring me a suffic[ient] custome; I find itt does already putt me to the charge off many a bottle but that I don't grudge, especially since itt gives an opportunity off remembering the scribe, to whom all health and happiness is wish'd to him and his by ....

1.   The Northumberland rebels left Hexham on 19 October to join a force from south-western Scotland which had reached Rothbury. They then marched north to meet the Highlanders who arrived in Kelso on the 21st.

2.   The *posse comitatus*, the 'force of the county', was the body of adult men which the sheriff could summon to deal with public disorder.

120

Oct[ober] 25th 1715

I can't well express the obligations you have laid me under by your constant correspondence, even att a time when your head and hands were so full off business off the greatest importance to the publick. Your accounts were allways so concise and perfect that my friend [Cowper] in Lincoln's in Fields took such a pleasure in [them] that he made the lady read them thrice over. My cos[in] L[iddell] has bin not altogether so forward in carrying the originals to the office as before; nay he has never desired itt since my father came from Bath. Last night in Sir H[enry's] presence I told Mr Fr[eke] the story. He knits his brows and upon't declared his mind frankly, which is not conven[ient] to insert. In short, I must desire you will continue the correspondence as usuall to me, and if you can learn anything remarkable pray inclose mine herafter to Charles Allanson esq[ire] in Bedford Rowe. What is contain'd shall goe no farther than Red Ly[on] St[reet] and the Fields, and the business will be as well don that way as the former, perhaps better. If att any time any thing very extraordanary should happen, if you wrote to the Lord T[ownshen]d, itt might not doe amiss. Last night I mett Sir W[alter] Y[onge] att the Colledge [and] imparted to him what you had wrote in relation to that board; nay I gave him a copy off what related to that concern as he desired, but without a name. He promised to acquaint his brethren this morn[ing]. He desires you will send him a copy off the affidavitt you took off the master that d[elivered] 17 instead of 23 *ch[aldrons] att the allum works, and then he says he shall be able to give him a lift [i.e. remove the customs officer responsible]. Suppose they should be att a loss whom to recommend, lett me know if you could any [candidate], as also a fitt supervisor for the coast in case they be att a loss. I only mention this as off my own head, and if itt should so happen that they did not know a proper man, to be ready to serve a friend. What do you think off John Bowes? These are random thoughts. The Dutch troops could not come till the barrier with the Emp[eror] be adjusted, which is now don.

[P.S.] 9 att night. Sir W[alter] Y[onge] sends me this paragraph: Mr W[illiam] Selby, riding surveyor att Whitby, is orderd to supervise the officers on the coast and to wait upon Mr C[otesworth] when he comes to Newcastle. Ly[onel] Colepitts I hear is dead. I gave a *bill on J[ohn] J[ohnson] for £100 payable to him by James Robert's order, who desires that itt may be paid to a safe hand, that is to the ex[ecutors] off which you will inform him. I sent to Ch[arles] S[anderson] about what you desired; he says you shall have a satisfactory answer by this post. Now my good friend lett me begg off you the continuation off this correspondence. Have an eye to what passes in your neighbourhood and the county of Northumb[erland] and depend that a perfect good use shall be made off the intelligence, perhaps to more advantage than under the conduct of the Member. I have bin interrupted by 2 of the dealers from Billingsgate, who satt with me from 3 till near eight; they have

disorderd me and incapacitated from answering yours as I
ought, which you will excuse from him who is att all times ....

[P.P.S.] past 10. I have just left Mr Fr[eke] who is your
serv[ant]. He is off opinion in reading yours that you should not
putt your self to any extraordinary charges, but continue as
above your correspondence to [us. My] father salutes you,
adjuring keep a watchfull eye on your neighbours.

                                    121

Oct[ober] 27th 1715

Your former mention'd my sending the inclosed to Cha[rles
but] there was none but what belong'd to my letter, which was
the novells your parts produced. If therfore you design'd him
any about business, you had mislaid itt; if none, you will excuse
me. Cha[rles] had one from you last night and I another. We
both mett att the Colledge, where happen'd to be Lord Ch[ief]
Jus[tice] K[ing]; he read his to the company and I mine. Do you
really think the keelmen right and tight and may be depended on
occasion? My cos[in] is not so zealous as att first, though there
is not one off yours that I have not read him or sent to him
immediately after the rec[eit] theroff. I percieve by him that to
gett you reimbursed will be a matter off difficulty, which I
complain'd off heartily. I spoke privately to Mr Fr[eke] on that
subject and reason'd upon't. He shrugg'd his shoulders, told me
we should certainly find itt so; probably iff any post should
offer that might suit, they may herafter readily grant itt as an
equival[ent], which makes me not a little uneasy. Upon this I
need not advise you what is fitting to be don; what intellig[ence]
you can have on reasonable and easy terms, one would not
want. This morning, one off my sis[ters] going to Kensington, I
sent your last by her with a desire to have itt again this evening if
possible. I drew a line as a ready mark under those passages
which were the most remarkable, such as concern'd the
informations [against the rebels] and the cruisers etc. As to the
first I have imploy'd Tom Wake[lin] who has an acquaint[ance]
in each off the offices to be appriz'd off any certainty iff any be
come up from your quarter; when itt is, then will I by some
means or other gett imparted to the two principalls the

advantage that will accrew to the publick by a proclam[ation] or other [action]. I hope to have an opportunity off seeing our friend in Lincoln's Inn Fields before I sleep. Tis not his immediate province, yet if itt come before the [Privy] Counsell itt may be conven[ient] he should be appriz'd. In short within my sphere I will not fail to make the best use off what you write and yet with all secrecy imaginable, without my appearing or you. Provided itt be but don, 'tis no matter by whom. 5 att night. Just now I rec[eived] a note from the party that went to the office; he inquired att both and finds they have not had an account off their names remitted, but if you could gett itt dispatch'd, doubtless speedy orders would be given accordingly. 7 att night. I am just return'd from Lord Chan[cellor's] who has bin much disorder'd by a fitt off his old distemper the strangury; this is the first day he has bin att Westm[inster] and went in a chair. Itt has affected his looks somewhat but God be thank'd the worst is over. He was going to the Cockpitt soon after I left him. When I took leave, he return'd me thanks for the very entertaining letter I sent him. I find by his discourse that his sentim[ents] off matters was much the same with yours. I will not tell you all he said in your commendation, but by what I could gather [it] was that he would be glad to see some more from the same hand. His Maj[esty] sent Duke Richm[ond] to Duke Somersett yesterday or day before to acquaint his grace that he had no further occasion for his service. 'Tis said 'twas on account off that duke's free expressions att Newmarkett: certain 'tis his grace has grumbled in the gizard ever since the committm[ent] of [Wyndham, his son-in-law]. Thus you see how people's tempers and dispositions are apt to change. There is no such in him who is semper idem ....

[P.S.] I forgott to tell you that I went into the Fields [Lincoln's Inn] to introduce Sir And[rew] Hume to my lord and were scarce seated till in came Sir Littleton Powis and him we left there. So that I had neither opportunity nor time to discourse on some heads off your last letter. You may direct mine to either off the Members in the Row as you think fitt, or sometimes to one, sometimes to the other, but lett me hear from you. Your speculations and observations please all tastes, I mean honest men's.

122

1 Nov[ember] 1715

I am in concerne that you should be depriv'd off the use off your pen, though you are so generous as to supply that defect by your deputy. Your intelligence is so much in vogue that no sooner [is] the post come but I have great men's vallets waiting for the produce off your packett. However I can assure you 'tis not to above two that I will trust them out off my hands; and 'tis a high fav[our] don to those I read them too and those are very few in number. My good kinsman ever since my father came to town, as I formerly hinted, is not so zealous; he is att present a housekeeper by reason off a sore throat, but he fails not once off seeing your dispatches. Herafter I shall make use off another hand. This morn[ing] my father and self went to Duke off Devon[shire] to impart [but] he was not to be seen; thence to Mr Walp[ole] who was not to be mett with; we took Lord Somers in our return and were there also disappointed. I do imagin they were all sommond to Councell. So we lost our labour. Pray send me the present supervisor's name, as also that off the person you would have succeed him.[1] I will not lett my friends rest from solliciting. Is he supervisor for our county or only our ward? Pray continue your early accounts. Our friend [Cowper] in the Fields has bin ill off the strangury for severall days but after the post came he found him self easier, which I attribute to the good account yours brought, though is not so well this day. But don't take the least notice off his health in your return. The parson recommended by Ald[erman] White, Matt[hew] Foster, your Coll[onel] and other friends has succeeded att last for Long Horseley, notwithstanding as I hear your magistrates join'd in a recommendation on behalf off Willcox, Sir J[ohn] Clav[ering's] chaplain, which makes the obligation the greater. Att the Grecian the talk is that the Dutch forces would be imbark'd last Sunday, so that now they wait only the wind. The cantoning [i.e. quartering] your troops as proposed, is look'd upon as the produce off a sollid judgem[ent]. A report is curr[ent] that Ja[mes] Buttler did putt to sea ten days ago from Ambleteux not farr from Calais and is said is return'd back to France, finding his scheme in the west was broke. Others will have that a man off warr gave chace to his ship, which obliged him to return; but of either off these reports I can't depend as what comes from the north.[2] When things come to calm and these burlys are over, you may assure your self a lasting security may be reasonably expected. I am summond to attend Mr Fr[eke] and am obliged to deliver up my arms, my pen and ink, and rest to my father. Both off them are much att your service and so is ....

1. Cotesworth was again trying to combine personal and public interests by pressing for Tory officials to be replaced by his own nominees. In this case he wanted his former apprentice, Edward Mawson, to become supervisor of the window tax.

2. Ormond in fact arrived off the coast of Devon on 28 October, unaware that the south-western rising had been foiled. He then returned to the Pretender at Saint-Malo.

123

8th [November] 1715

I seldom have fail'd writing to you every post save 2 or 3 since these troublesome times began, and even then I made my excuse by Capt[ain] or Peter, and last Saturday by reason my cosen undertook; so that I must need apprehend a miscarriage in some of mine, but which I know not. In yours off the 20th ult. you recommended to speak to Sir Walt[er] Y[onge] which I did that very night and gave his answer by Tuesday's post following, which was the very day after I rec[eived] itt. The substance was they had order'd one off their chief inspectors from Whitby side to visitt strictly and have a watchfull eye on the behav[iour] of the officers along the coast; that he had directions to wait on you and recieve your instructions. Att the same time he desir'd you would send up a copy off the information you took from the master that d[elivered] to Zach [More's] works. I likewise answer'd yours dated the 28th ult. in relation to the behav[iour] off supervisor off the windows; was advised to gett the man's name, as also the party's you recommend as his successor, before we proceeded. This was by our good friend Lord Will[iam's] advice, who told me itt would be referr'd to the comm[issioners] of the leather [duty] who have likewise the menagem[ent] off that off the windows and that they would appoint, therfore desired I would forbear till I gott your friend's name. I remember I wrote you a long letter, wherein amongst other things I mention'd this; but hearing nothing from you on those heads conclude that letter might miscarry, therfore att a venture recapitulate. Am much obliged to you for the many services you have don my relation's friend Mr Savern. I have laid by the certifficate till call'd for by the partys. My cosen would inform you that I carried his from you to the Fields though att an unseasonable time off night and when our worthy friend was much out of order. I had admittance for ½ a quarter off an hour, where was none but his d[octor]. He read itt; what related to a proclamation my cos[en] would inform, and as to your desire off having the managem[ent] off an estate in your neighbourh[ood], he express'd himself the request was very modest and the Gov[ernment] could not putt itt into such hands, according to the notion he has off your abilitys and sincerity, and he thinks that, though a reimbursem[ent] off your expences, by much too small a recompence for your zeal and good services.[1] But in answer to this you must not in the least take notice off his indisposition nor off what I write concerning his thoughts. He reads your letters with satisfaction and expresses himself very much pleased with your conduct. I must desire you will send for the H[igh] Sher[iff] and acquaint him that 'tis thought advisable hc should represent those that have not obey'd his summons etc., that he should sett forth particular cases when he mett with any that opposed his authority, and lett itt be transmitted in a paper by itt self which he may inclose. But charge him not to publish itt; you may readily guess the meaning. Mr Fr[eke] has desired he may be putt into commission [of the peace] as soon as he is out off his present employ: 'tis granted. I come now to thank you for your last fav[our] and am sorry Gen[eral] C[arpenter] should have mett with a foyle. Had he pursued the same rout the bogg trotters took, I am satisfy'd he could never have come up with them, must have ruin'd the young horse and indeed am apt to believe the men would have had much ado to have subsisted. They will lay wast wherever they come, but you may depend 'ere they be well in Lancash[ire] you will find Gen[eral] Wills ready to recieve them with 7 regim[ents] off regular troops, and 'tis supposed Carpenter will not fail pursuing his march towards them as expeditiously as possible.[2] I expect you will give us the [soonest] advice off the transports with forces, which I hope are upon the Yorksh[ire] coast already. A little piece off an intercepted letter could not be amiss. What will be don for intelligence in these remote parts? If you had any correspond[ent] thereab[outs] on whose representation one might depend on, if you could ingage him to send me a letter directly, I should be obliged to you and him. Now my good friend, I am much concern'd to see another pen, not your own, that you are obliged to make use off. Whence proceeds your pain? Your complaint has bin long; pray take advice about itt. Should any thing befall you, you can't imagin how the publick in gen[eral] as well as your friends in particular would be affected with itt. I am sure none more than ....

[P.S.] This wett weather has shaken me much and increas'd my complaints. The ministry have bin so taken up off late and still are with these rebells that one can't gett a word to them. However I have memorand[ummed] the d[octor's] bro[ther]: pray send the name off the person you would recommend to succeed.[3]

1. It took four years for Cotesworth to negotiate the purchase of the estates of Stella and Winlaton following their forfeiture by Lord Widdrington as a result of the rebellion.

2. After chasing the Jacobites north in October, Carpenter had returned to Newcastle before taking an easier, more southerly route to intercept their march through Lancashire. By the time that Wills attacked Preston on 12 November, Carpenter had reached Clitheroe.

3. Cotesworth was attempting to have one of the infamous Dr Sacheverell's brothers turned out of the customs administration: see below, letter 140.

124

10th [November] 1715

Though I wrote att large to you the last post and have little to say this, yet am unwilling to omitt the very first in making my acknowledgem[ents] to your young secretary [Cotesworth's son], who has given therby a hansome specimen off his improvem[ents]. His hand promises to be a masterly one, his letters are true cutt, and his lines att such an even distance that one would readily guess he had wrote them by help off a ruled paper. Pray thee honest Will what is the meaning off your militia disbanding att this time off day? Doe you think your selfs

safer without such an arm'd force? Or that the danger is over?
For my part I think there is as much reason to be on the guard
now as ever; att least till we have a better account from
Lancashire and that Wills is come up with the rebells. Is your
Lieuten[ant] in the miff? If so, what occasion given for his
dissatisfaction? This method of proceeding shocks people. The
affidavitt you inclosed I putt into Sir W[alter] Y[onge's] hands
within this hour; he has promised to lay itt before the board to
morrow. He had not heard off any representation from the new
supervisor but will inquire after itt, but you ought to have sett
down where he inhabits, as also Ed[ward] Mawson; the latter I
must recommend to Lord Will[iam] as also to gett information
off the officer, for he is intimately acquainted with the great
men to whom I am a perfect stranger, no further than by sight.
The teller goes shortly to Lemmington to be reelected.[1] This
minute my father is come in from putting in an appearance to
the Bi[shop's] cross bill [in their lawsuit]: he desired me to send
his services and referrs to Mr Sand[erson] for your affairs, I
mean the Ald[erman's], which is a new tryall att Y[ork] assizes
which Mus[grave Davison] cryes out as ruinous to his clients. I
am going to the Colledge where if I hear anything worth adding,
itt shall be don. I must conclude with my kind remembrance to
W[illiam] C[otesworth] j[unior] as well as to Mr May[or], whose
very humble serv[ant] I am ....

1.   Powlett's lucrative appointment as teller of the Exchequer meant that he
     had to seek re-election to the Commons.

125

Nov[ember] 12th 1715

I am still in great pain that you should not be yet able to make
use off your pen. Your last came safe and as I had an
oppertunity off seeing Mr Honeyw[ood] this afternoon, he
undertook to make the best use off itt he was capable off. But
before I d[elivered] itt to him, I took care to blott out here and
there what was judged needfull. He is very zealous and hearty,
and prudent withall. He came directly from the Secretarys'
office, told us that they expected by the first post news that the
transports were sail'd: long look'd for will come att last. Here is
a noble declaration off the Archb[ishop] Cant[erbury] and

which most other bi[shops] in and about this town have signed,
save the Bi[shop] Rochester who rudely refused, as did the
Bi[shop] off Bristol. If I can by any means compass a frank you
shall have itt. Pray make my excuses to the honest Capt[ain], tell
him his with the 2 *bills came safe; that for 20 guineas was paid
this day, the other I believe will not by a year and a day. We had
a consultation in Red Ly[on] Street this evening in presence off
Mr Fr[eke] and Mr Honyw[ood] in relation to Tynm[outh].
Both were off opinion that as matters stand circumstanc'd, itt
would not be practicable nor advisable to stirr for itt att present.
[There is] not a word off truth off the resigning off either off
those two great men and as to that worthy person who has bin
pretty much confin'd to his house on account of his
indisposition [Cowper], I can tell you to my own knowledge [he]
is next door to be perfectly reestablish'd. I am sorry to hear off
such misunderstandings in your county [just] when all ought to
be off a piece for the publick safety.[1] I can't enlarge having to
draw out my account off exp[enses] to transcribe to honest Pety
[Peter], which am to send by this post. Martinmas is now past
and no delay shall be laid to the door off ....

1.   This particular rumour was unfounded but it reflects the growing divisions
     among the Whigs, particularly over foreign policy, that rose to the surface
     once the domestic crisis had passed.

126

Queen Besse's day [17 November] 1715

I did not write the last post, having nothing worth troubling
you, so desired the Capt[ain] to excuse me to you. Since I have
yours off the 11th inst with a copy off a letter which my father
has not seen nor Mr Fr[eke] to whom I take the liberty off
communicating this evening, as I did last night to our friend in
the Fields and none else, after which shall keep itt under lock
and key. If I did not mention to you before, can't omitt taking
notice that when I went to Lord Townsend's levy, he was mighty
inquisitive if I knew one Ald[erman] Wise in Newc[astle] and
was very desirous off his character. I told his lordship that he
meant Ald[erman] White, who was as vigorous and active for
the present gov[ernment] as any within those walls. Again he
repeated Ald[erman] Wise; I then reply'd there was one Andrew

Wise an Irish papist (formerly bookeeper to Sir Will[iam]
Creagh who was the first popish may[or] in that corporation), a
man capable off insinuating himself with the meaner sort. I
presume from these repeated quaerys that att that time they had
something to charge him, which is unfolded by yours. Yesterday
came two expresses from Preston signifying that the rebells had
surrender'd att discretion; will not trouble you with repetition
but referr you to that off the *Flying Post*, which by what I can
gather is the fullest account off particulars and believe may be
depended on. Lord Carlisle wrote to town that after a short
campain off 4 hours, they had gott possession off Preston and
the whole nest off rebells, which wer computed by some at
4[000], others 5000 men; 1700 wheroff were the Highlanders and
Northumbrians, the rest what they had pick'd up in their rout
and were join'd by the disaffected off Lancashire. 'Tis said
there are severall h[igh] ch[urch] d[octors] among them, who are
order'd up immediately along with the chief off the rebells to
town. You see a joy through out the City which can't be well
parallel'd and the court shew no less satisfaction. This noble
action has nipp'd the designs off our enemys in the budd so that
they can't expect a plentyfull cropp, off which I wish you and all
friends hearty joy. Mr May[or] and his 2 sergeants being taken
prisoners is a pleasant adventure and as to the complaints
against a man doing his duty, itt will occasion mirth and nothing
else.[1] I can't say I am much concern'd that the late man in power
should be insulted in his turn and the less since the indignity was
offer'd by one off his own kidney. Both you and I have known
when a certain person was one who did not discourage such sort
off proceeding and could not see any harm or inconvenience by
itt, but when the insult turns upon himself, immediately crys out
their power is sett att naught etc. Much good may doe him with
itt. I should not be sorry if some more partys should serve some
others whom I could name the same sawce. Pray when you see
Peter [Bernardeau] tell him I hope he will secure me a
h[ogshead] off good body'd white Bourdeau for my own
drinking. I leave a little space to add what I can pick up this
evening....

1.   Cotesworth's zealous support for the Government was not universally
     popular in the north-east and his irregular exercise of authority left him

vulnerable to retaliation. He suffered considerable harassment in the aftermath of the rebellion, including a series of unpleasant anonymous letters: see Ellis, *Business Fortunes*, p.214.

127

19th Nov[ember] 1715

Honest and trusty Will, your last was by mistake deliver'd to my father which I retrieved this afternoon, when he was looking for the chapter in Ezekiell.[1] Within the libertys off Westm[inster] the justices have begun with their convictions by order off Counsell and had d[elivered] in their rolls to the clark off the peace, where it has laid sometime. An enquiry was made by the Counsell what was don by the justices and on Monday I think they design to make their representation. In Essex they began earlier, so that 'tis hoped these presidents will spread all over the nation. I remember my father as he read over yours, when he came to the particular off the caveat, said that was done. As to Ja[mes] Cr[aggs] and your assistant [Mawson], I must referr to my Lord Will[iam] who is very active and ready to serve his friends. Sir W[alter] Y[onge] is but slow. But indeed the confusion the whole ministry and nation has bin in makes that they can't lend an ear, or if they doe 'tis in att one and out off the other; but now 'tis hoped this hurricane is over, and shortly we expect a calm and from thence that recommending a fitt person to serve will be listen'd unto. What you propose about the militia would be of singular use att this time; they could not fail off picking up abundance off strollers, which though no corporall punishm[ent] were inflicted on them, yet were they but mark'd so as to be known, a watchfull eye might be sett on them again[st] another time. One would think that your Lord Sc[arborough] and Mr C[ar]r could not but see the necessity off doing itt and off what service itt would be. This account off the battle twixt Argyle and Marr is the confused'st account sure ever was given. It sinks our joy conceiv'd on the first report. Pray can you reconcile what became off the centre off our army? Had the first report we had come confirm'd, you would have had S[outh] Sea att near par this day and others in proportion.[2] Sure I am my friend had not so much as a finger in that narrative. Will, I just long for a better account from those parts. The officers here, not one off them can reconcile itt, nay

even his grace's best friends. Adieu, 'tis past 8; pardon me for I
am ....

1. The chapter concerned is unclear, the book of Ezekiel containing
    numerous passages which an old-style Whig like Sir Henry Liddell might
    have thought applicable to the current political situation.

2. On 13 November the Jacobite army engaged Argyll at Sherrifmuir.
    Despite the collapse of their left wing, the outnumbered government forces
    held their own and in effect won a decisive victory by avoiding defeat.

128

24th Nov[ember] 1715

Give me leave to make my acknowledgem[ent] for the favours
you have bestowed on me by your very valuable correspondence
ever since the troubles began, towards the quelling off which no
one person has contributed more than yourself, the fruits
wheroff I hope you will live long to enjoy and after that your
posterity will reap the advantage. I inclose you open this short
letter to honest Peter which you will peruse and deliver. The
whole produce off the colliery being in J[ohn] J[ohnson's] hand,
I thought itt not improper to advise with the persons therin
mention'd, and having gott their opinions, concluded itt would
be the most forcible means I could make use off towards
compassing your rightfull and legall demand. My good friend
you know there are allways some favorites who under hand have
frequent opportunity off skreening some off those who would
have destroy'd both [his] Maj[esty] and his friends had they
succeeded, and this seems to be the case att this juncture. A
great friend off ours [Cowper] is not a little disgusted att these
proceedings and indeed all I converse with are no less. I wish
you would draw out your thoughts on the circumstance off
affairs in your parts in half a sheet by itt self; I will promise you
no bad use shall be made off itt. Reading the *Postman* today
was struck with the paragr[aph] from Lancashire to see that no
greater care is taken off the prisoners off note than to lett them
slip through their fingers. You may if you please ground your
animadversions from that head.[1] Yesterday marched 1500 off
the Dutch northwards and as many followed this day. The
Prince reviewed the Blue regiment behind Mountagu house and

thence they marched to Barnett, in as lamentable weather as we have had this year. My curiosity would not lett me sitt att home by a good fire; I was over shoes before I gott to the Fields and then stood in the wett grass ankle deep. While I was a spectator did not apprehend the least inconvenience, but now that I am cool'd find a sore throat and a pain all over me. I can tell you for your comfort you will see a parcell off clever blades, middle stature but well sett and excellently well arm'd. I dare answer that your young secretary will not be kept in the house the day they march into your town. This day a proclamation is issued for the sitting off the Parl[iament], I think the 14th next month, its whisper'd to pass a bill off attainder ag[ainst] all those in rebell[ion] as well [those] as shall be hereafter.[2] The prints will inform you that the K[ing] of Sweden has bin soundly mauled and obliged to quit the island off Rugen and retire with a small number to Stralsund. I must tell you 'ere I close this that a statute ag[ainst] your friend Gil[bert Spearman] was putt into uncle All[anson's] hand the day before yesterday. The sollicitor desired itt might be superseeded by reason there was not the least ground since his client had swore himself worth better than £20000 beyond all reprisals. Have not heard how itt went since. Adieu my good friend, take the best care you can off your health, so as you may be in a condition to oppose the P[retende]r iff he should attempt any thing northwards. There is a flying report as iff he landed in Scotland, 2 days after the battle. I remain to honest Will ....

P.S. Mr Honeyw[ood] is just come in and says the wagers in Change Alley run 50 guineas to 30 that the Pretender was back to his old quarters.[3]

---

1. The total number of Jacobites who got away was surprisingly high although there were fewer, and less spectacular, escapes from the Lancashire prisons than from Newgate and the Tower.

2. The examination of the seven peers captured at Preston in fact began on 12 December and they were impeached on 9 January.

3. In fact the Pretender was on his way to Dunkirk, from where he hoped to sail for Scotland.

129

1st Dec[ember] 1715

Methinks tis a long time since I heard from Mr May[or] which makes me apprehend now that he has less troublesome business on his hands, that he is more sensibly affected with the late prodigious fatigues he underwent; too heavy a burthen fell to his share, I am satisfy'd a greater than any one pair off shoulders could bear. I hope my last with an inclosed to Peter came safe. Upon the oath taken by Spearm[an] that he was worth £20000 beyond all just demands on him, the statute formerly mention'd was suspended. However by this his cred[itors] will have a fair pull att him if they menage right. I am desired by Ba[rtholomew] Scott to know what steps you have taken towards the recovery off the £50 *bill I formerly sent you. He desires you would shew him no fav[our] and sends me word that the rest of number ten have had a meeting this week and are resolved to prosecute him for the money due to them, which is to a considerable value. Your countrey gen[eral Forster] with the chief off the N[orth] Britt[ish] Preston prisoners are to be bro[ught] to town to morrow. The inferior are distributed in severall off the county goals below. I can tell you for certain that this day Mr Masterman, father to the young gentlem[an] off that name whom you know, is appointed to goe down to Lancash[ire] and take informations, not only against those that were actually in arms but all who were any ways concern'd in aiding and assisting the rebells. On these informations the Attorney Gen[eral] is to frame his prosecutions. He rec[eived] his credentialls and instructions with recommendations to severall well wishers in the countrey this morning and setts out this afternoon. This gentlem[an] is very capable and zealous.[1] There lye now att the Tower wharf six vessells from 100 to 200 tunn each, on board which are to be embarked many pieces off heavy canon, 20 cohort [?] mortars and 4 others off the largest size, proportionable amunition off all sorts for Edinbr[ugh]. I hope soon after this you will see the van off the Dutch that marched hence beginning off last week. You will find Bucksnook in the utmost distress next year, they have not a friend att Gate will trust them a half peny piece. They will suffer unpity'd. Adieu honest Will, take care off your health, in doing which you will oblige the publick as well as ....

[P.S.] We were yesterday to visit our Lord Lieuten[ant] but he was abroad; we see his son but other company being with him we had no private confabulation.

1. A commission of oyer and terminer was established to set up a court in Lancashire to try the rebels there and commissioners were appointed to gather evidence as quickly as possible.

130

10th Dec[ember] 1715

I am obliged by 2 off yours and begin with that dated the 2nd inst. Am sorry that Mr Bern[ardeau] could not afford you any more than £300 especially att a time you want itt so much. The concern in its present circumstances is att a very low ebb and the H[igh] Sh[eriff] either has not moneys or no mind to part with itt. He has lately made a *return in *bills on J. Wiely to the tune of £250 but which will not be paid on this side midsummer att soonest. Could you not help to lessen your ballance by taking off *pan coal? I should be glad to hear off the success off your meeting with the Coll[onel] and Mr Ord. I should be glad to be freed off my troublesome post and attendance amongst a parcell off sad fellows att Gate. Your representation to Cha[rles] Sand[erson] was full. I have imparted to our great friend your 3 articles. Was told that the Reg[ent] had bin so decieved by numbers off lyes from hence that he began to shew himself in some measure a favorer off a certain person [the Pretender]'s designs, but very lately he is fully convinced off the contrary and we shall have something good from thence.[1] Your other 2 articles I believe there is very good grounds for and the Gov[ernment] has an eye upon them. Your diligence and care is much approv'd and you are desired to continue itt. Mr Fr[eke] says you must and shall be reimburs'd, though perhaps itt may not be so speedy as we could wish. Yours off the 6th came to hand yesterday. I sent Madam this afternoon to the Fields to shew that part which relates to Mr R[oge]rs; none was at home. What can be done in itt I can't tell; can only say that I am heartily concern'd that that gentleman could not pitch on a better deputy [sheriff]. T[homas] Gibson is out off order; when Cha[rles] and I shall meet [him], till then must expect no answer. Yesterday came the pris[oners] from Preston. I saw your

Bensham landlord Clav[ering] look'd pretty pityfully, Hall off
Otterburne the same. Foster was muffl'd up in a blew coat. 'Tis
near 11 a clock; if I save the post 'tis all I can do. Adieu, I am
....

[P.S.] I am in vast pain with this snowy weather.

1. The death of Louis XIV without an adult heir left the new regent, Philip of
    Orleans, prepared to negotiate with England in order to protect his
    position. This opened the way to eliminating the French threat to the
    succession.

131

15th Dec[ember] 1715

I am infinitely indebted to you that you will spare so much
time in conversing by letter with a person that makes such
indiffer[ent] returns. But 'tis not in my power to doe or gett
done what I wish. I attempt boldy, though not with the success I
could wish. Take the will for the deed. I expect every day a
summons from Mr Sand[erson] on yours to him, as soon as Mr
Gibson getts abroad. Yours off the 9th I show'd first to our
friend in the Fields, who return'd me thanks for itt; also to Lord
S[ome]rs and to Mr Fr[eke]. The latter had some discourse with
him on the subject, I mean the 2nd person, who I believe if his
health permitt will be very servicable. Neither off the 2 lords
affect to discourse or boast much, yet I flatter my self, when
matters come to a bearing they will both exert, nay I hope
effectuably in most off those points you recommend. They both
extoll your industry, zeal and clever way off expression. Mr
Fr[eke] said upon reading the first paragraph off yours that the
generall [Carpenter]'s visitt would be an additional expence,
which says he must be added to the £70. Lord Sc[arborough] is
not yet return'd from Sussex. Mr Masterman's son wrote to his
father the substance of what you desired should be
communicated the last post. Tis a pity your bad state off health
would not admitt your taking a Lancash[ire] journey. We are
sensible that no one living would be off such use att this time off
day, and to be coupled with the above nam'd gentlem[an] who is
a man of good law understanding, honest and zealous. I dare
venture to say that you two together would dispatch more

effectuall business in a day than 'tis possible now to be don in a week, and make more useful discoverys, for I know you would be able to lay open the wound to the bone and consequently probe the bottom off the sore. Who knows but the commission may be adjourned to Northumb[erland] and that you may meet there. Yesterday morn[ing] I went into the Fields to breakfast with that good lady [Cowper]; you were in a great measure the subject off our discourse. She was heartily wishing that you had bin able to have assisted att these examinations and lamenting the want off health to a person so publickly serviceable. I believe an inquiry will be made if the informations made be not sunk [i.e. concealed]. Such a remissness would be unpardonable. My good friend, 'twixt you and me, I doubt there is not so good an harmony 'twixt the 2 Secretar[ies] and our friends first mention'd as one would wish. By which means I am att a loss how to act. This is only my surmise, therfore don't take the least notice. These 2 are but young statesmen comparatively but yet rely upon their own notions much. I need say no more. This day I reminded Lord Will[iam] to deliver to Mr Walp[ole] the case off the glass window merch[ant] and to recommend your friend for a successor. My wife d[elivered] it to my lady who promised her care. I am glad you have drove St[ella] concern so near a bearing [i.e. right course]; if she keeps her head above water 'tis chiefly owing to your self. You have the liberty off recieving the £50 off Jemmy and give creditt in your account. That gentleman wrote me word near a month agoe that he had lodged that summ in your hands; you promised to return a *bill in lieu. The d[octor] has just left me joyfully att the success his prescription has had on me and by Monday's carrier you will have some off the same sent you. I am going into Red Ly[on] Street wher if I hear any thing, shall be added by ....

[P.S.] The B[ishop] off Lincoln is like to succeed the old rock [Canterbury]. The poor Dutch forces have undergon a fatiguing march: if your Corporation had any sort off zeal for the Gov[ernment] they might shew itt by expressing their charity to those poor souls.

132

Tuesday near 10 att night

I have bin obliged to attend our board all this day and a new commiss[ioner] off our [stamp duty] office, who invited us to dinner and with him we have bin ever since. However I can't omitt adding a few friends [*sic*] to my good friend. You must know that I am much out off constitution, upon certain intelligence that the Coll[onel] had not appeared so zealous upon the late disturbances as could be expected, nor my father's friends, by which itt plainly appears that a certain gentlem[an, Carr] would make his interest att court by taking all upon himself. He talks much off his indefatigable pains, such as his lying whole nights att the gates off the town ready to recieve expresses as they came from this town, and giving dispatchs to the scouts he sent out whenever they return'd, with much more off this nature to ingratiate himself. This a friend off ours had from a friend who heard itt told to the Prince himself. This you may imagin has not a little discomposed our old gentlem[an] after the hazard the Coll[onel] run and his friends, besides the expensive part, that they should be reputed rather as indolent and inactive att that time off day. Poor Lord Sc[arborough] I dare say had not the least hand in this misrepresentation for he has bin in Sussex almost ever since his coming from your parts and is there yet. My father is very inquisitive after the full particulars, which as soon as come to hand shall be communicated att large. This morn[ing] Lord L[umley] came and made a visit to my father. He express'd himself very frankly upon the matters of the north; told us that the saving off the town att first was in the greatest measure owing to the Coll[onel] and your self, who by means off the friends off your county kept the town quiet, and express'd himself very handsomly upon that occassion. By which I percieve from what quiver the malitious arrow was shott. I read him part of your 2 letters; he desired me to draw an abstract and send him, and he would take care that your desires be answer'd by laying before Lord Townsend etc. He says he will make some off your Newc[astle] people smart; he is very zealous, nay I may say extraordinary, from whence I expect something will be don. You would doe well to write to cos[in] L[iddell] and Mr Gibs[on] upon the subject you mention for they may be both serviceable. I can't omitt mentioning one passage that happen'd between a gentlem[an] of my acquaintance and another of yours and mine. Talking off the affairs off the north, he shew'd him severall informations that he procured, among which was that against G[eorge] B[aker?]. My friend was curious to see itt but he told him that itt contain'd nothing materiall and so took itt out off his hand. From this I conjecture many will be sunk, which is an abominable practice. I shall make the best use off your letters I can by imparting them to some I hope one time or other will make inquiry after such practices. I have not had time to consult a method for correcting the abuse committed by your being putt to the charge off shamm scoundrell packetts, but from those I have talk'd with their opinion is that you should seal them and return to the Post Office, who will be obliged to return you the charge. Lord L[um]ly was inquisitive if any officers either custome house or excise were not zealous for the Gov[ernment], that Mr Walp[ole] had desired to be acquainted with them and he would take care to sett those matters right. Do you think if you wrote a letter to him on this subject, I dare say itt would be the most effectuall method of having redress. Excuse this scrawl for I am above half seas over [*i.e.* almost drunk] ....

133

24th Dec[ember] 1715, past 9

Yours came to hand this day att noon. I had an opportunity of shewing itt to Mr F[reke] just before supper. I pass over the first part having but time to speak a word. We think an information might not doe amiss, suppose you send itt to the Lord Lieut[enant] and another to me. What sort off a trade is it that Alb[ert Silvertop] drives, for *ship or *pans? The above gentlem[an] is positive the Record[er] is quite wrong and he cant believe that person would give his opinion under hand. And whoever deals with any off my Lord [Widdrington]'s effects will be answerable for the value, besides the trouble they will meet with. His further opinion [is] that no sheriff after he has pitched on his deputy can remove any part off the power, therfore 'twill be necessary to advise him to a trusty well affected person and not depend on the reservation. He further adds that he differs in opinion with you in relation to forfeitures. By the statute in a county palatine all lands etc. escheat to the king in cases off treason, but in those off fellony to the bi[shop of Durham] and no otherwise. I mention'd your son's request off having his schoolfellow B[right] to accompany him to Sedberg. Our old gentlem[an] referrs the point to his father whom you may consult by the Capt[ain's] pen. I have bin severall nights att the Grecian without ever seeing T[om] Gib[son]; he has bin ill but told my father he would come and dine with us these [Christ]mas holydays and would summons me to attend. Sir W[alter] Young is a very devout man and that I could not give him any disturbance att present touching what regards the custom house, but will doe itt att a more seasonable opportunity. Excuse this imperfect account from an invalid, but at all times ....

134

4th Jan[uary] 1715/6

Itt is none off the least concerns that sensibly affect me, to find my kind friend's zeal for his countrey so little taken notice off. I found my interest after a short experience off no signification, which made me apply to my cosen and putt the letters off note into his hand in order to be communicated. This was kept on foot till latter end Oct[ober] that my father return'd from Bath, after which upon desiring him to introduce me to the 2 Secretarys and Mr Wal[pole], which he seem'd not forward to doe, but told me that iff I would shew him my letter by that post he would tell me plainly his opinions. He perused and said they would not allow themselvs time to read itt, upon which I reply'd hastilly if the[y] don't desire to be rightly inform'd off the state and disposition off ours and the neighbouring parts, they should not be troubl'd with itt, adding that I doubted not before they were a month older they would find the want of the intelligence. However as Mr Fr[eke] and my father advised I never fail'd sending them to our friend in the Fields, not as being part off his province, however we concluded itt necessary that when the northern matters came to be discoursed off in Counsell, that he might be appriz'd off the true matters off fact, for which I have had his thanks ofter than once.

In the next place what related to corrupt officers off customs, which way had I to apply but to a friend Sir W[alter] Y[onge] who being an old friend and acquaint[ance] and bears the name off a Wh[ig], I thought I might have depended upon him. I read to him your first complaints att Mr Fr[eke]'s of whom he stands in the greatest awe, and there before him charged him never to make use neither off my name nor my correspondent's, which he faithfully promised. From time to time he would be very inquisitive if I had any further to make; when I had I shew'd him them and he would be free in giving an account off what small matters past att their board. This past so till off late finding no effect from the representations one night as I wrote you word, I shew'd Mr F[reke] one off yours; he threw itt to that gentlem[an] Sir W[alter] and said itt was a shame or to that purpose. But I found by his answers that little effectual could be expected from that quarter. Yet being resolved to push for Ed[ward] Mawson, I then shew'd some off yours to honest Roger Gale, who told me that he would take an opportunity of discoursing freely Mr Walp[ole]; and least that should fail I drew out a short abstract in relation to Breakes and gave itt to Sir Rich[ard] Sandford, who d[elivered] itt to his own hand. I putt another off the same into Lord Will[iam]'s to be d[elivered] the same way; itt laid with him above a fortnight, after which he return'd itt to me, being obliged to goe to Lemington to be reelected. These offputts made me more uneasy than you would imagine, least you should attribute the miscarriage to my neglect. I spoke to Rob[ert] Hony[wood] and any prudent person to remind Mr W[alpole] and Lord Z[etlan]d off what related either off them but to take an opportun[ity] off doing itt privately. With those I could be free, I now and then read yours to them att large in order to make the greater impression. What I abstracted and left with Lord Lumley was only in relation to the Recorder, your proposed method off menaging the forfeited estates most advantageously to the crown, about exam[ination] off the Lancash[ire] rebells and about the window officers. These are the heads that I gave in writing to this lord and the chief persons to whom [I spoke]. That any off them should make a bad or indiscreet use off them such as should turn to your disadvantage, or were itt by my own carelessness or otherwise, which I proffess my ignorance off, att least I can safely swear did not doe itt with any ill intent, so that I may for

ought I know [be] the inocent cause off trouble or grief to you,
which to my knowledge would be the very last I should be guilty
off. As to Sir W[illiam Blackett] I was over and above cautious.
I was pump'd by severall to know my opinion how farr he was
ingaged; my answer was that gentlem[an] was in possession off
too plentifull a fortune I thought than to ingage himself.
Touching your coll[ector] I remember Sir W[alter] Y[onge] see
the letter where he was mention'd, but I caution'd him not to
take the least notice till he heard further; if he has bin so
imprud[ent] as to blabb any thing off that matter before his
brethren att the board, [it is] not unlikely what you suspect that
itt might come about by some clerk. Good God, what an age do
we live in. I thought that when we had what we wish'd for, a
Wh[ig] administration, that then all injurys cry'd out off before
would be redress'd. But itt seems some others besides priests are
still the same. I am resolv'd for the future not to sett my heart
on any thing and then shall not meet with a disappointm[ent].
Only this I will pursue till I see effected iff possible, that is the
procuring that post off the wind[ow] officer for E[dward]
M[awso]n, and then I have don with polliticks. People are apt to
exclaim ag[ainst] the corruption off the coal traders; there is no
comparison to be made. I shall return contentedly after what I
have seen to my old way off conversing. I have discover'd so
many tricks within these 2 months that there is no trusting save 3
or 4 off our friends. You might imagin by severall off my letters
in answer to yours that I could never give a direct one, and I had
not conversed long enough with a certain comm[issioner] off
your acquaintance [i.e. Carr] to disguise itt. But I will quit this
ungratefull subject and acquaint you that his Maj[esty] last
night rec[eived] letters from the Regent, wherein are mighty
cordiall expressions; that he will inviolably observe the treatys
made between the 2 crowns and that iff his Maj[esty] pleases he
shall appoint an officer in all the ports off France who shall have
liberty to inspect any suspected vessells etc., that [he] has given
effectuall orders to prevent shipping [Jacobite] officers and
men. Could not you recommend proper surveyors by pricking
out [i.e. marking names] from Tees to Berwick? Yesterdays
express from Scotland brought very agreable news to the court
likewise.[1] If things goe well there we have no just fears off an
impending danger, but if we meet with any considerable ruffle
we shall be in immediate confusion. Now my good friend 'tis

high time to release you from this sad scrawle and give me leave
to assure you I am semper idem ....

1. The Government position in Scotland had recently been improved by
   advances in Fife and by the arrival of reinforcements in Glasgow and
   Leith.

135

7th Jan[uary] 1715/6

I have but a word to say to my friend after wishing him a
happy new year and many. This afternoon I see a letter from Mr
Master[man] wherin he gives an account that he took young
Pierson's information, which he drew up fair in writing, gave itt
him to read over which he did and then sign'd itt, but when he
offerd him to swear to it, he absolutely refused. His opinion is
that he is a harden'd obdurate sinner and that nothing can be
made off him. He adds that Mr John Hunter off
Northumb[erland] who was in prison att Wiggan had made his
escape thence. I believe that Hunter is the same person that used
to carry wines from Scotland into our parts before the Union. If
itt be so his father and he liv'd att Shillow hill, as I remember, or
some such name. The Preston prisoners have bin very uppish
ever since their confinem[ent] on what account I know not; they
say Marr will be able to release them but those are distant views.
Phil[ip] Hodgshon is the most dejected; he says plainly we shall
be buoy'd up with hopes off a pardon till we are hang'd. I have
bin confin'd to the house these 2 or 3 days, seldom stir farther
than Red L[yon] St[reet and] am much fuller off complaints
than usuall. 'Tis a sign that age and infirmitys steal upon me
apace. I am prevented by this from solliciting. Adieu honest
Will, I am at all times and seasons ....

136

9th Jan[uary] 1715/6

Just after I had sealed and sent away my last, Sir W[alter]
Y[onge] happen'd to stumble in amongst us. He told me that
they had that day read at their board the Rockliffs man's
vindication off himself. He alledges as the case stood then that

so many shorts [*i.e.* short deliveries] might very well happen,
giving for reason that Mr Zach [More] had bought a bargain off
very ordinary coals off one W[illiam] C[otesworth] off
Newc[astle] who was to take a quantity off allum for paym[ent].
That those coals being sold extreemly cheap, that the said
W[illiam] C[otesworth] wrought off the coursest sort and (being
very wett besides) must needs sink the *keel extreemly; and
consequently what is taken in att Newc[astle] by weight can't
make out att the delivering port by *measure, etc. To which I
reply'd that there was a difference twixt coal off a finer and
courser mettle, perhaps one and half [*chaldrons] in the score,
but in this affidavitt they fell short above ¼, a pretty jest. He
adds that W[illiam] C[otesworth] was making room for a friend
off his. These particulars from Sir W[alter's] own mouth; if I
can gett a copy off the justifi[cation] shall send you itt, however
this is the substance. They have adj[ourned] the consideration
till another day, and as this gentleman is off opinion he will be
discharg'd, I reminded him of your recommendation. He told
me that in all probability their board would ballott [for the
choice]; you may depend on mine for your friend. In the next
place I can tell you that my lord's secretary had some
conversation with Mr Craggs concerning G. Thompson, the
substance off which was that G. T[hompson] came up the latter
end of this sommer att his own charge and made a proposall by
which the [postal] revenue in those parts would be considerably
advanced. This Lord Cornw[allis] and the other approv'd off,
and came to an agreem[ent] with him and his perform[ance]
likewise answers; but says in case he misbehaves or shews any
disaffection to the Gov[ernment], notwithstanding the
agreement he assures he shall be discharged. Dr Lloyd the
Bi[shop] off Worster's son desired to have a true character off
Mr Ly[onel] Norman who I think was a commiss[ioner] off
customs in N[orth] Britt[ain] by Lord Godolph[in's] means, and
he says was turn'd out off itt by the Earl Marr upon account off
his steady adherence to the protestant succession. Pray lett me
have his character by the very first opportunity. Inclosed comes
the most glorious speech that ever was spoke from the throne.
After itt was d[elivered] the Commons return'd and voted an
address and sent itt to the Lords desiring they would continue
sitting for they were resolv'd upon impeaching. Lechmer carry'd
up the message and told their lordships that he would undertake

to impeach one, which was the Earl Derwent[water];
accordingly the Commons did resolve to begin with the 2
English and 5 Scotch lords taken att Preston; I hear the articles
are drawn up and to be lodged this [day] with the Lords. But for
further certainty I must referr you to the votes.

5th Jan[uary]: about noon my father came in coach and hurried
me to wait on Lord Sc[arborough]. That gentlem[an] itt seems
came but to town the night before, though expected Friday last.
I find in him a sensible decay since he went into Sussex, which is
about 5 or 6 weeks since; pray tell your H[igh] Sh[eriff] from me
that I acquainted his l[ordship] the Northumb[erland]
association was in Lord Lum[ley's] custody and I desired his
l[ordship's] care off itt that itt be d[elivered], which I promised.
I have not heard from you these 3 posts yet am troubling you
with my impertinent scrawls; if I pick up any thing off this days
proceedings shall add itt, and remain though very full of
complaints and half starv'd ....

137

19th Jan[uary] 1715/6

I had almost possesst my self with the believe that the frost
had congeled your ink till I rec[eived] yours off the 13th inst
which lyes before me. The very morning after itt came to hand I
took courage and resolution to venture a walk as farr as Tom
Wakelin's (since going in coach was much more hazardous).
There I found my friend [Dr Lloyd] to whom I imparted the
character; no sooner had we read itt but the party himself
knock'd att the door, sends up his name. My friend return'd for
answer that he had an account from the countrey which did not
att all please him, and till he had a more satisfactory one would
not in the least meddle in recommending him. The message
Ly[onel] N[orman] return'd was that he had many enemies in
N[orth] Britt[ain] who can't indure that any Englishm[an]
should be employ'd, so could not expect a good one from that
quarter. You may depend my friend will not interest himself on
his behalf. I assure you I have bin provok'd as much as you can
possibly be att the slow proceedings ag[ainst] your Rock[liff]
merch[ant]. Monday night after rec[eit] I shew'd itt to Mr
Fr[eke] att his house, where Sir W[alter] happen'd to be; after

having perused itt, threw itt to the barr[onet] and with a frowning countenance bad him read it, told him itt was a shame that justice was so long in executing. In short he talk't so warmly that the poor gentlem[an] had not a word to say in vindication off himself and brethren than that itt would certainly be done. What relates to your other complaints I must find out another hand to make use of them to advantage. If itt be not too much trouble (when you have the most leisure) should be glad to hear from you; itt is not to be laid att your door nor mine if the accounts you give are not duly improved. Your friend Wakel[in] being intimate with one off the Secretaries' clarks, thinks he may procure a true list [of informations] which when comes to hand shall be transmitted.

Mr Gilroy was with the widd[ow] Cole about letting her 3 *pans and was told that Sir W[illiam] had the sole menagem[ent] off them, along with his own 3; that she has them as jointure. This he had from Maltis Ryall the dealer who is a near relation off the widdow's. I can't but admire that I don't hear the least syllable off Clav[ering] St[ella] from any hand, iff she be lett or likely to be so. The dealers about a fortnight agoe invited my father, uncle, cosin and self to a diner, after which they desired to know off me iff they might relye on the same *praem[ium] for C[lavering] St[ella] concern as this last year; I told them that I could not answer iff she were to be lett, or work in our own hands or *lye in, that depended upon directions from the court this next term. Itt seems within this week they (that is to say the chief off number ten) have hinted as if they would be obliged to take off the full quantity meaning 1000 Newc[astle] *tens from the *steath, and desired to know what price we could and were willing to afford them att *ledd down; they would send down ships. This is projected by the 2 Oldn[ers], Blunkett and Watts I think is the 4th. You must not take notice off this since they desired itt might not be divulged. Am att a loss what to insist on, not knowing how farr treatys in the countrey are advanced, and supposing those are vanish'd I must have recourse for your information what to insist on. Our friend in the Fields invited me to diner the other day and in discourse told me he hoped we had lett the colliery; I reply'd, not that I had as yet heard off, says he I wish she were disposed off to advantage. Tis confidently reported att Gate that Ald[erman] R[amsay] has agreed with Bucks N[ook] owners and as confidently talk'd that they are to lead down the same quant[ity] as last year; and that a certain friend off mine has liberty off leading down a quant[ity] from Brainslope and that he likewise is to have a share off B[ucks] N[ook] and have the joint menagem[ent] with Brum[ell], this last is to be sole *fitter.[1] Lady B[owes] has gott her injunction confirm'd upon Mr Wortl[ey] till a tryall att law determine. I am much, I may say very much affected with the weather which you may guess by the frequent blotts and blunders in this. However itt does not alter me in my disposition to Mr May[or] whose humble serv[ant] and friend I always remain ....

[P.S.] This day the 7 Lords were carried from the Tower to the House off Lords, where in their answers they confess'd the articles off impeachm[ent] and threw themselvs on the king's clemency.[2]

1. An agreement was certainly made with the owners of Bucksnook colliery but it failed to end the waggonway dispute because Lady Clavering continued to use it without leave.

2. In fact Lord Wintoun pleaded not guilty and was not tried until 15 March. The other six concerned were Lords Carnwath, Derwentwater, Kenmuir, Nairn, Nithsdale and Widdrington.

138

[January 1715/6]

[The delay in letting Clavering Stella is] a very unhappy circumstance I assure you. Gilroy is off opin[ion] that the dealers may afford to give 8s p[er] *ch[aldron] for them *ledd down but rather than fail they shall goe att 7[s] 6[d] or even 7s; and as they first proposed to send ships off their own, they might lay them on board for 6d or very little more. Had I [£]1000 lying by me, I would venture to *undertake her my self. Pray send for Dan[iel] and Peter; inquire off them if they be like to gett her lett to some others who had made offers. If they be near upon the point off concluding I desire they would forbear putting the finishing stroke till they hear from me what the dealers here will doe, for we must not lett twice. And how John[son] will be disposed off I know not, though doubt not he

has a view off ingaging and I wish itt be not to Tanfield or
B[ucks] N[ook]. One word off politicks before I conclude.
Depend upon't our Admiralty is in very good hands and who
work their work silently. As to the raising forces either att home
or to have some from abroad, you may be assur'd the ministry
have weigh'd well those matters. 'Tis not conven[ient] to alarum
the people with either at present; such handles give
opportun[ity] to enemys to the Govern[ment] to raise
formidable argum[ents] which poyson the subject, who is
readily to swallow any att this juncture. 'Tis true the ministry
have a vast deal on their hands, yet itt can't be imagin'd that
they neglect the main points. I need not inlarge. My stomack is
wonderfully impoverished; digestion naught, can't sleep, only
the last night had recourse to an opium pill, which did not
afford me above 3 hours disturb'd rest. Notwithstanding my
courage is not cast down; the greatest off impression thes[e]
complaints raise in me, that I am troublesome to those I
personally converse with as well as by letter, for my spirits are
much weak[end]. I am ....

139

25th Jan[uary] 1715/6

I am indetted to two off yours off no small size each, but how
to discharge is the difficulty. We have had a cold sort off a
thaw, which does affect me cruelly. There is no stirring abroad
neither in coach, chair nor foot without manifest hazard off
breaking bones, so that we are all in a great measure confin'd to
our respective habitations; from whence you will conjecture that
one has nothing to doe but answer letters, but that is not my case
for I am in pain from head to foot, sick att stomack and so
listless that I am not master off one clear thought, consequently
fitter for bed. However before I goe there will attempt to answer
as farr as I can your favors. Your town was unworthy off so
honest a man as Jurin; as you very well remark, posterity will
have reason to curse those who have had any hand in making
him uneasy in the post he was possessed off. But what other can
be expected from such a sett off govern[ors]? And to be
succeeded by such a wretch, who is not worthy off wiping his
shoes, is no less admirable.[1] By this they seem resolved that the

next generation shall continue in the same obscurity. Ignorance is the mother off devotion. Oh blessed moth[er] church! You have named the person that poysons all [Lord Crewe?] and yet I wish he can be outed. Mr F[reke] spoke to Lord S[ome]rs about itt but his bodily informitys disable him prodigiously from doing service to his countrey as well as particular friends. As to the forfeitures, you need not doubt they will be punctually and rightly apply'd. C[harles] S[anderson] you have describ'd to the life. I have press'd him by letter as well as word off mouth to send a petition drawn to the H[igh] Sh[eriff]; he pleads multiplicity off business in excuse and promises fair. Honest Gil[bert Spearman] is as great a master in his way as E[dward] M[ontagu?] was in his, with this distinction that the first does itt without mask, the other picks your pockett and att the same time smiles in your face. Pray push what you can to gett in that *bill; if money be not to be had, had you not best return the bill to Scott? You know how I am circumstantiated in Cl[avering] St[ella]. The season for opening the trade is att hand and to be att an uncertainty att this time off day may prove off the worst consequence. I hope 'ere this arrive that the gentlemen have come to a determination one way or other, for till I hear that would not exchange a word with the dealers. I am fully convinc'd that all your affairs have suffer'd much by your Lond[on] journey [for the Regulation] and especially the *vend off your coals. I should have thought the Gentlem[en] whom you were serving obliged to have lent you an assisting hand but when the business is over and done the benefactor is generally forgott. This is the way off the world. Your Chester friend [Hedworth] shews himself every day more and more in another interest. The barr[onet, Blackett] has kissed the hand, but you may rest assured that iff any thing can be made out ag[ainst] him he will not escape. This I had from undeniable authority.

I come in the next place to your bill [of complaint] in Chancery which bears date the 20th. I doubt you are too true a prophet concerning the reg[iment]. I have frequently shew'd that part off your letter dated the 2nd Dec[ember] where you pointed out correctly what has since happen'd in relation to that gentlem[an, the Pretender]. Our divisions att home have given him encouragem[ent]. The Governm[ent] has had a watchfull eye upon him. We have a fleet att sea or just ready, about ... sail, I can't say in a body as yet but you will hear off them

shortly. I am off your opinion that the cruizers have not bin so
diligent in their station as could be expected. We long to hear off
the march off our army towards Perth, which if itt please God to
prosper with success will be a vast strengthening off the K[ing's]
friends. If Sir Cha[rles] Hotham does not represent effectually
the usage some off his men have mett with he does not doe
justice, but as he is a man off mettle and hon[orable] I doubt not
in the least his seeing them righted.[2] As to the blew coat excise
man, I have bin speaking till I am weary. Lately I discoursed
Rog[er] Gale about him. Says he Mr C[arr] should doe that, I
am a stranger to that town and a young comm[issioner];
however if you would send him an information, he would out
him in spight off Will[iam] C[arr]. Had not that gentlem[an] this
man represented to him among many others? But he is a slippery
spark; my father has not bin able to find out to the bottom off
what he went in search off. As to the victualling and clothing
[contracts], 'tis my admiration what interest those gentlemen
have to [succeed] in it. By what underhand means they work. As
I take it those *undertakers are generally [recommen]ded to the
comm[issioners] by the Treasury, where I have not the least
interest, having bin solliciting [a]ugmentation off sallary as all in
that office have had save another and my self, but without
success. I d[elivered yours] about Breaks in favor off Ed[ward]
M[awson] to Sir Richard Sandford last Saturday and gave him
liberty to [make] use off my fathers and my name. He did itt att
the House that very day to Mr Walpole, had his promise itt
should be done. They are so overcharg'd with business that none
can gett a minute's discourse with them but some that are their
intimates. I doe my best towards improving your frequent
advices to the publick benefitt but am much concern'd that my
endeavors prove off no greater use: your indefatigable pains and
zeal is as good as thrown away. Itt happens that those people
who ought to inform themselvs of what passes I am a stranger
too, and am apt to believe that they take all their
representat[ions] from Lord Sc[arborough's] W[illiam] C[arr].
Were you not amaz'd to see in the *Gazette* that Lord
[Scarborough] had d[elivered] the address introduced by the
former. I abstracted part off your letter wherein you pray that
itt [be] discountenanced; left itt with Lord L[umley] who
promised his assistance and that he would remind his father.
Not [above] ten days ago my father and self waited on the Lord

Lieut[enant], brought that subject upon the board, told him itt was an affront to his l[ordship] that they would not accept off the association he left them; but you see to what purpose.[3] This makes me wary off transacting matters with people that blow hott and cold. But poor man he is directed by another [person] who never plaid a game but fast and loose. My father went this morning to the Lords to talk about the armies but came too late. Last post I see a letter from Leverpole with account that young Pierson has bin wrought upon by a sis[ter] who is with him to confess and has swore to as well as sign'd the information. Since that is, I believe they will [be ver]y nice off sending a copy (least itt should miscarry) till after the tryalls. However I will attempt itt. I design shewing the latter part off yours about the [suspension of] hab[eus] corp[us] to some friends off the House. I am perfectly jaded so fitt to take a napp. 26th Jan[uary]: this morn[ing] att 11 I was saluted by your last; have imparted what is most materiall to a particular friend, from whom I expect benefitt. Adieu ....

[P.S.] There is a flying report that to the west our men off warr had taken 2 ships loaded with arms.

1. Jurin devoted himself to medicine after his resignation and achieved a formidable intellectual reputation. His successor, Edmund Lodge, was better respected than Liddell allows.

2. The Pretender had landed at Peterhead on 22 December, nine days after Sheriffmuir, having evaded numerous naval patrols. Unfortunately, the Jacobite forces at Perth were already fading away and their weakness was reflected in Newcastle's growing impatience with the troops whose protection had been welcomed in October.

3. Many counties and boroughs presented loyal associations to George I at this time, usually through their Lords Lieutenant. In contrast, Newcastle's humble address was presented by Carr and only delivered by Scarborough.

140

2d Feb[ruary] 1715/6

Yours with the inclosed came safe. 'Tis full off mettle, I mean yours to G[ibson], yet considering the actions off the man you have drawn him to the life, no one can cavill att itt. I wish with all my heart that itt may be shewn not only to the person you fancy itt will [Walpole?] but likewise to the principall Secr[etary]; itt might be off use. All the information they listen too comes from a certain acquaintance off yours [Carr], off whose parts I have a very good opinion [and] wish could say the same off his integrity. I am jealous 'tis through his means that when we recommend a person that is capable and zealous to serve the Govern[ment], that there are such delays and difficultys; nay 'tis look'd upon as an obligation don to ones self. Which is a maxim I never did yet nor ever shall rightly understand. I should make a wretched courtier but God be thank'd my sole subsistence does not come from that quarter. We have too many saints among us which whilst they continue to act as they doe, I should wish rather for a sinner who acts according to his profession, an opcn game. If I proceed on this subject shall raise my passion, which is expressly forbid by my d[octor]. The Gov[ernment] expect great matters from N[orth] Britt[ain] upon which account they forbear giving out the commissions for the raising off the 16 new regim[ents] that were to be raised. I believe some time next week judgem[ent] will be pass'd on the guilty lords; soon after that Lansdown will be try'd and after him cunning Mortimer. This I think you may depend upon.[1] Gil[bert Spearman] is as notable a man as any off the profession; to find him taking in J[ohn] Dawson and such off his depth and head piece is not so much to be admired, but to gett beyond the Ch[ief] Justice [Wright], an old friend off his, is a pure merrim[ent]. I wish you a good conclusion in the affair that has bin so long depending: a York tryall would more than half kill you, especially if the weather should continue any time as severe as 'tis now. I am by itt little better than a prisoner att large, confin'd by the limitts off the next street and the Rowe, and that but once a day and rejoice when I return back. My old complaints are grievous to me, I need not say any more. I have discoursed all my female friends and relations on the subject off our Ovingh[am] friend's letter; what is admirable is that none off them are yet weary off a single life. 'Tis time enough half a score years hence, say they, to talk off giving away our libertys etc. Therfore had not my cosen best turn his thoughts on some off your country fortunes? You know off two very considerable ones, besides many others. Will you give your self the trouble off acquainting him with as much from ....

[P.S.] What becomes off poor Farnacres and our Whickham? Mr Clav[ering] sent me lately an information off one Hunter a Chopwell ten[ant] who had his horse taken away by Willson, Lady Bowes' *viewer and 3 or 4 others. It would not be amiss to take others, for if they escape Lancash[ire] you have a rod on them att your assizes. Sir W[alter] Y[onge] just now tells me that your officer Sachevrell is turn'd out by their board; they ballotted for successor, itt fell to Sir Tho[mas] Frankland's lott. Sir W[alter] Y[onge] told me that if itt had fallen to his, he would have taken one off your recommend[ations]. If charrs be in season, pray send me up 2 midling potts. I design one for Lincolns Inn Fields; shall thankfully repay all charges.

1. Cowper pronounced judgment on the six Jacobite peers on 9 February, condemning them to death. By this stage public opinion was running against retribution, making it unlikely that those who had been arrested before they could take up arms, like Lansdowne, would be brought to trial.

141

7th Feb[ruary] 1715/6

Yours by last post came to hand last night att 11 a clock and very wellcome itt was, though itt brought in substance what the express brought Sunday night. Your correspondent is a man off notable intelligence but to guess the person I am att a loss; my own thoughts lead me to some officer who you have entertain'd in passing. This day brings another express which confirms the first, with this addition that the rebells took 2 different routes, that Cadogan was in pursuit and doubted not giving a good account off them.[1] Your zeal in propagating the contents off your letter is highly commended, as also your obliging their [Newcastle's] great bells to ring aloud till next morning which sufficiently proclaims our success throwout that neighbourhood. Itt is a pity Sir W[illiam] W[illiamson] should not have what would please him since his expectations are but very moderate; and as to his militia officer I will attempt to morrow morning, though since I have had the misfortune off miscarrying hitherto in all my undertakings off that kind, yet any neglect shall not be laid to my door. In relation to the present circumstances we have the most difficult part to act. My

Lord S[carborough] ought to be acquainted with itt, as one off his under officers is the person that putts in and a word from his mouth to the Board off customs or Treasury would doe, but if we should impart to him perhaps he may think no more off itt, or iff he doe may send and acquaint his right hand [Carr] who probably may make interest for another. If you speak to the Treasury, there you have a saint who never fails off a friend ready to popp in: there again you are frustrated. If to the comm[issioners] you have seen the fate of that, so which way has one to steer? The only method that seems feasible is by applying to Mr W[alpole] who has his head and hands so full off publick affairs that you may make 20 fruitless journeys without seeing his face, and yet delays are dangerous. Now good friend consider what dificultys we labor under which makes desire you would not expect the success. If itt should come to pass, 'tis more than what we do. Rest satisfy'd our endeavors shall not be wanting. T[homas] G[ibson] promised but never did dine in Red Ly[on] St[reet]. Mr Ga[le] would either take your word or mine, but as he is a new commer does not know but that he might meet with opposition from a certain gentlem[an] whose place one would think obliged him to give an account of the disaffected within his own circuit, therfore had a mind to be back'd with an affidavitt. We drank your health att his house not many hours agoe. Wakelin's friend att the office has bin laid up by this weather for above a fortnight and I have in a manner bin confin'd to a very narrow compass as long att least, but I will sett some body to work in order to obtain itt. J[ohn] Hed[worth] is perhaps more steddy than you expected but less than I did imagin. We have severall ships upon the coast off France, a handsome squadron to the west, besides what are upon your coast, att least the number mention'd. No [new] regim[ents] but iff occasion we shall have foreigners. We shall send you p[er] first opportunity some St John's drops. Yesterday some off the Lancash[ire] people had like to have made their escape from Newgate by filing 4 iron bars but were timely prevented. Pray excuse this short account, my head is in great confusion, having had a late night. I have not had time to read over nor correct but you will make up the defects off ....

1.   Government forces had entered Perth on 1 February and were now pursuing the Jacobite army northwards, forcing the Pretender to embark

on the 4th. Argyll was still in command but, as this letter indicates, Cadogan succeeded in claiming most of the credit.

142

9th Feb[ruary] 1715/6

I must take things as they occurr to my memory. Lord Will[iam] has drawn a *bill on you pay[able] to Mr Gilroy's order, on account off coals he had laid in about a 12 month agoe and also for what was due to Strowd the waterman for Lond[on] duty on the 2 h[ogsheads] wine you sent him up about the same time. This bill is [£]48 9[s] 6d. Mr Gilroy desires I would inclose itt to the Capt[ain]. Ten to one if that lord has advised you off itt. As I promised in my last I would exert my self in behalf off your Northumb[erland] capt[ain] as also Sir W[illiam] Williams's friend, though God knows little able att this time to stirr abroad. Away went my father and I Wednesday morn[ing] to try if we could meet Lord Lum[ley]. When we came to the house he had not bin gon to bed four hours before from the Duke Mount[agu's] masquerade. Lord Sc[arborough] was gon out, but before our coach had turn'd from the door, in came the latter in his chair [and] took us in. We chatted over severall things; he readily undertook to speak to Mr Walp[ole]. I recommended you heartily to him and desired he would doe itt without loss off time, but least his memory should fail, I wrote him a letter this day and inclosed the persons' names with their characters etc. and the places vacant. We proceeded to Lord W[illiam's]; he had likewise bin att the masquerade and not stirring though past 11. Thence to Lord Sommers, who was confin'd to bed by the gout and see no company. I shall take the liberty to remind Lord Sc[arborough]. There is no getting speech off Walp[ole] by such chubbs [*i.e.* inexperienced rustics] as we. They have more bysiness on their hands than they can turn their hands to. I thank you for your very kind letter which came to hand just as I was going to bed. The news itt contain'd reviv'd my heart. I did not design to discharge you as my principall and sole officer off intelligence when I wrote to hear from your northern correspond[ent]; 'twas only on account off expedition for itt runs in my head that the Edinburgh letters came in generally the day after yours were sent to Lon[don], and

that was the sole reason. I can't say I should be sorry iff
Dougl[as] should carry his point in that county. Though I am
much so that the gentlemen should not have come to an earlyer
resolution to Clav[ering] St[ella]. 'Tis a great hardship on us and
lett me tell you 'twill be a greater on them selvs, since the dealers
will grow yearly in their dem[ands] off *praemium. There is not
one concern in the river save Team that gives less than 12d p[er]
*cha[ldron] and that I think is H[utton] and B[enwell] and theirs
is about 9d. Had I apprehended that they would not have
accepted Stella att a reasonable r[ent], I should have struck in
with number ten who were eager about her after our meeting att
the K[ings] Head. How farr they are since ingaged to Tanfield,
B[ucks]nook, Byermore etc. I shall not know till begining next
week. I sent Mr Gil[roy] down to inquire but they wer all
dispers'd before he gott there. If they be preingaged as above
and have reason to suspect (since they have wrote down to know
what quantitys those concerns have above bank [*i.e.* on the
surface] and what their dayly workings are), in such case I must
publish to all dealers little and great that they shall have 12d
p[er] chal[dron]. This seems unavoidable, though my father as
well as Gilroy seem very apprehensive that will considerably
lessen the *vend off M[ain] T[eam], otherwise they must
advance ....

143

25th Feb[ruary] 1715/6

I am much in your debt and doubt the arrear would grow
insufferably if I did not attempt to lessen itt as oft as my health
will give leave. Therfore accept off all imperfect accounts. I am
not without hopes off getting the list [of prisoners] you have so
long desired, also a copy off Piers[on's] confession; these am
promised from Mr M[asterma]n. When this gentlem[an] went
down to Lanc[ashire] he had no list, being told that the
commanding officer would give him one. When he came he
d[elivered] him in figures the numb[er] off prisoners, so that this
gentlem[an] was obliged to ride to Lancast[er], Preston, Wiggan
and Chester and there make one, so that I might have sollicited
long enough 'ere I got one here.

I have bin these ten days past more disorder'd than ever. This hum[our] from my leggs has got possession off my head and stomack, and for want off rest find myself feavorish. I kept in my close quarters for 3 or 4 days but not finding the least relief, I steal out now and then to the next street and the Rowe where I spend half an hour. I am so restless and uneasy that I cann't rellish conversation, nay a glass off wine does not goe down with a tast. This hinders me from seeing Lord Sc[arborough] though am not a little sollicitous to hear off his success, as also Tom G[ibon's] in behalf off your friend. I shew'd Mr Fr[eke] Dan[iel]'s about letting the coll[iery] and after itt was transmitted to the Fields. The first is much delighted att the prospect, and bid me by last post to write to Dan with orders to close the bargain and he would take care to gett the Master should certifye to the court the necessity there was off disposing after this manner; upon which an order will be made to justifye the [action]. You know that I am perfectly passive since that gentlem[an] has accepted the guardienship, and my business is to give my reasons pro and con and then leave itt to determination off superiors. What makes me the easier in this case is that the project (as Dan writes) has your approbation intirely. As we were before I never was free from continuall complaints from masters and *fitter during the summer season, and then in the winter plagued how to gett moneys from the fitter to keep the works going and men from starving. If I had proceeded with the Billinsg[ate] proposalls they might have raised objections ag[ainst] the coal, that they were not the same that were stipulated for; they would pin us down to ¼ Coleb[urn] and no other *mixture, and even off those a good p[art] they expected should goe to the *pans. Their *bills must be taken and sure I am the longest creditt must be given them. Further they would but ingage for a year. We were to find moneys to work and *lead. Wheras by Dan's we have nothing to doe but recieve the growing r[ents] as also for our dead stock [of coal] att pitts and *steath, allowing a reasonable time to the *undertakers to turn itt into money. I hope he has discoursed over the whole particulars with you; for my part I know only that the rent is to be £200 or 250 [a] year, know not the name off the party, iff one or more persons be concern'd. Mr F[reke] says that if she be not lett the court will certainly order her to be *laid in. Thus I have told you all I know on this head. Must add a word in relation to your coal polliticks. I think your notion

about deferring the granting to Wortley an additional term off
*way leave after the expiration off the 7 or 8 years yet to come
[is a good one]. Itt will be a good curb upon their lofty concerns
and iff success attend the tryall on the Swallwell wasts [*i.e.*
Whickham common], you will have them in a cloven stick. And
I hope 'twill be in my father's power to prevent laying a *way
over Blackb[urn]. My father told me he had severall times
recommended to the Coll[onel] care to secure any *p[arts] off
that concern as they were likely to fall, att any rate [*i.e.* price]. I
hope some of you will be able to strike in if my father or his
family can compass the half. I doubt not he would without any
previous stipulation make his acknowledgem[ents] and not act
so ungrateful a p[art] as the body off Regulators have don
towards somebody. Pray what have they don in your fav[our]?
Is there any one gratefull bounty that they have bestow'd? We
seem to live in a strange ungrateful age both from the publick as
well as private persons, off both which you have had a sufficient
tast. You may guess by the miscarriage off the officers'
representations from your parts when their coll[onel Hotham is]
a Member and may speak any day with the first ministers, that
want off success in matters off the like nature has not proceeded
from any supiness or neglect in your friends here. No I do assure
you, but 'tis more than probable that some body or other that
keeps behind the curtain comes by night and devours the seed
others have sown, so what cropp can be expected.

I have in short given you my poor thoughts on yours off the
19th. My head is so confused that I can but guess the meaning
off some parts off it. I come last to that off the 21st inst. Why
will you putt yourself to such a charge on my score? I am
perfectly ashamed; can say no further on that subject than that
you seem resolved I shall never be out off your debt. The potts
when come to hand shall be disposed off as you direct; when
they are broach'd, I will take the liberty off informing you off
their proof. I inclose a copy off yours to T[homas] G[ibson] as
you desired in one off your former. I wonder [a] gentlem[an]
who has the ear off the great men can't gett a certain person
call'd up to his post. Don't you frett your self to pieces about
the publick. What you hear from hence is generally false; the
faction have a new lye every day. I do assure you the Princess
[of Wales] would not so much as see the petitioning lady and the
Prince declared itt was not in his power to doe any service. The

lady way laid his Maj[esty] as he came from chappel Sunday last and upon her knees offerd her petition, which he refused to take and but told her he pity'd her unfortunate condition. You have heard that on Wednesday itt was caried up to both Houses. Lord W[illiam] promised to give you an account theroff by last post, as also the k[ing's] answer to the resolution off the Lords which was like to himself. You have here the dying speech. Have but patience and all will do well. My garden is overrun with weeds, this will require time to glean them and can but be don gradually. There is a plentifull cropp but few laborers.[1] If you heard but Mr F[reke] discours on the Reg[ent's] menagem[ent] I believe you would be off his opinion, which is that considering the disposition off the people off France in fav[our] off the Pretender, he could not avoid doing even more than he has done to secure himself and his own interest in that kingdome. There are secrett springs in all gov[ernments] which are not to be fathom'd. In short I shall conclude with this observation, that had he bin hearty for him he could have given him much greater assistance. There is a superior power above all and which governs and decrees future events; on that great goodness we must depend. So adieu, I scarce know what I write but remain always....

[P.S.] I see Mr Fr[eke] this day who has nothing to add to his former sentim[ents] and orders for letting, which you will acquaint Dan[iel] least I should not have time.

1. Frantic efforts were made to save the Jacobite lords from execution, ranging from private appeals to public intercession by the House of Lords. George I compromised by respiting three of the executions; since Nithsdale escaped, only Derwentwater and Kenmuir went to the block on 24 March. This hesitant approach to 'weeding out' Jacobitism had clearly provoked Cotesworth, never the most patient of men.

144

6th Mar[ch] 1715/6
past 6 att night

Ab[out] half an hour ago Mr Fr[eke] did me the hon[our] to smoak a pipe with me; told me he came on purpose to acquaint me that last night the affair off the wag[gon] way was brought to

a period, that not only Wr[ight] had withdrawn himself from
being a party, but also Lady C[lavering] and Proctor and as I
understood him all the rest acknowledge the Ald[erman's] title
[to Whickham]. For particulars I referr you to C[harles]
S[anderson] this post and congratulate you on your success. He
ask'd me if I wrote to you this post. If I did, he charg'd me to
make his complim[ents] for your kind present and thinks
himself not a little obliged by your ready complyance in
relinquishing your [*waykeeping] bargain, which otherwise
might have destroy'd the letting the colliery by which his pupill
will reap a certain yearly profit, and obliged me to acquaint you
with the above success. Last night I tasted your pott off charrs. I
have seen and tasted more than one from other hands, but not
to be compared to this which is perfection. I believe that which I
sent into the Fields made its appearance this day before the
Duke off Marlb[orough]. Lady Powl[ett] sent hers away to
Baron Bernsdoff, who was not a little instrumentall in procuring
a teller's place. My father sent down last week ½ pint St John's
drops for you in a box Mr Wait was sending to Ra[lph]
Feathersone. Lett inquiry be made after them. The town will
needs talk Lord Chan[cellor] out but I hope without grounds.
His misfortune is the want off the Fr[ench] tongue. His
Maj[esty] was att the House; what pass'd have not learnt but
Wakelin see him return thro' the Park att 3, never brisker nor
more lively. Were I but in plight once I would trouble that great
man (who has not dealt with you as he ought) till he did grant
my request, or rather sollicitt till they were weary off me. I never
heard a syllable off Lord Will[iam's] motion in the House. 'Tis
all a shamm. Ol[ey] D[ouglas's] petition is putt off *sine die*.
Lord Cornwa[llis] discovers; what the others doe I know not.
This much I doe, that I am more certainly ....

[P.S.] Dick R[idley] is the sole *undertaker mention'd.

145

4th Apr[il] 1716

   I am so taken up with phisicking night and day that I have not
so much as a moment's leisure to think off business. This instant
I am so grip'd that my face is enough to sower a barrell off bear,

so that I don't know how to sett about answering either off
yours. Accept off thanks in the first place for both your favors.
The proposed *way cross Darw[ent] I look'd upon as next to
impracticable, if itt were only the difficulty off securing itt
against sudden floods. I can't pretend to judge off itt, having
only a distant idea off the situation; however by your prudent
forecast in securing Anderson's and Thornley interests you have
so cast their bowle off its byass that there is no prospect off its
ever coming near the jack.[1] I concluded that Silvertopp had bin
so ingaged with his friends in [Octo]ber last that he would not
have bin able to show his head, but he is a cunning, crafty blade.
Lady B[owe]s tho' a timorous woman, yet will not part with a
penny to any friend unless she have att least its worth. Old
Wortley perfectly distracts her; she gives out that he is actually
working 8 off her pitts in the broken myne [*i.e.* cutting coal
from the pillars left to support the roof], that he will not suffer
her agent to view, that he will certainly thrust her [*i.e.* collapse
the colliery by weakening the roof supports] to the vengeance.
She adds that he and J[ohn] O[rd] are two off the greatest
r[ogues] that ever a county was blest withall; they will by right or
wrong come att means to purchase estates, but att last must goe
to the D[evi]l. I presume the new invention you went to see is
design'd to be fix'd above Ironside's house in the wood. The
Coll[onel] writes me word that they had sunk about 8 fathom
below the m[ain] coal att Farnacres and 2 fath[oms] att another
pitt. He owns she is troublesome and expensive, but att this rate
we shall loose this year before we gett a pitt coal'd. Why don't
we fall upon the Ald[erman's] liberty (who I rejoice is better)?
The m[ain] c[oal] must be drain'd there I should think, as much
as ever will be. When I am ingaged I don't love to sitt still. Tis
above 3 weeks that I wrote to Peter for closing his books this
year to clap [*i.e.* place] the £260 to Coal Chamber account,
which we hope sooner or later will be reimbursed. I had a letter
last Monday from Dan[iel]; he is sadly in the miff and hup't
[hipped?]. He wishes he had never ingaged in the matter. I am
sure to have my head in my hand if this bargain miscarry. Mr
Fr[eke] never sees the post but inquires iff an end be not putt to
the lease. Therefore must begg off you to lend your assistance in
forwarding. I write to Dan this post and incourage him. I tell
him that J[ohn] Bull[ock] is the man I propose to take a view
every 14 days in the Inf[ant's] behalf, that the charge may be 5

or 6 guin[eas]; that if Weatherly would take a moderate sallary as steward I thought itt might not do amiss. He is used to the ten[ants], knows perfectly what allowances and bargains were made with the ten[ants] etc. and what were the terms to be perform'd. If £10 or 12 would doe, he might deserve that. There is a good deal off writing etc. As to a gen[eral] liberty to the ald[erman Ridley] off *leading any coals, I never did consent but for leading down that pitt which was led from the Gr[and] Lease and those from Hedley Fell, provided our ten[ants] were to be employ'd in the same, and no farther. I read the ald[erman's] letter to my father and Mr Fr[eke] as also Daniell's; they both did agree that such a liberty might enable the lessee to make our Chopwell reputation and the better to perform his bargain. Upon this the Guardian orderd me to write to the ald[erman] and Dan[iel] to that purpose, but they are to be restrain'd from the use off the way for any other coals, save as above.

When the new act comes into the house, Mr Fr[eke] will discourse and inform his friends with the reall design and I hope some way or other to gett Mr G[ibson] possess'd.[2] My Lord Will[iam] has appointed a day every week for severall by past to wait on Mr W[alpole] by this gentleman's own appointm[ent]. When we came, the day was putt off till that day 7 night, and so from time to time till he kept his bed and I am affraid will never gett abroad again.[3] If he doe he shall see your inclosed; if not one off the Secretarys shall, tho' I wish to better effect. Dear friend had I had yours before had given an answer to the ald[erman], your sence off the matter would have influenced me. But after having given the word, honour does oblige, tho' it does not a certain lady [Clavering] with whom you have a contest. I don't see that we shall be thank'd scare for all our pains and endeav[ours] to preserve this scurvy trade and that is but sorry wages. Adieu honest Will, lett me begg off you to dispatch this lease for I shall be teaz'd to death by the Guardian till itt be don....

1.   Lady Clavering's apparent acquiescence in the Chancery ruling that upheld Ramsay's rights over Whickham Common concealed a determination to circumvent the disputed territory by constructing a parallel waggonway west of the Derwent. The practical difficulties to which Liddell refers, however, still made it necessary to use part of the old way and so the dispute continued.

2.   This represents the early stages of legislation passed in 1717 to improve the navigation of the River Wear.

3.   Walpole had fallen desperately ill of fever and was not fully recovered until well into May.

146

10th April 1716

Believe me I am in very bad circumstances off health. I have a constant and violent pain in my right kidney as also in my bladder, insomuch that I am obliged to take quieting potions without which can't gett to sleep; that added to my old complaints is enough to confound any constitution. My life is very uneasy on this score and I can't think off business, much less transact any. Though I seldom fail you. I read over yours this evening to the Guardian as also Dan[iel's], who bids me return thanks to both for the zeal express'd on behalf off his pupil. Your observations which relate to Weatherly make itt intirely necessary that a *viewer should be appointed; as I think I told you before, if J[ohn] Bull[ock] would accept he was the man we approv'd off. Mr Fr[eke] thinks the article which fixes the *way the nearest to the certainty by leaving itt in the same condition as to quantity and quality, a very good one, but desires that the lease be proceeded upon with all expedition and dispatch. If Sand[erson] and Colson will not be concern'd upon these terms or such like, what will become off the ald[erman], who will he apply to? I remember 4 years agoe Weatherly proposed our taking Hedley Fell. Mr Clav[ering] had meetings on that subject with Mr Cole every audit but was putt off from time to time till the duke's intentions were known, which never could be had. Att that time Weatherly was off opinion that we might work 2[00] or 250 [*tens] good *ship coal. I remember Mr Cole, when press'd by Cha[rles] S[anderson] to lett, said that his lord expected 10s p[er] ten rent and to be bound to work yearly what would make the rent certain [£]150 a year, which we could not comply with. If the ald[erman] has any way [out?] off the bargain, in what a condition would the heir be? Or even if itt ingaged us in a Chancery suit, what would become off the ten[ants] etc? You know my short hints. I can't add more than wishing you success in your affair and remain ....

147

19th April 1716

Your last was the most disagreable I have rec[eived] from you
for a long time, since itt brings the news off the departure off
that worthy honest man the Ald[erman], who to the last
withstood the evill designs off the faction and approved himself
a true friend to his first principles, I mean the present
establishm[ent], even in the most dangerous times; and to his
family he shew'd but a just regard, by his kind remembrance off
you and yours, to that which you had so well merited att his
hands. May you and your descendants long live to enjoy what he
has intail'd upon you.[1] You have lost a dear relation and give me
leave to say I have likewise [lost] one who honour'd me with his
friendship, which I mightily valued, and to whose memory I
shall allways pay the greatest veneration. Last night I gott to Mr
Honywood's [election] committee for an hour. I was scarce well
seated till was accosted by your Chester Member [Hedworth].
He began to complain that he was represented as a T[or]y to
which I gave little answer; after this succeeded a complaint that
you never had taken the oaths to this Gov[ernment] nor to the
last, that he had told the same to Lord W[illiam], who indeed
inquired off me if you had. I told the lord that doubtless you
had and on the other gentleman's persisting in the contrary, I
acquainted him that you were not a stranger to the penaltys you
incurred by the want off qualifying as the act directed, and
desired he would excuse me if I did not come into his
sentim[ents] off your neglect. From this he turn'd his discourse
upon the colliery off Chester wasts, in which he heard the
Coll[onel], you and I were ingaged, as he told me about a month
agoe (off which I think I touch'd either to the Coll[onel] or
yourself; am sure did to my father). He gave me to understand
that he had compremis'd differences with Mr Allen, that he had
secured the *way leave, yet was willing to treat with the
Coll[onel] (but would never with W[illiam] C[otesworth]) about
terms off taking the leases off his hands etc.; ask'd me if I had
wrote about itt. I reply'd I thought I had but was sure no answer
came. He press'd me to come to visitt him before he sett out for
the countrey, which he propos'd to doe in 3 weeks. I believe the
gentlem[an] was a little in his cups for I could scarce gett away
from him. I wrote to Dan[iel] two times last post att 11 at night,

wherin I told him that the view of sleepers ought to be made and computed, as near a valuation putt on them as possible and that there ought to be a consideration enter'd from the time the first view was taken. He mentions Dryden only on our part [as *viewer], which I represented wrong, because a case off mortality there ought to have bin 2 att least for us. I knew mine would not entirely please him. Pray continue as much as you can to bring these matters to a conclusion; itt will be great ease and comfort to me during my present very bad circumstances, which are much aggravated from the great pains in my kidneys which the d[octor] and apoth[ecary] both seem to apprehend to be some stone. I paid £25 for a horse today, they tell me trotts hard but there was but Hobson's choice. Adieu, I remain ....

1   Ramsay left the bulk of his estate to Cotesworth, with relatively minor legacies to his other relations. This transformed Cotesworth's social standing and he began preparations to turn over his business as a merchant and tallow chandler to his clerk.

148

10th May 1716
past 12

Yesterday was the first day I gott into the Fields for a mouthfull off fresh air since Tom Shafto and I walked in Kensington Gardens. I have struggl'd with a stout feavor ever since which still hangs upon me. I was in hopes had gott the better off itt but last night I did not gett 2 hours sleep, and this minute the d[octor] is come to visitt and order'd me to swallow a dose off opium, which is don. I am extreemly faint in spirit, swett vastly and in short almost dissolv'd. This made me lay hold off the opportunity (though my letter does not goe till to morrow) least I should be disabled then, to return you my best thanks for your last as well as former fav[ours], which must be ever acknowledged with a gratefull sense. Yesterday was the first time I sett pen to paper, when I wrote to honest Peter and inclosed him Mr James Clav[ering's] *bill on you for [£]50 [payable] ten days after sight. Itt has laid by me ever since I have bin ill. I desired him to discount itt with you on account off wagg[on] way. Dan[iel] is much in the miff and desires to be excused from acting further in the affair of the view off the *way. This made me desire Peter that he would wait on the Coll[onel] some day att your house, and I did not doubt but your 3 heads would be able to putt that matter upon a sure foot. He will read you what I wrote. I earnestly covett to see an end made; Mr Fr[eke] presses upon me why I don't execute the lease. What I wrote to Dan[iel] related to a former I wrote him a month agoe att least, wherin I incouraged him to proceed; that as the ald[erman, Ridley] was obliged to leave the way in every respect as he finds itt, what had his new *undertakers to apprehend iff they did perform their part? If they did not design to doe itt, we must come upon the lessee and he upon them. I shall be glad to hear from you. Your lines revive me much; are much more so than a cordiall blister, to use the d[octor's] words, that Wakelin clap't on my back a foot square. I leave this open till to morrow, when you shall hcar further how itt fares with ....

[P.S.] What tydings from Farnacres? Is any good to be expected; if there be I shall be agreably balked [*i.e.* disappointed]. Adieu. 11th: I have had but another scurvey night. The feavor lyes in my head and stomack and a load on my spirits. The d[octor] talks off sending me to Hampsted for the air. I have bought a horse att Smithf[ield] att the d[octor's] pressing instance, which cost me [£]25. I don't approve of him, he trotts hard and a very plain nagg.

149

24th May 1716

I thank you for your last fav[our] but tis impossible I should keep touch in answering. ['Tis] the morning or indeed till 4 a clock before my German spa be wrought quite off, during which time am neither to read nor write; they don't pass as formerly neither doe I reap the like benefitt. Every other afternoon att 4 my horse is att door and I ride out till near 8. The other days I must return a visitt with the old gentlem[an]. Thus you see how I am employed and iff I did not trespass sometimes on my d[octor's] rules, I should never have an opportunity off the least correspondence with any friend, and when I am drove to that extremity, farewell to one off the comforts off life. I can barely keep on foot, though have followed pretty strictly my doctor's prescriptions. He ordered me to take a new house which is just on the back off where we are, called East Sreet. We have a little more room, a better neighbourhood but I can't say so much off the air. We enter att Michaelmas to inhabit though our term begins from Midsummer. The rent [£]45 p[er] ann[um] besides all manner of taxes etc. If I hold out this year I shall not fear a [bankruptcy] statute herafter. You have abundance off people that don't wish well to your undertakings, but your success in this great commission for the Wear will make some off them frett like gumm'd taffety. Farnacres you know I never had a stomack too. The expence will goe near to break us, which made me in severall off mine to the Capt[ain] and your self press beginning with Whickham, which might in some measure help to alleviate the exp[ense] off the other. As to Blackb[urn's] 8th [*part] with the other fields, I was press'd hard for my thoughts theron. I said itt was better to referr itt to those below but that would not pass for an answer; so then I told my mind which was that if Blackb[urn] could be had upon a dearer rent single [i.e. without a partnership with the Wortleys], I should preferr itt but still desired itt might be recommited. Pray who were the persons that viewed the *way with you? I thought itt had bin one of them when I see by Dan[iel] that he had employ'd one off our old wrights. I wrote to him that I could not approve off any one that had bin employ'd by Lowry, since we were so abused by him and them. You had I dare say a great satisfaction in the company off your favorite gen[eral, Cadogan] which could not fail off proving a mortification to some people. I believe I could tell you a secrett relating to that gentlem[an], for which all true Brittons must ever have a due regard to him, but I have not time. Our Were water friend ought to be remember'd when an opportunity offers. I have discoursed several Members about the forfeitures; they all agree a clause should be added but none I hear off will undertake to bring itt in. They say 'tis the business off the ministry, who have not fail'd being advised and recommended off itt. Such coolness makes me sick. Adieu honest Will, I am always....

[P.S.] If any choice white Lisbon be to be had in your town pray send me up 3 doz[en] and I shall be accountable. My distemper is gott such hold off my stomack that the strongest wines seem not such to me.

150

7th June 1716

I thank you for yours by yesterdays post and the pains you
have taken about that unfortunate concern off Chopwell. I have
not heard a syllable from the Coll[onel]; perhaps Fryday's may
bring a line. Ba[rtholemew] Scott has had an account from
Brummell that the £50 *note sent to you some time ago on
Snowden would be paid; if on tender itt be not, he desires the
originall may be return'd. I don't see but the money due for
*way keeping during the intervall off the 2 views belongs to you;
that you will discourse over with honest Peter for Dan[iel] is not
well pleased. But lett us consider how that may affect the first
view, for will itt not be an argum[ent] for setting that aside if
ever itt should be contested, since by the article when they are
enter'd on the lease we were to appoint *viewers? Perhaps there
may not be the least weight in this objection. I must own I am a
perfect stranger to the schem's off our great men; they surpass
my understanding and that off all I converse with. Our friend
[Freke] att the Colledge knitts his browes and grows very
peevish. That worthy gentlem[an] can't forbear laying about
him even in the publick coffee houses. Two, at the most 3, off
our great men who preside att the helm rule the roost. I believe
our friend in the Fields [Cowper] has not great sway in matters.
'Tis only my own conjecture, therfore don't mention. I wish
that letter you design for the Lord [Scarborough?] may have a
better effect than former, which deserv'd another return. I don't
doubt the inclination off the [Tory] party. I waited on Lord
Parker yesterday about a small commission he gave me some
days ago, to lay him in ½ h[ogshead] off Peter's wine. I sent
him 2 pints that morn for a tast, which he with a Lancash[ire]
gentleman had gott before them and were passing their
judgem[ent]. He inquired how all friends in the north did and
how we stood affected. I told his lordsh[ip] that I had just then
rec[eived] my letters and had an account that the disposition was
the same there as itt was in Sep[tember] last; and the other
gentlem[an] assured him that itt was the like in Lancash[ire]
and other adjac[ent] countys. That lord said that if they were
resolved off giving fresh disturbances, he could wish they would
begin before Parl[iament] be up. What relates to the town off
Newc[astle] I communicated all along to some whose interest itt

is to stirr in that affair [of Walker estate], as also to severall Members, and don't fail reminding them. I am perfectly sick to see matters thus menaged. I paid your complim[ents] to the Essex [Member, Honywood] immediately after he was admitted. Nobody knows iff the K[ing] goes [to Hanover] or not. The lady who was sent up in custody has no reason to boast off fav[ours]; our relation is civil to her, but every advantage she can make by her new alliance [with Pitt], depend upon't she will find her self mistaken.[1] The weather is exceeding hott. I need not tell you how itt affects....

1. Lady Clavering had refused to renounce her claim to *wayleave over Whickham Common and had therefore been committed to the Fleet prison for contempt of court.

151

19th June 1716

My good friend's afternoon sermon as also his by the following post lye now before me, for both which fav[ours] I own my self under great obligation; but in a more particular manner for the inclosed from the Lancashire travell[er] which is wrote with so much good judgem[ent] and observation that one may readily guess att whose feet he had bin bred. In short I shew'd itt to severall off our friends who were so taken with itt that they seem'd to question my veracity in affirming that itt was wrote and pen'd by a north country school boy, not above 14 years off age.[1] But I shall forbear inlarging upon this head least you should accuse me off flattery. Therfore shall proceed to answer yours off the 10th inst. I wrote some time ago to Peter and told him that the money for the *way ought to be placed to your creditt, and desired he would call on you about that affair. I have not to this hour heard a syllable from Coll[onel] who has both hands and head full off business, and to want off opportunity 'tis I attribute his silence. Lady Cl[avering] has mett with a ruffle in her last motion; I hear from a friend off hers that she designs to send down an agent to wait the issue off my father's tryall with the bi[shop of Durham] att York assize. Baron Montague is the sole judge that goes the northern circuit, which would make my father very uneasy but that he relyes on the goodness off his cause and ability off his councell. Could you gett a fair gripe of Fellon and that the water *undertakers be able to perform their part, I say that and the Park, I should think, att this time off day would be full out as valuable as H[utton] and B[enwell]. I fancy when once you begin with them, you will goe near to see the bottom off her as soon almost as we shall that off our present undertaking in Farnacres. I can't mention that word but itt putts me in mind off the obligations you have loaded me with in providing for my interest. My father told me the Coll[onel] had secured for him some excell[ent] new Lisbon whites, which was the reason I gave you the trouble off spurring out a little for your old friend, but since there is no good [wine] to be had we must make a shift with a little good sherry to supply the defect.

The particular account you give off the disturbance in your adjoining corpor[ation] between the D[utch] soldiers and the keelmen, looks as iff there had bin a design laid by the [Tory] party to have fomented fresh disturbances. God be thank'd that itt ended so well, and as for the case off the coif and his pinner [*i.e.* the serjeant-at-law, Cuthbert], I should not have bin displeased had both been besh[itted] up to the ears. Pray thee dear Will take a particular care off your self, gett home betimes and never travell without a sturdy blade and an oaken towell [*i.e.* cudgel]. The party are insolent to a degree; they seem resolv'd to try if they can bully our most gracious and his well wishers. I hear he is not to be disswaded from going to Hanover etc. and setts out this day or to morrow 7 night. He certainly has some great projects in view off settling and acquiring new people. Will, I want an evening's King's Head converstion with you. Pray read the B[ishop of] Ely's thankgiv[ing] sermon and another off Bi[shop] Hoadley's before his Maj[esty] the 29th ult. Your friends [the clergy] I perceive left the prelate to end his collation without, though itt was usher'd in with, church musick. Frank Gast[rell, bishop of Chester] has bin visiting within his diocess, your archb[ishop] has bin doing the like. Arch[bishop] Thom[as Tension] was a rock and a stout one; I wish I could say half as much off his successor. By the account your last gives off the proceedings in your town the 10th June, by oak branches etc., itt is plain itt has bin concerted aforehand all over the nation more or less.[2] Att York they were so insulting as the Lord May[or] and his brethren were forced to use their autority to disperse; they have secured 4 or 5 off the principles, which 'tis to be hop'd will not fail off having their reward in due season. What has the Gov[ernment] gott hitherto by itts superabund[ant] clemency? We are dispised by the criminalls themselvs. I am invited to Sir John Colebatch's to diner; iff have time shall send you a copy off p[art] off a letter which relates to you. P.S. I inclose you the paper promised. We are drinking your health in a tast off the best claret I have mett with this year. A h[ogshead] was sent him directly from Ireland. Adieu, I am ....

[P.P.S.] 7 att night. I just now see Lady B[owes] who then came directly from Lady C[lavering]. She told me that the latter had promised to join interests with her, but she look'd upon't so very chimericall as would not hear her story out. She vows as soon as she getts into the countrey will pull up the way that lyes in Fawdens field. And added that Mr P[itt] had bin with her and desired to know if she would grant him *way leave through her liberty; she told him yes, if she lik'd the terms. He gave her a week's time to consider off demands. When he came again, the consideration expected was £1000 a year; the gentlem[an] turn'd upon his heel and walk'd out off the house, since which she has neither seen nor heard from him.

1. Cotesworth's son had taken advantage of a school holiday to go on a tour of Lancashire with some friends; on his return he sent home a detailed account of the Preston campaign and Jacobite activity. He was in fact about 16 years old at the time.

2. May 29, 'oak-apple day', commemorated the restoration of the monarchy in 1660. On this occasion it was marked by both clerical and popular wrangling over the legitimacy of the Hanoverian succession.

152

26th June 1716

I rode out off town yesterday about half a doz[en] miles and din'd with our friend Mr Tomson, and in the evening att my return was wellcom'd home by yours, which came safe and brings Scott's *bill; which I was glad to see for that fellow made such a noise and complaint ffor want off itt as was not to be indured. The mistake off calling itt a £50 bill was soly mine. I doe assure you Mr Walp[ole] is no stranger to your recommendation. I had employ'd severall off my friends, att

certain distance off time, to lay before him Ned M[awso]n's
case; nay even since his last illness gott cos[in] Honyw[ood] to
remind him, but these great men will bide [*i.e* resist] teazing.
However this your last supplication by Lord W[illiam] I hope
may prove more effectuall. My father and I design waiting on
his lordship to morrow where ten to one he shews me your
originall. I shall perhaps see Sir W[alter] Y[onge] this afternoon
and shall speak to him as you desire about Selby. This knight's
son is upon the point off committing matrimony with a niece off
Sir Gil[bert] Heathcote's. The information I gave you was as I
had itt but since have had a more certain account; therfore you
will correct itt and read Geo[rge] Pitt instead off Lady
Clav[ering]. What relates to colliery, I mean the bringing to
reason the great man [Wortley], deserves a due consideration;
and as my father and uncle are partners itt will require a joint
meeting, which I shall take care off before the first leavs the
town and I shall putt them both upon speaking their minds
freely and openly. Your opinion off Fellon and the Park, and
the ability off the water catchers to perform what they
undertake, is my sheet anchor in the coal trade and on what I
soly depend, as also on Whickham upper seams off which I all
along entertain'd a favourable opinion; but as to Farnacres I
never could, and have not as yet any reason to alter my first
conception. I have seen Sir Walter and tooke notice off what
you recommended; he assured me itt should be done. I shew'd
likewise our friend Roger [Gale] the copy off yours to Lord
W[illiam]; his advice was to lay itt before the Board off
Treasury, Mr Wal[pole] being taken ill off his old distemper the
stone. While I was discoursing that gentlem[an] att the Grecian,
in came Lord W[illiam who] immediately took out yours which I
read without taking any notice. He was att a loss what to doe. I
proposed laying itt before the board, which he seem'd to
acquiesce in and promised to doe itt. There it was I mett with the
capt[ain's] son off Hexham, who rec[eived] a letter from
Newc[astle] with an account off John Bell's death; this was so
remarkable a piece that I believe if true you had not omitted itt.
I have made your complim[ent] to Sir John Coleb[atch] who
rec[eived] it very kindly and desired to return his best thanks.
The Parl[iament] is prorogued this day to the 7th Aug[ust] next.
His Maj[esty] I believe will sett out next Thursday for
Holland....

[P.S] I don't know if the Cap[tain] had gott any Lisbon [wine] or if he had only the prospect off getting.

153

3 July 1716

I wish I had better news to send my good friend but such as itt is you shall have. I think I have often in my former told you that I was sorry to see that our great men att helm did not draw steddily together. Those breaches were soon after made up and I heartily wish that the present, which threatens not a little, were well blown over. His Maj[esty] thought fitt on Fryday or Saturday last to dismiss his grace off Argyle from his service, which has inraged the North Brittains to a degree; the Earl off Ila laid down att the same time. I can't learn who joins in with them. This perhaps may deferr his Maj[esty's] voyage till itt be known what the consequences.[1]

P.S. Just now 'tis talk'd as iff Lord Orford would lay down, but I hear since that he is resolv'd to continue steddy to his friends in this extremity and therfore will not quitt. Lord Devon[shire] has resign'd his staff but, 'tis given out, in order to be made Presid[ent] off the Councell. We are all in the dark; but certain 'tis that these things must give his Maj[esty] a very great disturbance and a shock I doubt to the Whigg interest. The Torys are very uppish and flatter themselvs they shall come into play. But there is an overruling providence that governs the world. His Maj[esty] setts out on Saturday next. I have dwelt too long upon so mellancholly a subject. Nay I have I doubt lost the post. However was resolved that so zealous a man should not be ignor[ant] off what passes, as farr as comes to the knowledge off ....

1. Argyll was dismissed from his official posts on 29 June because he, like his brother the earl of Islay, opposed George I's determination to limit his son's powers as regent during his absence. The Prince's court began to be a focus for discontented Whigs, widening the splits within the party and the ministry.

154

19th July 1716

Tho' this rainy weather has affected me much, yet I can't
forbear giving a short tho' imperfect answer to your favours off
the 13th and 15th and shall begin with the first. Since a word off
publick affairs please you, I must tell you as a secrett that my
great friend [Cowper] and yours with whom you have
sometimes corresponded by letter [Townshend?] have not for
some time sett up their horses together; the reason I can't tell,
only guess att. Our new Secretary Mr Methwin is a person
universally respected; is a man off great abilitys and entirely
honest. Itt was told me as a secrett by a great lady that we should
(notwithstanding the endeavors of a party) find our guardien
George firm and reveted to his principles, which is no small
comfort to us, and if you will come up the next term I doubt not
you will see his Maj[esty] gayer than ever. As to the 2 justices'
behaviour [*i.e.* Ellison and Clavering] I don't so much admire
their conduct, especially his with whom I am intimately
acquainted. Tis all off a piece, equally unaccountable; but
indeed this instance is more flagrant the circumstances
consider'd, and when you had done him such a signall piece off
service and so lately that itt could not lapse his memory. As itt
has bin in former days as farr as those off our Saviour's, so itt
does discend to ours, some are for laying burthens upon their
neighb[ours], etc. I have all along thought you highly to blame
that you did not act from the begining. Pray to what purpose
was you putt into commission? Sure I am none can sway the
sword off justice more deservingly in every respect. I have long
and many years agoe thought that Ra[lph Lambton?] grew every
day more insupportable than other; off this I have given gentle
intimation to our friends here but no notice taken till the case
came to be their own.
Lord Will[iam] and the Royall Haberdasher din'd with me
yesterday; the first is almost reconcil'd to your advice and we
drank your health in a bumper off clarett. I shall doe what I can
for young Pierson; tho' wish my endeavors prove more
successfull than those in behalf off poor Ned, to the shame be itt
spoke off some in whose power itt is if they will but give the
word. They have heard off itt in both ears and I don't fail to talk
freely on that subject whenever I see people who are likely to tell

it again. Nay insomuch that itt was surmis'd by some off my friends that I should have a rebuke for so doing! I should not be sorry if a distress [*i.e.* official seizure] was made for then itt will be brought to a publick hearing, when the present supervisor's conduct will be sufficiently exposed. I meant nothing by P[it]t's having an agent att Yorke tryall further than iff the b[isho]p should prevail, how farr itt might be off service to his and Lady Clav[ering's] interests. Lady B[owes] sent for me and begg'd I would come to her. Am this moment return'd; found her full of rhumatick complaints. After the usuall manner rails against pious John [Ord], his masters and all the other agents. Hard names are very plentifull. She tells me that the court has orderd a number off *viewers to be chose, off each side an equall number, to represent the damages that have accrued by working the walls [of Hutton]; and to make use off her ladyship's own words, she says that Ant[hon]y L[eato]n told her that they had thrust her so close [*i.e.* caused so much subsidence] that he defy'd any body to gett farther than the shaft and consequently what report can be made? She can't gett one viewer that has not already bin corrupted by the adversary. That out off the 4 commiss[ioners] she had named, the other party had fix'd upon one off hers viz. Natt Hargrave, which she attributes to the neglect off her clerk in court or rather an underhand understanding. She blames sometimes her coz[in] By[ro]m. In short she makes herself one off the uneasiest creatures imaginable. My father and Mr Fr[eke] and Cha[rles] Sand[erson] I believe decamp on Monday; the latter goes no farther than York, the other 2 will continue in your neighb[our]hood as many months. Adieu, I am going to meet them in Red Ly[on] Street ....

[P.S.] Tom Gibson off your town complains heavily off his usage here.

155

Hamp[s]ted 6th Aug[ust] 1716

I am indebted to 2 off yours but before I begin to answer either off them, must have recourse to that of yours off the 15th ult. to the article which relates [to] young Pierson. As to Mr Cratcherode I have not the least acquaintance with him, which made me imploy Cha[rles] Sand[erson] to discourse him; but

finding I had not a satisfactory answer from that quarter, I gott
my cosen Pye one off the commiss[ioners] off our office to talk
the matter over with h[im], as I had done Mr Masterman before
fully. They both did agree that no such warr[ant] or order was
ever sign'd for his transportation but that if there had, the
young man had deserved richly by trifling with the k[ing's]
soll[icitor] in spending severall hours in taking his informations
which after he disdainfully refused to swear too. Therfore was
remanded to Chester goal, where he lay a week and still
persisted obstinate till the jury found the indictm[ent] and then
he craved leave to be admitted as an [king's] evidence; which
had itt not bin on account off my letter to Mr Masterman would
not have bin done, and in all probability he had swung for itt,
for they were highly provoked att his insolent behavior. Att
length Mr Mast[erman] admitted him but he was never made use
off as an evidence. I allow'd all this and told them he did not
deserve the least favor, but as he was ready (tho' not till the ax
was lifted over his head) yet I thought he should not meet with
harder usage than the others in the same circumstances (viz)
evidences, besides he might be servicable to them herafter.
The[y] both did assure me he would not be transported, but if
they heard off any fresh order for itt the[y] would endeavor to
putt a stopp to itt, at least acquaint me therewith.

I come in the next place to a word in answer to yours off the
22th ult[i]mo which does not please me att all. I don't admire
that Sir W[illiam] W[illiamson] should think off laying down
[his post]. Your Lord Sc[arborough] will undertake for every
thing and very free off promises, but yet I don't find any one
thing he compasses; 'tis not want off ability or interest to effect,
but I can't but suspect his grand privy councell[or, Carr]. Tis
ever since or before Christmas that I putt poor Ned's case stated
by my own pen into his hand as he desired, not daring to trust
his memory. After severall weeks expecting every day the success
and hearing nothing from him, I d[elivered] the like paper to his
son, who faithfully promised speciall care; from which time
have never bin admitted to see him, the answer was he was just
gon abroad or not stirring. But for further particulars must
referr you to my father, who was a joint soll[icitor] and
advocate in the case, and lastly Lord W[illiam] will give you an
account off what reply Mr W[alpole] gave him after reading
your letter; I think he answer'd and said nothing. Itt fretts me

not a little to see my maugh [*i.e.* brother-in-law, Ellison] side in
so much with the Lamb[tons] and their kindred in the favoring
injustly those who, had they itt in their power, would not fail to
sacrifice him and all his family. His flights are frequent and very
unaccountable, and itt is no less to find another gentleman
[Clavering] who I know you have bin extreemly servicable to,
even in time off greatest distress, that he should strike in with
them. I had a letter from him lately, part off itt amaz'd me; you
must promise me faithfully never to impart or divulge itt to no
man living but to my father. Trusting this preliminary is agreed
to, I shall give you that part off his letter word for word, as
follows. 'I think when Mr Fr[eke] is in the countrey had also
best lay before him that matter off the w[aggon] way which you
very well know was undertaken soly on my behalf and itt was;
and it was by your recommendation on that account it was not
lett to other *undertakers at less price and what I believe am able
to prove was [a price] more than what yearly was expended upon
itt, and therefore the advantage and proffitt was to be mine. As
I can prove under Mr C[otesworth's] own hand, there will be a
considerable summ due. And as you formerly wrote me, if I
desired itt [you] would write to him on this head; and that I
think may not be amiss now, for he's a person I willingly would
not have a quarrell with all. I can not compare this case better
than to the working the upper seams att Bensham, where a
certain friend off mine advanced moneys for carrying on the
works but he best knows what return he had.' This I must own is
extreemly shocking but such as 'tis you have itt, depending
upon't that itt shall never be discover'd. I have not given the
least answer, but when I doe itt shall be that since he thinks off
laying itt before Mr Fr[eke], I desire that you may be present so
that the case may be truly stated and that gentleman may not be
troubled with a rehearsing etc. I am glad we are likely in the
spring to have your company in town; before you come, I will
bespeak a box att the K[ing's] Head .... I come 3dly and last to
yours the 31st July, which by the bulk off itt att first frighted
me. The scheme of Capt[ain] Hall's seems grounded upon good
reason. All my friends are out off town, especially the family off
Lincoln's Inn Fields, who are gon into Hartfordshire for the
summer and when business calls them to Hampton Court they
goe cross country. Prince Eugene intends to attack the Turks
without loss off time. Pardon hast ....

156

6th Sep[tember] 1716

I made a tollerable shift during the continuance off the good weather but now that rains begin to fall in plenty, attended with a storm off wind, I find my old complaints revive apace, which putts me in mind off hastning to my winter quarters; and am come to a resolution off decamping hence next Saturday, proposing to lye that night in my new house in East Street, where you may direct your next, near Red Lyon Square. I know that in your own thoughts you blame me extremely that I am not more punctuall in my answers to yours. You know that there is but one friend that I can pretend to advise with on any occasion [Cowper] and that person spends his time altogether in the countrey and att Hampton Court, so that I could never meet with him; but hope a favorable opportunity will offcr now that I goe to town, and as soon as I have his thoughts on the subject you desired, you may depend shall be transmitted. I had a short congratulatory letter from Lord W[illiam Powlett] upon my father's success at York. He then was in dayly expectations off recieving a summons from you to meet att Richm[ond]. Poor man his money is generally spent, or the best part, before he recieves. Want off a little forecast and consideration must make him uneasy in his present circumstances. My lady sent me a message desiring when I wrote to his lordship that I would press him to lease out his myne. I believe this time 2 years both you and I urged him upon that head, but his terms were so high as no *undertaker would make an offer. I hope you will find him now more tractable. When he shew'd Mr W[alpole] your letter, that gentlem[an] made no other reply than by a smile. Patience is a noble virtue but such usage would make one believe that there was none left in the nation. G[eorge] Nix[on] is as profligate a wretch as any in Britt[ain]. Tis a pitty that a mistake in [proper] forme should skreen such a villain from having his deserts. The curate was nicely handl'd. I should have expected from the baron [Montagu] a loyall charge; that man is perfectly honest. If poor Ald[erman] W[hite] should happen to dropp, then the current off that corporation will goe in the [Tory] channell free and undisturbed. I should be glad to have an account off Farnacres' view with your observations theron. Your friend Mr Pitt setts forwards to morrow for the north and takes along with him Sam[uel] Deagle, the attorney. This last has a very fair character. I doubt not you will make that great man sensible off his former usage. You may make your own terms with him. Poor Hebdon will be a loss to more concerns than that off the Parke. A lady off my acquaintance was att Hampton Court last Monday; saw the Prince and Princess [of Wales] att dinner, who have wonderfully obliged all that part of the countrey by their civill demeanor. I do assure you now that the good lady is with child and is expected to lye in in Nov[ember] next, which must be very agreable to every true Britton, to none more than you ....

[P.S.] I believe our Chopw[ell] lessee [Ridley] is sick off his bargain; am sure his menager here is, Ald[erman] Featherston, who can't gett off their coals but att the price off Cully's, nay the masters will not load them.

157

East Street, 2d Oct[ober] 1716

For this fortnight or longer I have bin extreemly bad; a constant diziness in my head, sick att stomack and am apprehensive off a touch off the pallsy, being held much after the same manner I was 3 years ago. This makes me wish Sir John Coleb[atch]'s return. The other day I took away 21 ounces; the blood had not bin out off the vein 2 minutes till itt turn'd all blew and yellow. I took hiera picra every day but gave no relief. Yesterday T.Wakelin sent me a potion which had no great effect. To morrow he has order'd to drink purging waters with manna [a laxative] or some other equivalent. Believe me my good friend I have had much ado to keep afoot the latter part off the summer. I wish I be able to doe the like this fall. I am now sensible that a constitution when once broke thoroughly, as mine has bin, can never be united again. The learn'd with all their skill can but make patch'd work on't. Within this fortnight I wrote twice to you and transcribed in each a long paragraph from a quondam friend off yours; since which I have not had a line from you, which makes me apprehensive one or both might have miscarryed. By the same post I wrote to Peter to lett you have the ball[ance] off your account but before he did itt, that he should advise with the Guardien [Freke] and have his approbation, without which, as he is on the spott, I know itt would be reckon'd a presumption off the highest nature. I happen'd to fall in with Jemmy Clav[ering] att the coffee house last Sunday; he told me that he had heard that Mr Pitt and the Lady [Clavering] were upon a close treaty with you, which he hop'd would succeed. I replyd that if they did not stand in their own light, I doubted not off your inclinations and ability to serve both the gentlem[an] and lady. I hear Geo[rge] Old[ner] is upon his return, *re infecta*. However his project has obliged the Sunderland owners to admeasure, wheras if I mistake not that was in a great measure disused off last year. I wrote lately to the Coll[onel] about Farnacres and desired him to consider, now that he has a fair prospect off getting down a pitt about [Christ]mas, if some provision should not be made out off Whickham topp coal to help off with those stone coal, without which depend upon't they will not be marketable. I hope your Park water catchers have no diffidence off compassing what they proposed in relation to that concern. I again must repeat my thankfullness to you for all kind offers. What provocation was given the knight, att a late sitting, to [abuse] the honest chanc[ellor] to that degree? Has there bin any old grudge lying latent 'twixt them? No coals goe off so currently all this year as Mr P[itt's]. The dealers say that Bucks Nook comes fowl, which is occasion'd by *mixture; H[utton] and B[enwell] much crestfallen; M[ain] Team not much to be complain'd off; Clav[ering] St[ella] in worse repute than ever, seldom comes within 13d off Team; the Grand Lease abominable; Scotsw[ood] and Fellon att a low ebb; and Elswick not so much as once nam'd. Our friends are still in Hartfordshire and don't return till middle off this month; I hear nothing off the motion of those from your quarters, they like their entertainm[ent]. But if the weather be the same with you as 'tis here, they will have reason to repent they did not move sooner. I always forgett my self when I converse with you; I find no end till I come to that off my paper, which now calls on me to conclude ....

[P.S.] The [French] Regent seems very desirous off cultivating a strict frindship with us and there looks to be a good disposition towards peace in the north. When I can learn the certainty you shall hear further. However these have off a sudden raised stocks very high.[1]

1. Anglo-French negotiations were in progress, urged on by George I who wanted to concentrate his attention on the Baltic conflict. Much to his displeasure, the treaty was delayed by the ministers left in London.

158

9th Oct[ober] 1716

By yesterday's post I had a letter from a person who is a sort off a confident off Mr Cl[avering] wherin he expresses himself to this effect: 'Mr Clav[ering] shew'd me Mr C[otesworth's] letters to him about Chop[well] w[aggon] way and told me in gen[eral] yours ran in the same strains off assurances in his fav[our]. I represented to him (adds my author) and advised him to avoid noise, but after having bin with Mr C[otesworth] without being able to doe any good, he was resolved to come to extreams.' He talk'd over the matter with him. This gentlem[an, Clavering] own'd the greatest obligations in the world to me and that nothing else should have stopp'd his proceeding so long; but his circumstances were such that he could putt off no longer his just claim, intreating him to represent his case once more to me and that I would use all my interest with you to procure him a reasonable satisfaction, declaring that if he had itt not he must go on, whatever comes on't. This is the substance off the letter. I never knew nor have heard further off his demands than what I have sent you, which to me seem very imperfect, so that I can't tell what to say. I do believe he has a mind by this quarrell to expose not only us as much as he can but the Regulation in gen[eral] and lay open that [agreement] off [stopping] the Whickam *way. This surmise is from my own head only. If things could not be compremis'd upon reasonable terms, I should not stick att [*i.e.* be deterred from] throwing in my mite, and recommend itt heartily to your consideration and most earnestly request that you would be so kind as to lay the whole matter before my father before he leaves the countrey. I don't remember what I wrote to Jemmy att the time but this I will adventure to say, that what I did was first with a view off no disadvantage to my trust [as guardian] and in the next I propos'd [it] as a service to my two friends. I declare before God that I doe verily believe am not less than £600 out off pockett, never took any bribe directly or indirectly from any person whatever, allways preferr'd the welldoing off my friends to that off my own; notwithstanding which itt seems that I must be blackn'd and have dirt cast on me in publick court. This seems to be the case and a hard one 'tis. I must bear itt but can't with any patience. Itt has broke me many a night's rest. This minute the lady in the Fields [Cowper] is come to town and there found a letter from Hampton Court, to which place she is summon'd by the Princess, who is not well. The women will have that she begins to cry out. Adieu and excuse the trouble my letters on this subject have given you. I remain att all times ....

159

18th Oct[ober] 1716

How many letters have I wrote to you without an answer? This is the 5th as I take itt. But I know your hands are always full off business and therfore I freely forgive. The occasion off troubling you with this is that I have had a quarter off an hour's discourse with a friend off mine [Cowper] concerning a paragraph in 2 off your letters, wrote above 2 months agoe. The first relates to Tinmouth: his advice is that the worthy gentleman [Hall] who gave himself the trouble off sending you the particular state off that fortress, should draw up the same representation and his proposalls with the reasons and inclose them to my Lord Hartford. When that is don, if he does not take notice off them the major [*sic*. captain] has don his duty and shew'd all the respect that is due to the gov[ernor]; and so [he] can't take itt amiss, iff his lordsh[ip] does not think fitt to stirr in itt, iff somebody else should. The other para[graph] relates to a certain person lately come from Holl[and]. My friend says that he may be assur'd off fav[our] iff he can make out any thing clearly so as to deserve [it]; that his name shall not be discover'd iff possible to be prevented, meaning as far as the nature off the thing will admitt. Therfore what you learn from that quarter, if you will transmitt itt, shall be d[elivered] to his own hand.[1] I must lett you into a secrett but such as you must never divulge. Itt is what comes from his own family, consequently must goe no farther least it be traced. My fr[iend] thinks himself not well used by the great men in power, and now he finds the publick safe he talks off retiring into the countrey for good and all, not being pleased with some people's menagem[ent].[2] All I can say on this head is I wish he has not too much reason. All things abroad goe on successfully, which off consequence must have its good effects on us att home .... Adieu, I am to you ....

1. This represents yet another attempt by Cotesworth to bring evidence of Jacobite plotting to the government's attention.

2. Lady Cowper was always inclined to believe that her husband's abilities were not properly recognised and this report may be misleading, especially as Cowper stayed in office until 1718.

160

27th Oct[ober] 1716

You have always a disposition to serve your friends which can never fail off bringing custom. You have had mine for many years and I don't think off changing hands. You must know that as Rav[ensworth] concern draws itt self into a narrow compass, it behoves those who are immediately interess'd to be informing themselvs what course is to be taken next in order to [secure] a fresh supply [of coal]. As Chowden lyes contiguous, your friends here would willingly have your thoughts off her; iff itt be feasible to *winn the m[ain] coal, and iff itt be comattable how advisable, for one would not be att 6d exp[ence] for a pye not worth a groat. Then wherab[outs] would be the properest place to make the essay, if in Dixon's and Wilson's farms or att the south end off her near Birkley Lane. If att the former, you have her but by the nose but then you will *lead cheaper; if the latter you will win her in the most effectuall manner. You may form a scheme off the charges off wining by your observation on Bensham, as also by Catcheside who sunk a pitt in the inclosed grounds three years agoe. What was the reason that more coals were not wrought there I don't know; iff overburthen'd with water, the badness off the upper seam or want off *way leave, I never heard. Our request to you is that you would be so kind as to give your genuine and naked thoughts, without any restraint or reserve, upon this subject. My cosen, who is present, joins with me and will own itt an obligation on him, my uncle, as well as ....

[P.S.] The answer you will direct to my coz[en] and save postage.

161

6th Nov[ember] 1716

Yours off the 16th last month came in its due course and very
wellcome itt was, tho[ugh] I negligently omitted in my last to
acknowledge the fav[our]. But itt can't be expected that a
Will[iam] C[otesworth] is to be found in every place, a person so
indulgent to his correspondents as to allow them the liberty to
break in upon his busy hours. Wittness my last letter, to which
yesterday's post brought his answer and so full and well digested
a one as to please all that have read itt. My cosen and I redd itt
over last night with pleasure; we drank a pint off Fr[ench] white
[wine] and in itt remember'd a black Mr May[or] of Gateshead.
This afternoon I left yours for my uncle's perusall. I will
adventure to say that as ours was a joint request, so likewise are
our sincere return off thanks. You have heard from one hand or
other that the travellors gott up [to London] well and in good
plight; what is more, the town seems to agree with them. I was in
hopes to have sent you by this post an account off the Princess's
being safely d[elivered]. If itt should come before sealing you
shall have itt from ....

162

17th Nov[ember] 1716

Yours off the 12th with the inclosed came safe, but before I
begin to answer must observe that the 3d off this month I drew
on J[ohn] J[ohnson] a *bill off £174 odd pay[able] to you as the
ball[ance] off the wagg[on] way as p[er] our accounts. I spoke to
Mr Fr[eke] about itt and he order'd my drawing on our *fitter.
So much by way off prelude. In the next place I come to answer
yours by a short method. I am confirm'd in my opinion that
what I wrote formerly in relation to a great friend [Cowper] will
prove true, either before or soon after his Maj[esty's] return. I
own I am not a little concern'd att itt but this amongst our selvs.
I have bin twice to wait on him, but either came too early when
he was engaged in his station or was gon abroad, so could not
read him the substance off yours. Have since gott [it]
transcribed, which will be d[elivered] in a day or two by a trusty
hand. I make no doubt the Gatekeep[er, Carr] has had a hand in

transacting what you suspect, nay and a deep one too. This affair shall never be divulged to the person you except against, and for that reason I will for once disobey your orders and shall not impart itt to T[homas] Gib[son] nor C[harles] S[anderson]. One must have Argus's eyes about them; nay even Roger [Gale] himself shall not know any thing. As to the commiss[ioners], I now don't know one I could recommend. They are all well affected but a more than ordinary prudence and discretion is necessary. I am not personally, that is to say intimately, acquainted with any of them but by what I can learn Sir Tho[mas] Hales is as proper a person as you can apply to, with a strict injunction off secrecy and you may introduce your self by the acquaintance my farther has with him. Since I began this 2 gentlemen came to visit me, which has taken up the time I had sett apart for this employ, and itt being late obliges me to conclude from ....

163

24th Nov[ember] 1716

This morn[ing] the cause with the bishopp [of Durham] was brought before the court. His councell threatn'd they would move for a new tryall, which they grounded upon some new discovery made. But itt prov'd to be an empty boast, for after half an hour's debate the boundary [of Ravensworth] was amply confirm'd in every respect according to the deed, and the diocesan is to pay costs both in law and in equity. I went to a certain lady this morn[ing] who told me that her gentlem[an] had yours with the inclosed to me and had weigh'd itt; that I might expect shortly a summons from him now that the term draws to a conclusion, so that I should have his thoughts from his own mouth. She told me in substance that the ambassad[or] may impart to you or any trusty friend the chief off what he can tell; that iff itt be judged when laid before him that itt be meritorious enough, he may expect what he insists on as a praelim[inary]. Iff itt does not he may depend upon't no use shall be made off itt to his prejudice in the least, no name made use off, so that the ambass[ador] may remain but where he was. This is what was mention'd to me but I am referr'd for some exactness to the principall. I left her with your last which she

promised, nay press'd me to leave itt, that itt might be seen by
the same person. Ask'd iff the under master off M[orpeth
school] was in orders. She is zealous. Pray act with all caution
and secrecy, which is needless to recommend to you. Pray who
were the providores [*i.e.* contractors for naval provisions] last or
this year? I hear they made a complaint to the board that they
had great quantitys off pickl'd provisions by them and desired
they would take itt off their hands; upon this they order'd a
vessell down to bring itt up [to London]. Upon the return off the
ship they order'd that itt should be examin'd in what
circumstance itt was and that the contractors' friend should be
present. Itt was reported that itt was not as itt should but on
further application itt was resolved that some off the
commiss[ioners] as well as masters would be present att the
tasting. Nay they gave leave to the proprietors to take a piece off
the best if any were better than other [and] had itt dress'd. One
off the commiss[ioners] had enough off the smell; some off the
masters said the best off itt might be used on occasion. I need
say no more. The victor [Sir Henry] hopes a relation off his has
return'd you his thanks for your good services att Wh[ickham]
upon a late occasion. I have severall letters to write this night;
must therfore begg you will assist in getting a valuation made
and in the disposall off your friend's share in Paul Holday's ship
the Begining of New C[astle], and you will much oblige ....

[P.S.] The minutes off the decree are just come from C[harles]
S[anderson]; you will see them in cos[en] Grey's hand.

164

27th Nov[ember] 1716

I have bin confin'd to my house ever since my last to you,
which was Saturday's post, and very ill I have bin and att
present my spirits so sunk that I can scarce speak to be heard.
Yet am sensible that a man off industry ought not to be balked.
In relation to the affair off M[orpeth] and misapplication off
the moneys for charitable uses, some honest gentlemen in the
neighbourhood or substantiall freehold[er] or inhabitant I
believe might file a short bill off complaint against the
menagers, and if they can make out their allegations that very

charitable gift may be obliged to make good the charge off the suit. You know that my Lord [Cowper] can't be advis'd with because itt may come before him; but I know a parrallell case in some measure to this where the partys prosecuting succeeded. I was directed as most proper to take the opinion off some learned counsell, which is the best way off proceeding if as above or by information in the K[ing's] Bench. If you think proper, draw up the state off the case as full yet as brief as you can and I shall lay itt before some able off the learn'd. To have his opinion will not cost above 2 guin[eas]. As to your former inclosed I can't yet come att itt to gratifye your desire off having itt return'd, neither can I give you a farther insight than what has bin hitherto done. If you will take my notion tis this. Suppose you should gett the gentlem[an] who is willing to signify the substance off what he knows, without any name, transmitt itt and I will lay itt before you know [who], who will be better able to judge off the meritt. You know we are cautious how we promise, but when we have done, a punctuall performance may be expected and above all a secrecy from that quarter may be depended upon. I need not inlarge. Pray is not a new undertaking [Farnacres] near bottom'd? Tis about the time proposed. Adieu ....

165

6 Dec[ember] 1716

I think I am born to be a trouble to mankind but in a more particular manner to your self. The last post brought me a long letter from our quondam [friend, James Clavering] wherin he expresses himself to this effect. He blames me for passing over in silence severall articles off his former,

> 'particularly as to your former generous kindness in relation to a share in Bensham upper seams, for I do suspect W[illiam] C[otesworth] plays the same part in that affair as he does about Chop[well] w[aggon] way, where he trifles and prevaricates with me in such a manner 'tis impossible to express itt. When I am with him he says as you mention, if [I] would communicate his letters to my bro[ther] Gr[ey], [he] would determine that matter. I not only communicated them, but also gave him copys and what he left with W[illiam] C[otesworth]. Now when talks to him, bids him

tell me when [he] comes to town desires to see me and then
would end itt. When I goe, then putts itt off to bro[ther]
G[rey] again. So that I am now fully resolv'd, by the advice
off friends, if [he] does not determine by the next time I go
to N[ew] C[astle] to send the papers up to my bro[ther]
Tho[mas Yorke] and Mr White with instructions in the first
place to advise and consult with you; for as I have acted
hitherto with the uttmost regard to you and I still desire to
continue the same, that iff possible no reflection may occurr
to you. For I am highly provoked att a story was told from a
good hand the other day att N[ew] C[astle] and what I
percieve has bin industriously spred with a design off
making a breach between our 2 familys, att least a shyness,
and what I doubt had an effect by some remarks when Sir
H[enry] was in the country. The case is this, that I should
threaten you with a bill in Cha[ncery] for tho' I could gain
nothing therby would do itt to expose you.'

He appeals that never such a thing enter'd into his head and
intreats that no credit be given. I design to answer that about
Bensh[am]. Itt was true I did make him an offer off p[art] off
my share but I understood that he had come to some
agreem[ent] since with you wherby he had quitted; in case that
were not so, he should be still wellcome to a share in the
proffitts, if any such were, after I was reimbursed the severall
summs I had advanced and the interest. That for my part before
I left the north, finding so much trash wrought which without
*mixture J[ohn] Colson could not make use off to his *pans,
and the other part commonly called *ship was so fowle that they
would not be taken off but att a very low price, and when the
masters brought them to this markett were forced to undersell
and great *praem[ium] paid: when I see that, I wrote to you to
think off lessning the works, for as my notion was att that time
that if we could save our selvs itt was more than I did expect. In
the next place I must thank him for his civility and must express
my sorrow for the differences betwixt you, and as you were both
my friends I should stand neuter, unless obliged in my own
justification and defence. And lastly that I was a stranger to the
report spred. I thought itt not improper to give you this account;
make what use you think fitt but privately. John Cay is come to
take leave. I hope you rec[eived] my 2 former letters. Adieu ....

166

11th Dec[ember] 1716

The excessive cold weather off late and the heavens that threatens us with a prodigious storm off snow has made me very uneasy in my body corporate; my blood does not circulate, especially towards the extream parts, which obliges me to rubb my legs every morn[ing] with camphyrated spirit off wine to bring me to a sense off feeling. My head and stomach are likewise both much out off order. These just complaints influence me to that degree that I can't read, neither dare I venture to sett pen to paper to any but intimate friends, who will have the goodness to overlook and conceal the imperfections off the scribe. Upon which I adventure this to you, tho' I can't inlarge as the subject off 2 or 3 last letters doe require. I begin with what you recommended severall weeks agoe, upon Sir Will[iam] Will[iamson] being teaz'd out off measure on account off moneys due by his [militia] subalterns to severall during the late disturbances. Last Sunday I had ¼ off an hour's discourse with my friend [Cowper], who upon hearing the case and being appriz'd off the merits off that gentlem[an] told me itt would be a difficult matter to compass, but the most likely means off obtaining the desired end would be that that gentlem[an] should draw up a representation off his case addressed to Mr Walp[ole]. Suppose that Ra[lph] L. should gett some Member to introduce him and itt to that gentlem[an]; att the same time that he acquaint Lord Sc[arborough] with itt, or may trye iff his lordship will introduce him because his lordship can speak to his own knowledge, and I doubt not prevailing with my friend to second the motion. I must have a copy off the representation sent to me, but neither my friend nor I must be known to be privy to this advice least we bring an old house over our heads [i.e. get into trouble]. What relates to the [Morpeth] free school I can't say more to than what I formerly wrote. I read yours off the 4th inst to a certain person, who said advising with councell etc. was perfectly right but you must name and apply to a sollicitor to menage and draw up his brief. I believe I can prevail for [altering] your commission [of the peace] as you desired. If there be any other friend to the Gov[ernment] in the county, lett me know his name etc. and estate and I don't know but may obtain for both or more perhaps; this must be done without loss

off time. I believe the comm[issioners] off forfeitures have done
as much as was expected by many; pray who are Slaughter and
Fletcher? While upon the school, I almost forgott to tell you
that iff the new ones [*i.e.* teachers] don't take the oaths to
qualifye them, they subject them selvs to the penalty. I doubt
the defeating off Jeni[son] will not be feasible. My papah
appear'd early to gett Rob[ert Bowes] off Thornton excused: he
apply'd to my Lord Ch[ancellor] and Lord Towns[hend] and
prevail'd. Who named Jenis[on] I know not. Itt would not look
well that my father or I should appear in this matter. If Mr
C[harles] Wai[te] gives us any advice off the method he
proposes, he shall not want our opinion.[1] This is a long epistle,
much in a little, if you can but comprehend the meaning. 'Tis
plainly mine that I am ....

1.   Ralph Jenison may have been attempting to evade his appointment as
     sheriff of Northumberland, the office of sheriff being more of a burden
     than an honour except in election years.

167

20th Dec[ember] 1716

I am obliged by your fav[our] the last post, which had itt
brought better tydings off your health would have bin much
more acceptable, tho' I think towards the end off the first
paragraph you seem to prick up. Alass Will[iam], I am pester'd
with an old humor which haunts a great toe. I have bin in
Small's hands almost every day this fortnight; you can't readily
imagine the pain I undergoe by having the nail even to the very
root forced out, and the surgeon's design seems to leave me
none. Besides his cutting and slashing, he never leavs me
without an application off precipitate corrosive powders which
keep me warm day and night: this last I did not sleep an hour
from the time I went to bed till I rose this morn[ing], and that is
a melancholly ditty. The Coll[onel] wrote me word off the
coaling Farnacres and promised a further account in a post or
two; nevertheless should be glad from time to time to hear from
you the cracks [*i.e.* news] off her. In answer to his I told him I
expected to have a *chal[dron] for a tryall gratis (save I would
pay freight) as soon as he had gott well into her. In the next
place must tell you that neither my father nor I ever heard a

syllable from Cha[rles] W[aite] on the subject [of Jenison]; we
had bin att his door two or 3 times, insomuch that I advised my
father to send this morn[ing] to know what he had done in the
matter. The answer was that he was wrote to to sue out the
pattent, for Mr Jen[ison] I presume, but when he apply'd he
found some other person had bin imploy'd in that affair and
that they had sent itt down by Tuesday's post; by which I
apprehend that Mr Ledg[ard] must have miscarry'd. Had I not
bin confin'd in a manner to the house by this toe I would have
had from his own mouth the particulars. Mr Roper was the
person sent, and he can neither recieve nor bring an answer to
satisfaction. No more on this till I am better informed from
Cha[rles] himself, save that I am given to understand that the
Gatekeeper [Carr] corrected the mistake [in the patent] by
inserting Wolsington instead off Elswick, but these matters for
your self. I delay'd answering your quondam [friend]'s for a
fortnight att least and then did itt in a few lines. The 4 names I
sent to my friend [Cowper] this afternoon in a letter, since which
have had no account than that itt was d[elivered] to his own
hand and that is enough. One would think that an evill spiritt
was gott into a bro[ther] off mine [Ellison]. My father had an
account off itt before but chose to conceal itt. You have
business enough for a doz[en] off tollerable heads on your
hands besides that off the publick. We are all mortall and
suppose you should dropp, would not your family be strangely
bewildred? Could Mr May[or] intail on his posterity his head
and genius in business well and good, but when all is don
experience is a great matter. Excuse this freedome, which comes
from him that is not capable off advising, yet is a perfect well
wisher to you and yours. Adieu ....

[P.S.] We dont know what to think off the dismission off Lord
Townsend. The Torys crow.[1] Mrs Mount[agu] having obtain'd
a commission off lunacy ag[ainst] her husband, the
commiss[ioners] mett this day. I heard her councell. By what
pass'd 'tis guessd'd she will prove him such.[2]

---

1. George I intended to appoint Townshend as Lord Lieutenant of Ireland,
    which effectively sacked him for his opposition to favoured royal policies
    while minimizing the risk of a split in the ministry. The situation hung fire
    until the Court returned from Hanover.

2. There was a definite strain of insanity in the Montagu family, although the subject of this particular reference is unclear.

168

Xstmas day 1716

Yours dated 18th came not to hand till yesterday with the 2 inclosed papers. That which belongs to C[harles] S[anderson] shall be d[elivered] to him, that is to say the Morpeth case. The other shall be shown to our friend [Cowper] att his return from the countrey where every body is gon during this week off recess from business. That gentlem[an] had the 4 names your former brought laid before him; we must wait time and opportunity. I gave the Philosopher yours to peruse; he is willing you should be accommodated with the 2 parts off ships you desire since you are willing to give as good a price as any other. I wrote some time ago to John Walker off Whitby to take an inventory and appraise our shipping as soon as they came to lye up but have not heard off him since. Perhaps some off them may unrigg [for the winter] in your river. I can't much apprehend from Hedly Fell. Am sure the trade has nothing to fear from Cl[avering] St[ella]: this last year has so surfeited the glass houses that they will not touch. Kitchingman is the only vessell that is come up loaded with those coals in the last fleet and here he lyes, for no body asks the price. Sir W[illiam] W[illiamson] is in the right to forbear till itt be known who will be out [of office] and who not, which I believe the greatest person in the land does not. Mr F[reke] advises that you send up the information in a cover to Mr Sec[retary] Methwin and inclose itt to Cratch[erode] with whom you have a correspondence, which he thinks the most proper method. In case you send me a short account off any further you take herafter, I shall be able to lay them before my friend, who is as ready as any I dare say to join in and second; itt will be paying him a complim[ent] however. No-one has or shall see the contents off your last save this gentlem[an] and my father. As to the menagem[ent] off the com[missioners] by their deputys, 'tis surprizing but I desire to know iff most off publick matters are not so. The Coll[onel] to my father gives a lively representation off that matter wheroff perhaps good use may be made. The Gatekeeper [Carr] has not yet made the visit I formerly mention'd. I have bin for above a fortnight under Small's care and wish I be free from him in the like time. A hum[our] that is fallen on my great toe gives him many opportunitys off distressing me with his crook'd shank'd sheers and eating powders. I am not intirely confin'd to the house but the next door [to] being so; 'tis with great pain that I can suffer an old shoe or slipper on that foot. 'Tis so great that after having laid awake for 2 nights together, was obliged to take a quieting pill the last. This added to my old complaints, I assure you makes the burthen almost insupportable. Adieu. Take care off your person.

[P.S.] Mr Fr[eke] who perused the Morp[eth] case bids me give you his opinion and advice. He says 'tis not seasonable att this time and if itt were he is pressing positive itt would not bear [*i.e.* succeed]. Therfore advises desisting att present.

169

1st Jan[uary] 1716/7

This comes chiefly to usher in my complim[ents] att this season by wishing you and yours health and prosperity for such a number off years as providence shall allott. My bodily infirmitys flow so fast upon me that I can't expect any off them. Life itt self under my circumstances is a daily trouble. I had like to have said a burthen. I am now confin'd to the house. I have daily three dismall visitors, the d[octor], apothecary and surgeon. The first prescribes, the 2d prepares and administers for my complaints off head and stomack in order to prevent that flying goutish hum[our] settling in those parts. The 3d has bin near a month in hands with a hott fiery toe, where there was a swelling. He has raised the nail and cutt half off itt away, root and all: thought he had pursued with his corrosives so sharply that he would needs perswade me a fortnight ago that there was no further occasion, which I could not readily come into finding still a sharp pain, but he persisting I paid him off. In 3 days time, finding my pains increase, sent for him again. When he open'd itt out, he found my suspicions too well grounded, renew'd his sharp applications with more vigor and has every day since ply'd me off with his crook shank'd sheers, lancett and incision knives, besides his fiery oyles and burning powders, and is raising the rem[ainder] off the nail in order to clear me off it root and branch. I can't propose getting out off his hands this month att soonest and tho' I have gon thro' one fiery tryall, yet a sharper is to follow. You will excuse this ungrateful detail. Itt is some allay to the affliction when one has told the story to a friend. I have but one word to add (before I conclude) in answer to a quaery of yours. By my bro[ther] (which you desired to be explain'd) is meant the Hebb[urn] Just[ice] and his proceedings att Whickham. You are in a good method in your paper proceedings. I believe you transact with 2 honest patriots, Sec[retary] Methw[en] and Mr Cratch[erode]; inclose to the latter the papers for the former and you need not fear secrecy. The affairs off the justices for Northumb[erland] lye before the proper person; we must wait the issue, which will be in due time I believe. As to publick matters I am in a mist, as I fancy are the chief off the whole nation. Some will have (what the Torys expect) a thorough change, others say (att least hope) itt will goe no farther, but I am satisfy'd none will know till little before or upon his Maj[esty's] arrivall. Be that as itt will, I am apt to believe that itt will not be auspicious to your present undertaking. For iff people suspect they may be out before what is proposed can effectually be bro[ught] about, itt must certainly make them the less zealous att least; it would be such to me. These are my own genuin notions, which I have not had I protest the least glim[m]ering from any hand, therfore you must not take notice and expose therby the little conversation I have with polliticians. The case about Morp[eth] is in C[harles] S[anderson's] hands. I desire you will write to him and give him your directions, for I having shewn itt to the Philosopher, perhaps iff I did not follow his advice I might be blameworthy. I need say no more on this subject, nor have I on any new one to discourse you. I am att the latter end as well as the begining ....

170

5th Jan[uary] 1716/7

Notwithstanding my growing complaints yet I can't forbear conversing with you tho' itt be but by a line or two. As to the change att court, there is no other than the Secretary. Each party give out as they would have itt. The Torys say there will be a medly ministry att first and after the whole will be in their hands. On the other hand the Whiggs flatter themselvs that itt will goe no farther, nay some will pretend that the Secret[ary] will be reinstated; but I dare be bold to say that all is but conjecture and matters will lye in embrio till his Maj[esty's] arrivall. If the Whiggs don't take pett and break among themselvs, I should yet think they might make their party good but there are reports spred about industriously to make them jealous off each other in hopes off dividing them. These are only my own suggestions and what I offer to your consideration. You have upon the anvill some matters off great importance, which wer the present ministry to continue in, yet itt will require some time before you can bring matters to bear. And as there is a very great ferm[ent] among the great men, one does not know who and who is together, neither can any judgem[ent] be formed till the scheme be known. I must leave you guess how itt may influence the affair you are prosecuting. I protest to you these are only my own thoughts which crowd into my head while I lye in bed and can't sleep. But methinks I should be sorry to see your zeal balked and those who have apply'd to you exposed. If the present sett hold their feet, you are in as fair a way to succeed as you could wish, but iff itt should be otherwise (which God forbid) I can't answer for itt. Within these 10 days the Gatekeeper [Carr] has attempted 3 times to visitt my father and this morning they mett. He was sent by your Lord Lieut[enant] to prevail that the lieut[enant] coll[onell, George Liddell] should accept off Sir W[illiam] W[illiamson's] commission (but this to yourself), which was modestly refus'd. This gave a handle to discourse off Sir W[illiam's] case and the old gentleman press'd him home on that subject. He promised to speak to Lord Sc[arborough] about him. I believe the noise some off your friends made has reached the earl's ears and I almost fancy he has bin told off itt by some great men. I should be glad itt have the [desired] effect. Your quondam friend [Clavering] has favor'd me with another letter, dated Christmas Eve, which I have not yet answerd. There is this parag[raph]: 'I must repeat my former request that you may be att ease as to my particular claim off a share with you att Bensh[am], for ingratitude I abominate and less [it] certainly could not be should you suffer for your generosity and friendship to me. If you have not gott those accounts in, 'tis high time you should. Remember 4 years before the w[aggon] w[ay] account could be gott in, which I have reason to curse. I don't know but I may see you my self and sollicit my own affair; I am so advised.' But all this under the rose. You would doe well to haunt And[rew] Dick till he finishes the account; lett him draw itt up as short as he pleases. I have now tyr'd you, so will release you. This winter has visibly a bad effect upon your old friend and serv[ant]. Adieu.

171

17th Jan[uary] 1716/7

I think I have wrote four letters to my good friend since I have had a line from him, which makes me uneasy and I can't but attribute itt to his thinking that what business he has recommended has bin neglected. Depend upon't itt has not in the least. But great persons' leisure and opportunity must be waited. Were you but with me during the smoaking off a pipe, I could give you full satisfaction. When I tell you that Mr Fr[eke] who upon his arrivall from the north sent into the Fields to lett them know he should be glad to wait on them when they would sumons him to give an account of his transactions and how he found the young gentleman [John Clavering]'s affairs; yet from that day to this he never has had one. This does not proceed from any disrespect, I assure you, but if you will have my thoughts freely their heads and thoughts have bin and are taken up about the divisions among the ministry that those and only those lye att heart. Could the severall parts be cemented (and what I believe is zealously endeavor'd by our friend) we should be yet happy. I am credibly inform'd that his Maj[esty] is steddy and will not desert his friends, but if they by their fallings out among themselvs break and can't be able to support him, he must unavoidably fall into other measures. But am not near so much under apprehensions off a breach as I was ten days agoe. His Maj[esty] has made a glorious alliance with the Regent and what I heard from a great man was that none but a profess'd enemy to the present establish[ment] could find fault with.[1] Being in company last Monday, I heard from one that was in company off old Wort[ley] and discoursing on the subject off Elswick coll[iery] he express'd himself to this effect; that coal will answer in every respect that off Benwell, adding that he had a letter from J[ohn] O[rd] who is a partner and wrote him word he would not take £1000 a year for his share, which is an 8th *p[art] I think. You would do well to try privately if you could gett a certain account off the concern. I hear J[ohn] Bowes and Ra[lph] Ellison have each gott a tyde survey[or's] place in the port. Lord Sc[arborough] told itt me an hour agoe. Adieu, I have not time to read over. H[enry] Pierson's ship is valued att £700 besides the stock.

1.   Liddell did not live to see the failure of these frantic efforts to heal the Whig schism. In April the Townshend-Walpole group in Parliament refused to support hostile moves against Sweden. Townshend was dismissed and his friends, including Walpole, Pulteney, Methuen, Orford and Devonshire, left the ministry.

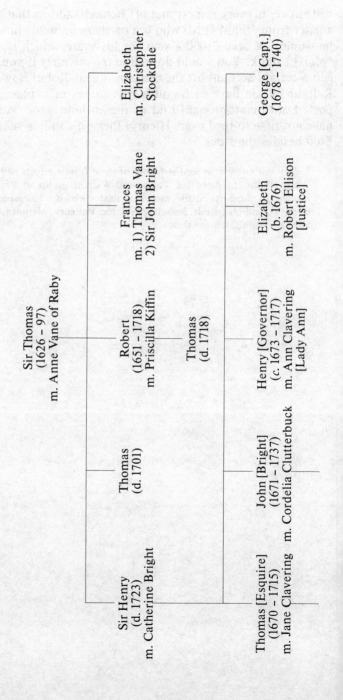

THE LIDDELLS OF RAVENSWORTH

Sir Thomas
(1626 – 97)
m. Anne Vane of Raby

Thomas
(d. 1701)

Robert
(1651 – 1718)
m. Priscilla Kiffin

Frances
m. 1) Thomas Vane
2) Sir John Bright

Elizabeth
m. Christopher
Stockdale

Sir Henry
(d. 1723)
m. Catherine Bright

Thomas
(d. 1718)

Thomas [Esquire]
(1670 – 1715)
m. Jane Clavering

John [Bright]
(1671 – 1737)
m. Cordelia Clutterbuck

Henry [Governor]
(c. 1673 – 1717)
m. Ann Clavering
[Lady Ann]

Elizabeth
(b. 1676)
m. Robert Ellison
[Justice]

George [Capt.]
(1678 – 1740)

Collieries and Waggonways on Tyneside

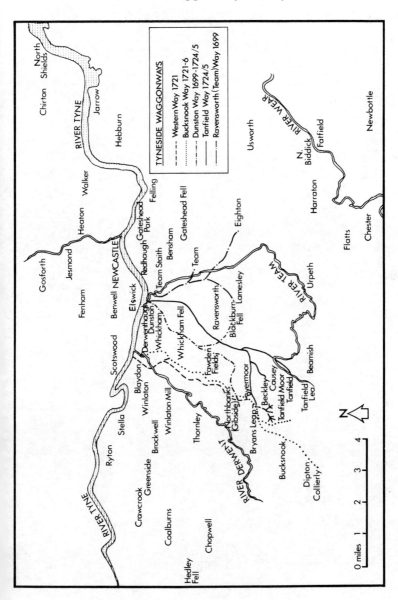

bill (of exchange): credit instrument ordering the drawee to pay a specified sum to the drawer or named payee on a given date; by far the most common means of payment among traders. [8, 21, 27, 28, 30, 34, 35, 42, 48, 63, 65, 68, 72, 74, 100, 101, 102, 113, 120, 125, 129, 130, 131, 139, 142, 143, 148, 152, 162]

bords: underground coal workings, separated by pillars left to support the roof. [59]

bowl (boll): coal measure officially containing about 35 gallons and used to determine the capacity of waggons. [38, 42, 57, 61]

branch: temporary extension from a main waggonway, serving an individual pit. [5, 86, 94, 101]

carriage: collective term for men and equipment used to transport coal from the pithead. [5, 11, 26, 37, 74, 81, 94]

chaldron: measure by which coal was sold; official measures amounted to 28-29 cwt to a London chaldron and 53 cwt to a Newcastle chaldron but in practice the latter was often exceeded; see also double coal, measure. [11, 18, 31, 38, 43, 46, 49, 52, 57, 67, 70, 71, 87, 97, 98, 101, 102, 120, 136, 138, 142, 167]

crimp: intermediary between shipmasters and dealers on the London market. [67, 95]

dead rent: fixed rent paid during the initial development of a colliery; sometimes paid to prevent exploitation of coal deposits. [21, 57, 96]

double coal: result of market pressures which pushed the 53 cwt Newcastle chaldron up to twice the London measure. [38]

drift: passage driven along the coal seam for access or drainage. [83, 92, 93, 94, 96]

fitter: agent employed to arrange sales of coal to shipmasters and to supervise transport downstream in return for fittage payments. [1, 7, 8, 10, 12, 15, 22, 23, 27, 30, 31, 37, 38, 43, 61, 67, 71, 74, 83, 107, 137, 143]

fother: coal measure containing about 7 bowls. [38,57]

gift coal: allowance of several extra chaldrons for every 20 bought, designed to encourage sales without lowering the nominal price. [31, 51, 67]

groats: subscription to the Regulation levied at 4d on every chaldron sold by members' collieries. [4, 10]

keel: coal lighter, manned by three keelmen and with an official capacity of 8 Newcastle chaldrons; moored at a rented keelbirth. [3, 7, 8, 12, 18, 26, 28, 38, 46, 59, 76, 136]

keep: to maintain waggonway track and waggons in repair, either for a flat fee or for 'tentail' payment, that is according to the number of tens carried. [12, 37, 77, 86, 93, 144, 150]

lead: to transport coal by wain or waggon. [12, 19, 26, 27, 33, 49, 57, 81, 84, 103, 137, 138, 143, 145, 160]

lye in: to close down a colliery. [2, 48, 54, 55, 67, 137, 143]

making out: dividing tens into chaldrons at the steath, usually producing 15-20 chaldrons; higher figures favoured the vendor since working costs were assessed on the ten and selling prices on the chaldron. [11, 38, 57, 101]

measure: coal was sold by statutory measure rather than weight; however, sluggish demand could force up the actual content of the chaldron so that coal was effectively sold at a discount; see also double coal, gift coal, making out. [11, 12, 18, 20, 57, 101, 136] mixture: blending coal from different pits or collieries, usually to upgrade poor quality coal which might then be sold under the more popular name. [1, 7, 25, 38, 92, 94, 143, 157, 165]

mount: ramp built at the railhead to load coal into waggons. [55, 74]

note (of hand): credit instrument with less legal protection than a bill. [11, 13, 34, 72, 76, 95, 113, 150]

pan coal: inferior, broken coal supplied at reduced prices to the salt-pans. [2, 7, 10, 11, 80, 88, 94, 95, 100, 101, 102, 108, 130]

pans: cast-iron pans in which sea-water was boiled down to obtain salt. [5, 11, 22, 25, 26, 36, 132, 137, 143, 165]

part: agreed share in the costs and profits of a colliery or ship; used to diffuse risks and regarded as a disposable asset. [7, 18, 31, 58, 61, 66, 110, 143, 149, 171]

praemium: commission paid to London dealers for buying coal from particular collieries; outlawed in 1711 but in practice maintained by market pressures. [5, 11, 13, 15, 16, 19, 27, 32, 36, 37, 38, 43, 46, 48, 49, 51, 52, 63, 67, 70, 96, 97, 102, 137, 142, 165]

quantity: either quota assigned to individual coal-owners within a partnership or cartel, or estimated yield of a colliery on which rent was calculated. [10, 19, 23, 34, 43, 44, 81]

return: to remit cash or bills to make a payment. [8, 15, 27, 32, 130]

ship coal: larger, better quality coal suitable for shipping to London and commanding a higher price than pan coal. [3, 5, 7, 11, 67, 132, 146, 165]

steath: wharf or quay where coal was loaded into keels under supervision of a steathman; riverside sites were rented in the form of steathrooms. [11, 15, 25, 26, 27, 31, 32, 38, 55, 59, 66, 81, 83, 86, 94, 101, 137, 143] ten: measure on which working and leading costs were calculated, varying in size according to the colliery concerned; distinctions also existed between wain and waggon tens, leading and delivering tens etc. [1, 2, 12, 23, 38, 41, 42, 43, 57, 66, 70, 71, 77, 91, 93, 96, 137, 146]

trunk: covered steath. [28, 31, 33, 45]

undertaker: term used for both entrepreneurs and small sub-contractors (also known as operators). [15, 43, 44, 57, 67, 77, 93, 102, 138, 139, 143, 144, 148, 151, 155, 156]

vend: total amount of coal sold either during a certain period or from an individual colliery. [5, 12, 15, 16, 26, 31, 38, 45, 49, 67, 77, 79, 139]

viewer: colliery engineer, responsible for surveying and inspecting the workings. [7, 38, 101, 103, 140, 146, 148, 150, 154]

way: abbreviation of waggonway, a horse-drawn railway constructed with wooden rails laid along a prepared track. [12, 14, 23, 26, 31, 33, 37, 38, 40, 41, 46, 48, 49, 50, 55, 56, 57, 62, 66, 67, 69, 77, 78, 81, 83, 84, 86, 90, 91, 93, 94, 95, 96, 99, 113, 143, 145, 146, 148, 149, 150, 151]

wayleave: right of way across private property leased to move coal to the river. [13, 15, 21, 23, 24, 30, 33, 36, 38, 39, 40, 41, 44, 47, 55, 57, 58, 59, 60, 67, 69, 71, 73, 74, 75, 78, 81, 91, 96, 137, 143, 147, 150, 151, 160]

win: to bring a colliery into production; particularly appropriate considering the risk of failure. [23, 38, 41, 42, 56, 57, 59, 83, 108, 160]

INDEX

285